Culture and the Development
of Children's Action

WILEY SERIES IN
DEVELOPMENTAL PSYCHOLOGY
AND ITS APPLICATIONS

Series Editor
Professor Kevin Connolly

The Development of Movement Control and Co-ordination
J. A. Scott Kelso and Jane E. Clark

Psychobiology of the Human Newborn
edited by Peter Stratton

Morality in the Making: Thought, Action and the Social Context
edited by Helen Weinreich-Haste and Don Locke

The Psychology of Written Language: Development and Educational Perspectives
edited by Margaret Martlew

Children's Single-Word Speech
edited by Martyn Barrett

The Psychology of Gifted Children: Perspectives on Development and Education
edited by Joan Freeman

Teaching and Talking with Deaf Children
David Wood, Heather Wood, Amanda Griffiths and Ian Howarth

Culture and the Development of Children's Action: A Cultural-historical Theory of Developmental Psychology
Jaan Valsiner

Further titles to follow

Culture and the Development of Children's Action

A cultural–historical theory of developmental psychology

Jaan Valsiner
Developmental Psychology Program
Department of Psychology
University of North Carolina at Chapel Hill

JOHN WILEY & SONS
Chichester · New York · Brisbane · Toronto · Singapore

Copyright © 1987 John Wiley & Sons Ltd

Library of Congress Cataloging-in-Publication Data:

Valsiner, Jaan.
   Culture and the development of children's action.
   (Wiley series in development psychology and its applications)
   Bibliography: p.
   Includes index.
   1. Developmental psychology—Philosophy. 2. Child development—Philosophy. 3. Cognition and culture—Philosophy. I. Title.—II. Series. [DNLM: 1. Child Behavior. Child Development. 3. Child Psychology. 4. Culture. WS 105 V214c]
   BF713.V34 1987   155.4   86–18925

ISBN 0 471 90523 2

British Library Cataloguing in Publication Data:

Valsiner, Jaan
   Culture and the development of children's action: a cultural–historical theory of developmental psychology.—(Wiley series in developmental psychology and its applications)
   1. Child psychology—Cross-cultural studies 2. Child development
   I. Title
   155.4   BF721

ISBN 0 471 90523 2

Contents

Preface

This book is a result of an intellectual journey—its author's experience with different traditions of psychologists' thinking in different countries. That experience had its beginning in Estonia, a country that due to historical coincidences has been a part of the Soviet Union over the last four decades. The intellectually stimulating and non-conformist atmosphere that characterized the Psychology Department of Tartu University in the 1970s, where I received my higher education and subsequently became involved in research, served as the background for my later endeavours. I am indebted to a number of the 'angry young men' of Estonian psychology of the 1970s with whom I shared ideas, collaborated in joint research projects, and wrote papers. Among them, Jüri Allik constantly challenged my thinking, so that I began to try to transcend ideas that at any time happen to be popular in psychology literature originating in any particular country, Peeter Tulviste introduced me to the cultural–historical thinking in psychology which is one of the foundations of the theoretical perspective outlined in this book. Mati Heidmets and I undertook a number of efforts to understand how the society and personality are interdependent within environmental contexts. My original interest in the organization of human social interaction and its development was greatly facilitated by joint work with Henn Mikkin. He, together with Peeter Tulviste, also provided me with my first exposure to the relevance of the history of psychology for better understanding and improvement of its contemporary state. I may have, somewhat stubbornly, refused to understand that 'modernizing function' of history at that time. However, it will be evident from this book that the historical roots of the suggested theoretical framework are of primary importance in my contemporary thinking.

After my luck in gaining an opportunity to leave the Soviet Union for good in 1980, my experiences in Western Europe and North America have had a profound impact on the development of the theoretical structure that is described in this book. My six-month stay at the Justus-Liebig-Universität

x

in Giessen, arranged by Klaus R. Scherer and Paul Ekman, provided an opportunity for an insider's look into the theoretical inclinations of the contemporary Continental-European psychologies. My subsequent work in the United States, first at the Institute of Child Psychology of the University of Minnesota, and then at the University of North Carolina at Chapel Hill, has provided me with ample opportunities to contemplate the relationships of psychological theories (and empirical research traditions) with the cultural–historical contexts of the researchers. Interaction with many friends and colleagues on both sides of the Atlantic Ocean has been very important for the development of ideas that are in the core of this book. Frequent meetings with Robert B. Cairns, devoted to discussion of basic developmental ideas, have been particularly rewarding and pleasant. The multiple opportunities for working at the Istituto di Psicologia of Consiglio Nazionale delle Ricerche in Rome during a number of summers, and continuing collaboration and friendship with Laura Benigni, have significantly contributed to the formation of ideas presented in this book.

The function of this book is to present to the readers a systematic and thorough overview of the present author's theoretical system, its methodological consequences, and the empirical data that follow from those. I have deliberately covered all the levels of analysis, from the most abstract (philosophical) to the most concrete (empirical phenomenology of children's development in their everyday life contexts). The focus of the coverage is on the interdependence of the levels of the system. Therefore, this is primarily a theoretical book, furnished with empirical illustrations of some of the aspects of the theory. In this emphasis, it is deliberately out of place among the majority of contemporary publications in developmental psychology which suffer from the ethos of empiricism, and that often reduce theoretical discourse about 'the data' to some relatively simple set of ideas, derived from the socialized intuitions of members of the given culture at the given time. As I argue in the book, the epistemological status of 'empirical data' as the foundation for an 'objective developmental psychology' is no simple matter, and depends on the theoretical system within which the data are constructed from observable phenomena. The conceptual difficulties with the idea of development that child psychologists have persistently encountered make it imperative to address difficult issues first theoretically (although in close connection with the observable phenomena), and then proceed to construct scientific methodologies that fit the developmental nature of the phenomena that are studied. My motivation to undertake the difficult task of working towards a better theoretical and empirical understanding of developmental processes stems from the growing dissatisfaction with the oftentimes dogmatic ways in which the most interesting phenomena are turned into highly uninteresting and inconclusive 'data' by conventional application of strategies of 'data analysis' that are meant for the use of stable (not developing) phenomena.

A number of people deserve my great gratitude in conjunction with writing this book. Kevin Connolly provided very helpful feedback on the first draft of the manuscript, and has encouraged my work in many ways from its beginning. The empirical research reported in the book was performed thanks to a grant from the Foundation for Child Development (located in New York). The help of Debra Skinner and Kathryn Luchok in the work with participating families, as well as the readiness of parents to participate in the study, is acknowledged with gratitude. Albrecht and Elzbieta Lempp helped me out by doing the photographic work. The Editorial Staff of John Wiley & Sons Ltd, and especially Michael Coombs were helpful in many ways in scheduling the writing of the manuscript, and in bringing it to its final state. The book itself, of course, constitutes a milestone on the author's way towards better understanding of development. It is not meant to be a final or 'absolutely true' system which is published with the aim of converting readers into a new faith. Instead, it will hopefully raise more questions than it provides answers for. In this case, the whole writing of the book will be considered by its author not to have been in vain.

Chapel Hill, North Carolina
July, 1986
                                                          Jaan Valsiner

Foreword

Science touches the lives of us all and in advanced industrial societies it is a familiar and powerful feature of our world. And yet it is not easy to define or even to capture its essence. For many, science seems to be about facts, hard facts, facts that are in some way better than those of history, literature or philosophy. Science is associated confidently with knowledge and progress but as Lewis Thomas has so elegantly pointed out in his *Late Night Thoughts on Listening to Mahler's Ninth Symphony*. 'Science, especially twentieth-century science, has provided us with a glimpse of something we never really knew before, the revelation of human ignorance'. In reality scientific conclusions are much more tentative than most non-scientists and many scientists think. Even a brief examination of twentieth-century science will show that dogmas come and go with astonishing rapidity even in those areas designated the exact sciences. Scientific progress is commonly talked about and institutions and societies of various sorts exist throughout the world to further it. But what is scientific progress and how do we measure it? The usual indicators are in terms of money attracted and expended, numbers of papers published, or citations scored, etc., but the validity of these is so obviously questionable as not to require further comment. The task of science is to provide us with a better, fuller and clearer comprehension of the natural world in which we live.

To do science, particularly good and original science, requires a mix of some seemingly conflicting qualities. It requires at one and the same time confidence and iconoclasm. It demands a mind which automatically doubts and questions but which at the same time has the confidence needed to pursue, develop and press home ideas. The practice of science needs a mixture of rigour and imagination. It requires that ideas be put to the toughest tests that can be devised and at the same time it requires vision and the courage to cut loose from the constraints of currently accepted dogmas. Most of contemporary scientific activity in psychology consists in carrying out empirical investigations whose purpose is to add to our store of 'facts'. But facts exist only within a theoretical context and there is consequently a danger that the activity of science, the conduct of investigations, becomes an end in itself. The activity takes on a life of its own and the primary purpose of furthering our understanding of the natural world is subordinated to organizational needs.

In this important book, Dr Valsiner argues that many developmental psychologists have lost their way and this he illustrates by his quote from Wittgenstein, the essence of which is that one cannot sort out conceptual confusions by experimental methods. Science like any other human activity is influenced by the culture in which it is embedded. In Western industralized societies the predominant and most influential branch of science which forms the 'scientific culture' in which other branches are embedded is that of classical physics which lays stress on things. But is the world of things, the Democritean world, a satisfactory model for psychology and developmental psychology in particular. Valsiner thinks not and argues persuasively that if we are to understand development then a better, indeed a necessary, starting point is a Heraclidean view of the world as composed of processes. The envy of physics and mathematics, which have been held up as the goal to which other sciences should aspire, has often mislead and ill-served the social and biological sciences.

There are three features which make this book unusual. First it is unashamedly and primarily concerned with theory. As Valsiner sees it, epistemological progress is the key to evaluating scientific progress, to deciding whether we have a clearer comprehension of nature. From an examination of basic assumptions underlying psychological research, Valsiner proceeds to a consideration of several theories of development and on to the presentation of a theory of his own about the development of children's actions and thinking. The second major feature of the book is that it deals with behavioural change taking place in the natural, normal, socially rich and varied contexts of children's everyday lives. The way in which culture shapes the behaviour of infants in some quite specific settings such as that of a meal is thus explored and described. The joint action of adult and child in the setting of a meal is brought out vividly in three longitudinal cases which are analysed. The third feature which distinguishes this work from the bulk of what is published in developmental psychology is the range of the author's scholarship. He draws on sources in ancient and modern philosophy, on several branches of psychology, on neurobiology, genetics, mathematics, anthropology, political theory, history, sociology, philosophy of science, education, artificial intelligence and theoretical physics. He integrates work from European, American and Soviet traditions and most important through his meticulous scholarship he shows us that many of the central questions and approaches are not new, we had simply forgotten earlier work. Drawing attention to important and still today highly significant work done 50 or more years ago is a valuable corrective in an age obsessed with what might appear in next week's *Nature* or *Science*.

The foreword to a book is not a place in which to do the advertiser's job, rather let me congratulate the reader on his good fortune in having obtained the book; I am sure that its message will be important.

Kevin Connolly

Acknowledgements

The author wishes to acknowledge the use of copyright material from the following sources:

M. Rutter, *Scientific foundations of developmental psychiatry*, 1980. Reproduced by permission of William Heinemann Medical Books Ltd.

J. Shotter, 'Duality of structure' and 'intentionality' in an ecological psychology. *Journal for the Theory of Social Behaviour*, **13**, 19–43, 1983. Reproduced by permission of Basil Blackwell Limited.

Excerpts reprinted from *The concept of activity in Soviet psychology*, edited by James V. Wertsch, by permission of M. E. Sharpe, Inc., Armonk, NY 10504.

T. R. Williams, *Socialization and communication in primary groups*, 1975. Reproduced by permission of Mouton De Gruyter, The Hague.

Excerpt from pp. 145–146 from *The Sociology of Child Development*, Fourth Edition, by James H. S. Bossard and Eleanor Stoker Boll. Copyright 1948, 1954 by Harper & Row, Publishers, Inc. Copyright © 1960, 1966 by Eleanor Stoker Boll. Reprinted by permission of Harper & Row, Publishers, Inc.

A. Freud, The concept of development lines, *The Psychoanalytic Study of the Child*, **18**, 251 & 252, 1963. Reproduced by permission of International Universities Press, Inc.

CHAPTER 1

Introduction: developmental and non-developmental psychological research in Western cultural history

> The confusion and barrenness of psychology is not to be explained by calling it a 'young science'; its state is not comparable with that of physics, for instance, in its beginnings. (Rather with that of certain branches of mathematics. Set theory.) For in psychology there are experimental methods and *conceptual confusion*. (As in the other case conceptual confusion and methods of proof.) The existence of the experimental method makes us think we have the means of solving the problems which trouble us; though problem and method pass one another by.

> Ludwig Wittgenstein (1968, p. 232e)

It is sometimes said that psychology as a science is in its infancy. This use of a term borrowed from stage descriptions of children's development may imply that the discipline is destined to develop fruitfully in the future, as the transition from infancy to childhood and adolescence, and later to adulthood, is an inevitable part of growth. Science, however, does not progress along simple, linear developmental lines. Instead, it may move slowly, often making circles rather than proceeding directly towards a more advanced state. Furthermore, scientists themselves are human beings who may dearly wish that their discipline advance, and devote their energy to it—but to no avail! It is only natural that under these conditions progress in science (and of scientists) may become evaluated by some external (but easily 'measurable') criterion (such as the number of members in a professional society, or the number of published articles). It may be easy, and very tempting, to measure 'progress' in a scientific discipline by such external criteria. Such measurement makes it easy to bypass the need for serious analysis of the advancement of the knowledge—the epistemological progress in a scientific field.

Psychology at large provides a good example of how its progress can be mismeasured by organizational criteria. Undoubtedly, the number of psychologists in almost any country of the Western hemisphere has increased. However, the increase in the number of people in a profession need not necessarily lead to highly innovative discoveries or inventions. Instead, the increased size of professional organizations may give rise to much social politicking in the given discipline, formation of groupings and subgroupings, fights for dominance in the professional societies, and so on. All these very human activities are the results of progress of scientific organizations and not science itself. In the rush of professional social interaction in the framework of their organization, scientists may be left little time and energy to ponder about the really crucial epistemological issues their science needs to confront. However, it is only in that latter domain that 'progress', 'regress' or 'stagnation' of a science can be diagnosed.

The main goal of this book is to analyze the epistemological state of affairs of the 'young' science of psychology from the perspective of how developmental issues are treated within its realm. I shall emphasize that careful explication of the ways of thinking that are used in psychology is crucial for the development of that discipline. In their frequent quest for more 'empirical data' psychologists have taken an easy way out of the complex conceptual issues that the discipline has struggled with from its inception. No empirical data that are collected (constructed) without a careful analysis of the thinking of the investigator can solve the discipline's theoretical problems.

It is the general epistemological issues that are of central relevance for the study of developmental psychology. The present book analyzes the question of how children's actions develop within culturally structured environmental settings. These settings are purposefully set up by other people who surround the children, and guide the children's relationships with these settings and themselves in directions appropriate for the goal of socialization. The task of capturing the development of children's acting and thinking requires new theoretical perspectives in psychology that are built upon carefully explicated epistemological bases. The aim of this book is to make these bases explicit, and to advance a theory of child development. The theoretical perspective is illustrated with empirical research materials linked with real-life phenomena of development.

1.1 Developmental and non-developmental approaches in psychology

Much of the conceptual confusion surrounding developmental psychology originates in the failure to separate non-developmental and developmental aspects of child psychology from each other. Investigators often use the term 'developmental psychology' as a *de facto* synonym of 'child psychology', and as a result developmental and non-developmental research questions are easily fused and confused. For example, in contemporary discourse in child psychology Piaget's stage description of children's cognitive development is often referred to as 'Piaget's developmental theory'. However, Piaget's description of stages *in* the process of development is not a *theory of* that development. The former is a descriptive classification of homogeneous stages that are assumed to follow one another in a rigid sequence in the process of children's cognitive development. Such description does not explain by what mechanisms the transition from one stage to the next takes place. It only describes the outcome or product of the process of development. Piaget's actual *theory* of development is his theory of equilibration of structures through continuous assimilation and accommodation processes. His equilibration theory is a theory of development, but his stage description of cognitive development is not since it does not explicate the processes that are involved in the course of change (see 3.2 for more elaborate analysis).

The process/outcome distinction can serve as a useful starting point in the present effort to separate developmental and non-developmental approaches in psychology. Without the need for being more specific, we can say here that certain psychological processes produce different kinds of psychological outcomes. Both these processes and their outcomes can either be thought of as stable, immutable, entities, or as variable, changing, and developing phenomena. Table 1.1 presents the four possible versions of the process/ outcome relationships.

Table 1.1. Developmental and non-developmental aspects of the study of psychological processes and outcomes.

Processes	Outcomes	
	Static	Dynamic
Static	1.1 Non-developmental	1.2 Non-developmental
Dynamic	2.1 Developmental	2.2 Developmental

From this simple table it is easy to see that different combinations of the nature of psychological processes and their outcome provide for the developmental/non-developmental split as it is conceptualized here. The 'static' verses 'dynamic' distinctions here refers to the principal (qualitative) modifiability of the process or outcome over time.

Let us consider the first case (cell 1.1) where a particular psychological process is thought of as being stable and unmodifiable, and generates stable and invariant outcomes. This is the case of non-developmental thinking *par excellence*. This example is represented by a psychological process which may be likened to a simple computer program that works exactly the same way on every re-run, and always produces the same result (e.g. a program that adds numbers 2 and 3 always produces the outcome equalling 5). A psychological process of that kind is clearly non-developmental, since no dynamic change in the process itself, or its outcomes, is expected from it. If such change nevertheless occurs, it is appropriately explained as 'error'.

The remaining three versions of the process/outcome relationships are potential candidates for consideration as exemplars of the developmental approach. The case where a static process generates variable outcomes (cell 1.2 in Table 1.1) stands at the boundary between the non-developmental and developmental approaches. it refers to a stable (unmodifiable) process that may produce a number of potential results. If that happens in a random fashion there is no need to consider the outcome distribution as pertaining to development. However, when the process starts to generate outcomes that differ from the previous ones in some consistent way, then the phenomenon is approaching the condition when it could become developmental. However, because of the axiomatically unchangeable nature of the process it cannot become developmental. Therefore, the cell 1.2 remains designated as 'non-developmental'. The possibility that the process itself can change after it has begun to produce novel outcomes is theoretically ruled out in this case.

An example of unmodifiable processes with potentially variable outcomes can be taken from the contemporary health fad of jogging. When a person runs, his (or, possibly, her) heart rate increases beyond the level that it ordinarily has in a resting state. That variable increase in the outcome does not alter the cardio-vascular system in the direction of making the heart work in a qualitatively different way. The system may become quantitatively better trained as a result of the jogging exercise, but it does not change qualitatively as a result of that activity.

Another case illustrating the non-developmental nature of the 'static process–variable outcome' condition is the classical 'Crick's Dogma' in biology that specifies the information transfer in one direction: DNA→ RNA→ protein. This conceptualization—the cornerstone of much of the history of genetics—involves the stable genetic code (DNA) that can produce a variety of outcomes (proteins), but these outcomes themselves do not modify the DNA code in any way. This classical-genetic perspective represents the theoretical consideration represented in cell 1.2 in Table 1.1. However, the closeness of this condition to a developmental one is illustrated in this example by the increasing knowledge of the possibility of reverse information transmission (from RNA to DNA), even if it takes place on a small scale. The possibility of reverse transcription (i.e. the possibility of feedback into the process from its products that modifies the process) immediately moves the example from the non-developmental condition (cell 1.2) to a developmental case (cell 2.2).

The third cell (condition 2.1) is a case of development where the process changes qualitatively while the outcome remains the same. Many control systems where the goal is to maintain the outcome of a process under certain stable conditions can be used as examples of that case. If a shop-assistant has to add numbers 2 and 3 to arrive at the sum 5, it can be done in his mind, on paper, using an abacus, or a calculator. Most certainly the invention of the calculator and its replacement of the abacus is a qualitatively new development in the process of arithmetic operations, which leaves the outcome (sum of $2 + 3$) the same. More generally—the process by which the same result is obtained may undergo development, but it cannot be revealed when observing only the outcomes of the changed processes, since the latter remain the same.

This condition illustrates the danger of inferring development of the process from the study of the outcomes—although abacus and electronic calculator can be used to reach the same outcome, it is not possible to infer from the outcome itself how these two different tools accomplished that.

Finally, there is the version where a dynamically changing process relates to dynamically variable outcomes (cell 2.2 in Table 1.1). This is the most clear case of thinking where the developmental approach is demonstrable. Finding examples of this in the realm of physical objects is complicated. Even efforts to make computers learn need not provide very rich examples (see chapter 5—discussion on learning automata theory). In contrast, examples from the cultural development of children and societies (see also section 3.5 in this book) illustrate the dynamic nature of the process $<==>$ outcome interaction. A child learns to speak. This involves the acquisition of the acoustic form and semantic function of the first words. Once these signs have become parts of the child's lexicon, the child's action is qualitatively transformed by the use of signs. The use of signs was previously an outcome of the child's learning process, now it becomes a means that is used by the child to reorganize his cognitive processes (see Luria, 1979). What previously has been an outcome of a process has now fed into that process and changed it qualitatively, offording the production of novel outcomes.

A similar process $<==>$ outcome dialectic relationship is present in the development of cultures. Consider the invention (or introduction) of literacy in a previously illiterate society. This innovation makes it possible to guarantee the fulfillment of some important tasks—e.g. memorizing of the culture's corpus of mythological texts—in a novel way. Instead of being preserved in the process of oral retelling and learning, these texts now can be preserved in writing. As a consequence, the demands on memory skills of individual persons within the culture may be reduced and changed in a qualitative way. Whereas the possibilities of accurate preservation of texts are enhanced by literacy, the high-level memory skills of the preliterate (so-called 'primitive') people may gradually be replaced by very limited memory skills of contemporary (so-called 'modern') people living in highly industrialized societies (see Vygotsky and Luria, 1930, chapter 2). The outcome—invention of external information storage devices— has modified the process of internal-psychological mechanisms of memory.

More generally, the condition 2.2 in Table 1.1 represents the developmental approach *par excellence*: a certain outcome in the course of child development leads to the reorganization of the process that produced it. That process in its turn generates new outcomes which lead to further reorganization of the processes. This dialectical relationship between processes and outcomes continues all through the lifetime of the developing system. In this respect, there exists a fundamental difference between non-developmental (as represented by condition 1.1) and developmental approaches in psychology. However, in the discourse of child psychologists that distinction is often overlooked. As a result, some non-developmental cases (e.g. as of cell 1.2) may be presented as if they were developmental in their nature, or the importance of some developmental cases (e.g. as in cell 2.1) happens to be overlooked because they seemingly result in no novel outcomes.

The majority of the instances of the non-developmental approach in psychology concentrate on the study of the static aspects of psychological phenomena. For example, the traditions of psychological testing have been based on the quantification of subjects' responses to some test items which constitute *outcomes* of these subjects' psychological processes that were functional in generating these responses. This emphasis on the static (ontological) aspects of the phenomena elimintes the dynamic aspect of these phenomena as either irrelevant, or 'noise', or includes that aspect in the 'error of measurement'. This tradition follows from the positivist effort to carry over research methodology from classical physics to psychology. In that transition the basic difference between phenomena in classical physics and biology/psychology—namely that the latter are capable of development—is overlooked. This example fits into cell 1.1 in Table 1.1 (stable process/invariable outcome).

A more subtle version of the non-developmental approach in psychology goes beyond looking only at the outcomes of psychological processes and tries to conceptualize these processes themselves. Such an approach is representative of the problem-solving research in the cognitive sciences, where the question of *how* a certain problem gets solved is a central one. On the one hand, the dynamic aspect of the phenomenon—movement from a state of no-solution to the state of a solution—is included in the studies of problem solving. On the other hand, it is often expected that the psychological processes involved in problem solving are stable and fixed, rather than amenable to change and development. In terms of the cells of Table 1.1, this approach fits the cell 1.2 (stable process/variable outcome).

In contrast, the developmental approach addresses the issues of how an organism changes from one ontological state into another. These ontological states are relevant as intermediate 'anchoring points' for the study of development. Instead of the non-developmental question—'What is the true nature of a child's state of age X or Y?'—the developmental question is asked: 'How does a child's state change from X to Y?' It is obvious that any developmental research question includes the use of the time dimension as an integrated part of the theory, rather than just a dimension along which developmental events unfold. Therefore, explicit study of the temporal organization of developmental events is a necessary aspect of any empirical study of development. Developmental psychology studies psychological processes of children that give rise to different outcomes, and that themselves undergo transformation in the course of their functioning. This conceptualiz-ation of developmental psychology is close to that of Heinz Werner, who emphasized the necessity that 'development should be conceived as a trans-formation of one pattern of processes into another' (Werner, 1937, p. 360).

To summarize, at the most abstract level, the developmental approach deals with the transformation of an organismic (systemic) phenomenon from one state into another. Its aim is to reveal the rules and laws that underlie such transformation, as a result of describing the processes that keep the organism functioning and produce its change. Table 1.2 provides a direct comparison of the developmental approach with its non-developmental counterpart.

It should be emphasized that even though the developmental and non-developmental approaches are in many ways opposite to each other, this does not mean that they are independent of each other. The developmental approach is complementary to the non-developmental one, and vice versa. Non-developmental descriptions can serve as the background that the devel-opmental approach uses to study the processes of change. In this sense, Piaget's descriptive taxonomy of stages in children's cognitive development provides the background for his explanation of the process of cognitive development in his developmental theory of equilibration. Likewise, knowl-edge about the processes of development can be used within the non-develop-mental paradigm for different applied purposes. For example, tests of cogni-tive development based on Piaget's description of the stages in that develop-ment are usable within the non-developmental paradigm in child psychology for selection purposes.

There is, however, one domain of scientific activity in which the two approaches are better viewed as irreconcilable. That is the domain of research questions set for empirical investigation. Here the two approaches differ—it is in principle impossible to explain development on the basis of non-develop-mental theories and/or data. For instance, a static 'picture' of how a child functions psychologically at a certain stage tells the investigator nothing about the process of development by which the child is going to advance to the next stage. Developmental questions cannot be answered on the basis of non-developmental research methods and data. On the other hand, non-developmental questions (e.g. 'Why is this 14-year-old girl extremely aggressive?') can be answered if the developmental data are available about

Table 1.2. Comparison of developmental and non-developmental approaches in psychology.

Topic	Non-developmental	Developmental
(1) Object of investigation	The 'being', i.e. the constant and stable aspect of psychological phenomena	The dynamic, 'becoming' aspect of psychological phenomena
(2) Source of 'noise' in research	The dynamic, unstable aspects of phenomena. These are often dealt with as 'error' and eliminated from the study	The static, stable aspects of phenomena, since these do not pertain to the issues of 'becoming' and can obscure the dynamic processes hidden underneath the static appearance
(3) Source of concepts for theories	Platonic philosophical concepts that emphasize the stability aspect in phenomena and eliminate the time dimension (and time-related change) from scientific discourse	Different philosophical backgrounds, all of which emphasize the variable aspect of phenomena (Heraclitus, Goethe's romanticism, Hegel, marxist theoreticians of different kinds)
(4) Dominant research design	Cross-sectional accumulation of data, excluding any information on time-related change in the phenomena	Longitudinal—awareness of the danger of eliminating information about development through aggregation of data over time and subjects
(5) Emphasis in theoretical discourse	Theoretical discourse often operates with concepts that capture some outcomes (products) of psychological processes. Processes are expected to be revealed through investigations of their outcomes	Theoretical discourse concentrates on the analysis of the processes (that produce outcomes), attempting to study these processes directly, rather than through their outcomes

the personal history of the given person. Thus, the two approaches have an asymmetric relationship; it is possible to explain outcomes (non-developmental aspect) by the processes that have led to these outcomes in the course of time (developmental aspect), but not vice versa. It is impossible to explain the functioning of a psychological process by the study of its outcomes only.

1.2 Cultures and psychologies: the emergence and selective diffusion of developmental ideas

The emergence of developmental ideas in occidental philosophy can be traced back to ancient Greece, to the philosophical system of Heraclitus of Ephesus (*c*. 500 BC). Heraclitus' thinking was based on an emphasis on the permanence of change in nature; things were considered never to remain the same over time. An emphasis on change of things across time is an essential prerequisite for any developmental perspective on the nature of things. Once such emphasis is present, a developmental theory of the particular phenomenon can follow. If, on the other hand, the emphasis on change-with-time is not prominent in a thinker's philosophy, no developmental perspective can emerge. Within ancient Greek philosophy, both the developmental and non-developmental ideas were concurrently present. The non-developmental frameworks of thinking were prominently represented by Parmenides' (*c*. 470 BC) theory of being, and Plato's (427–347 BC) theory of forms. In general, the conceptual problem of how to deal with issues of change occupied the minds of many ancient Greek philosophers who quite often tried to find 'the real' that constitutes the permanent something which underlies change. In other terms—the cause for change was conceptualized as not changing. For example, Aristotle's reduction of the idea of development to a category of being illustrates the efforts that were made to understand the changing world in terms of static causes rather than dynamic processes.

One possible way to let the non-developmental perspective on the world prevail is to separate the qualitative nature of phenomena from its quantitative aspects, and assume the constancy of the quality while ascribing all the change to quantitative aspects of the phenomena. That tradition is deeply ingrained in psychology (see Valsiner, 1986), and can be documented already in Aristotle's thinking:

> for that which is losing a quality has something of that which is being lost, and of that which is coming to be, something must already be. And in general if a thing is perishing, there will be present something that exists; and if a thing is coming to be, there must be something from which it comes to be and something by which it is generated, and this process cannot be *ad infinitum*. But leaving these arguments, let us insist on this, that it is not the same thing to change in quantity and in quality. Grant that in quantity a thing is not constant; still it is in respect of its form that we know each thing. (*Metaphysicas*, Book 4, 1010; quoted via Smith and Ross, 1908)

The separation of quality (the permanent essence) and quantity (the extent of the appearance of that essence) by Aristotle served as a conceptual means for fitting together both the constant and changeable aspects of the world. The primary relevance of the former was emphasized by Aristotle in his insistence on the permanence of the 'first mover':

> Evidently again those who say that all things are at rest are not right, nor are those who say all things are in movement For if all things are at rest, the same

statements will always be true and the same always false,—but they obviously are not; for he who makes a statement himself at one time was not and again will not be. And if all things are in motion, nothing will be true; everything therefore will be false. But it has been shown that this is impossible. Again, it must be that which is that changes; for change is from something to something. But it is not the case that all things are at rest or in motion *sometimes*, and nothing *forever*; for there is something which always moves the things that are in motion, and the first mover must itself be unmoved. (*Metaphysica*, Book 4, 1012; quoted via Smith and Ross, 1908).

Aristotle's dualism about change—accepting its presence in reality on the one hand, but on the other explaining it through reference to permanent essences—emerged in the cultural context of Greek mythology which has provided the basis for much of the philosophical and scientific thinking. A very similar duality seems to be present in the thinking of contemporary child psychologists—on the one hand, the issues of development are recognized as those central to developmental psychology, whereas on the other hand the theoretical concepts that are used to explain development are often non-developmental in their nature. It is often the case that psychological explanations of development make reference to some static essence which is treated as if it were the cause of the particular developmental phenomenon. For example, the attribution of causality for an infant's fussiness to its belonging to the temperament type 'difficult baby' is often made as an explanation of the child's behaviour: 'This child cries because s/he has a difficult temperament'. Or—a 2-year-old's temper-tantrum may be explained through that child being 'insecurely attached' to the parents, and a whole series of future developmental problems may be predicted from the assignment of the child to the class of 'insecurely attached' children. In both of these examples the explanatory concepts—'difficult temperament' and 'insecure attachment'—are non-developmental concepts, which are used to explain the presence of phenomena that occur during the children's development (fussing, temper-tantrums) as well as the basis for predicting the children's future development.

Even though the majority of Western societies (and sciences within them) have been influenced by the ancient Greek heritage in one way or another, the particular cultural systems in contemporary Europe and North America have developed along somewhat different lines. The social sciences that have emerged in Western societies at the intersection of social ideologies and basic sciences have likewise been affected by the cultural ambients in which they emerged. That influence of the culture on science need not be observable at the surface level of different social sciences which have largely imitated the use of methods borrowed from classical physics and some branches of mathematics. However, at the level of the 'deep structure' of the Western social sciences—i.e. in the domain of basic axioms on which theories are built—the intertwinement with the cultural system is evident. One of the purposes of this book is to analyze that deep structure of the assumptions on which most of contemporary developmental psychology is based, and to demonstrate how different basic assumptions of research that make up this deep structure either afford, or prohibit, the study of development in psychology.

Developmental psychology is an area that is perhaps more vulnerable to cultural influences than any other field of psychology. The reason for such vulnerability may be similar to Aristotle's dualism in conceptualizing change. On the one hand, the everyday thinking of people (based on their 'common sense') usually captures the constant, static side of the world. This includes thinking about children—in many respects, adults' discourse about children in any culture emphasizes the static side of children's 'being' and only marginally touches upon their 'becoming'. On the other hand, developmental psychology aspires to capture the basic laws of 'becoming'—the dynamic aspect of children's existence.

It would of course be an oversimplification to assert that the cultural common sense fully excludes knowledge about change in children. However, the relative emphasis on change versus stability contrast can vary in the culture over time. For instance, emphasis on change may become more widely spread in a culture that itself is currently undergoing change at a quick pace (e.g. during a revolutionary social change), and may decline in eminence once the period of rapid cultural change is over.

The history of developmental thinking in psychology is intimately related to the history of evolutionary biology and to German natural philosophy of the eighteenth and nineteenth centuries (see Cairns, 1983; Cairns and Ornstein, 1979). Developmental ideas that emerged in the framework of the German culture gave rise to the study of child development, as well as to all psychology. Psychology as separate from philosophy was historically initially a German invention which was actively exported to other countries, where it acquired a fate of its own in conjunction with the conditions in the particular culture (Cairns and Valsiner, 1982). The presence of cultural 'folk models' (see Holland and Quinn, 1986) that structure people's everyday knowledge about children and their growth sets the stage for acceptance, rejection, or modification of the set of ideas and practices that are imported under the label of 'child psychology' from another culture. The cultural salience of children makes the study of child development open to the cultural guidance of the discipline in ways that are not possible in the case of other sciences that deal with some subject matter which is less influenced to culturally mediated rules. For example, two disciplines—physical chemistry and experimental psychology—were imported into the United States from Germany in the last decades of the nineteenth century (Dolby, 1977). The import of physical chemistry (which is not particularly close to basic cultural patterns of social life and thinking in American society in the last century) resulted in minimal modification of the conceptual sphere of the discipline. The fate of psychology in the webs of American culture was very different.

Psychology was imported selectively—those theories and methods that fitted the cultural–moral values and perceived needs of American society were taken over and started to develop on their own. In contrast, many aspects of European psychological thought that were alien to the American culture were never imported, or vanished soon after their arrival in the New World.

Furthermore what was imported from Germany (and Europe in general) was also changed as it was integrated into the existing cultural system. Thus, Binet's practical testing methods were imported into America in the beginning of this century and quite soon became a widespread school of psychological practice of intelligence testing. In contrast, Binet's theoretical ideas were paid little attention. Such selectivity in importing and assimilation of European psychological ideas in North America was not limited to the beginning of the present century. It has continued over the past up to the present time. The history of the dissemination of Gestalt psychology in the United States is noteworthy as an example of the culturally restricted acceptance process of a social science in a culture (see Henle, 1977).

In contrast to the slow and complicated process of entry and survival of developmental ideas in the American social context, the dissemination of these ideas eastward to Russia proceeded along a very different line—but in ways likewise organized by the cultural conditions of the recipient society. The entry of developmental ideas from the nineteenth-century German philosophy was facilitated by the import of the whole marxist world view into the society that went through a quick and turbulent reorganization. Once the marxist philosophy was set up as the ideology for the new society that was developing towards goals similar to those of different social utopias of the previous centuries, the emphasis on the issues of *development* was a natural side issue of the social discourse in the 1920s in the Soviet Union. It is in this social-utopian context that 'Soviet psychology' emerged (Kozulin, 1984). From its very beginning, 'Soviet psychology' that was built on marxist grounds was declared to be developmental in its nature. In reality, some of it indeed was—the contributions to developmental thinking by Vygotsky and Luria date back to the 1920s or early 1930s. However, most of the rest of Soviet psychology became developmental only in its declarative side, without corresponding breakthroughs in theory and empirical research (see Valsiner, 1987).

Similar cultural guidance of developmental psychology can be observed in any other country in which that discipline has put down its roots. Although developmental psychologies in Italy, France, Switzerland, and other countries share some common aspects with the discipline in the USA or USSR, the particular way in which the discipline is related to the background culture has its own unique history and present structure. This cultural embeddedness of developmental psychology is not unique—in any social science, its assimilation into a society depends on the previously existing cultural knowledge structure. For example, psychoanalysis was accepted into the French culture on the basis of its similarity to the religious practice of confession (Moscovici, 1961, 1984). Once it was accepted into the knowledge structure of the culture as a social representation, it became possible to view its basis (religious confession) as an analogue of psychoanalysis! What had historically facilitated the acceptance of a system of ideas subsequently became explained by these new ideas. Such inversions in cultural explanatory practices illustrate the change of the cultural knowledge system as new ideas are imported into it and 'fitted' into the existing system in such a way that both the incoming ideas and the recipient system are changed. The process is largely an analogue of Piaget's assimilation/accommodation process (see 3.2.3), only at the level of the cultural rather than of the individual person's mind.

The inevitability of the dependence of psychologists' thinking on their cultural surroundings at a given historical period leads to the central question of this book—*how to conceptualize issues of development of children's actions within their culturally structured and dynamic environments, accepting at the same time that these conceptualization efforts themselves are necessarily dependent upon the present cultural knowledge?* An answer to this difficult question is sought in the analysis of children's actions and their development at three levels. First, the basic assumptions that underlie the thinking of developmental psychologists are analyzed in chapter 2. Related to this is the theoretical analysis of existing approaches in developmental psychology (chapter 3). These analyses allow us to eliminate different domains of thought from further consideration in theory building since they do not fit the present goals. The second level of analysis involves the explication of the concepts used in the present theory (chapter 4) and the discussion of their nature, as well as of different possible ways of using formal systems in the service of the present theory (chapter 5). Finally, at the third level, the theoretical system is illustrated on the basis of the empirical material of infants' and toddlers' mealtime settings. The organization of these settings is analyzed in chapter 6, and observational data derived from the author's longitudinal study of children's actions at mealtimes follow suit in chapter 7. Chapter 8 summarizes the proposed theory in a general form.

In this book my aim is to treat the theoretical system and the psychological phenomena as interdependent and mutually important, rather than emphasize one over the other. Neither theory, nor the empirical reality, is more important than the other. Instead, theory and the empirical reality are mutually related—a theory cannot be built without having the reality as the basis. Likewise, no empirical study without a clear explication of its theoretical bases can result in new knowledge.

A note of caution is in order at this point. While I emphasize the relevance of the 'empirical reality', that term is not to be considered as synonymous to 'the data' in psychology. The 'data' are the result of a transformation of the 'empirical reality' in accordance with a theory—implicit or explicit. In this sense, the data are never theory-free or 'objective' in themselves, but constitute results of the investigator's social construction process. Traditionally the data have been talked about in psychology as the ultimate proof of the objectivity of theories. This position itself is based on some basic hidden assumptions in the scientists' culture, as it assumes the independence of the object of investigation from the investigator. Thus, the reader of the present book will not be able to view the 'data' in the traditional sense of the word. Instead, the reader is introduced to the theory in a process of gradual deductive analysis moving from the basic assumptions to the concepts of the present theory, and is only after that provided with different analyses of the empirical reality using the conceptual system that is presented in the book.

1.3 Summary: towards a relativistic theory in developmental psychology

Both children and developmental psychologists act and think within their cultural frames of reference. Usually the axioms that psychologists take from their culture's knowledge base remain implicit in the mode of how their particular theories relate to phenomena of child development. My aim in this book is to suggest a theory of child development that includes the interdependence of two dynamic processes—the development of children and the development of cultural contexts within which the children live. Such relativistic theory of development has to be context-sensitive—it specifies for each statement it produces the contextual (cultural) conditions under which these statements are applicable. A hypothetical comparison of a relativistic and a non-relativistic theoretical statement about child development is provided in Table 1.3

The main difference between non-relativistic and relativistic approaches to theory construction is in the way in which they treat the interdependence of the theory and its cultural context. In the case of the non-relativistic approach, the constructed theory is assumed to be culture-free, and its possible cultural roots are not explicitly studied. Secondly, a non-relativistic approach is likely to consider the empirical data to be the ultimate proof of a theory, downplaying the active role of the investigator and the constructive nature of data derivation. In contrast, the relativistic approach to theory construction makes the cultural (historical) roots of the theory explicit and proceeds to analyze each new level of the scientific discourse as being embedded within the more general one, and interdependent with it. From that perspective it becomes possible to acknowledge in explicit ways how the core concepts of a theory in child psychology stem from axioms that are accepted in the given culture at the given time, rather than from universally true axioms. Likewise, the specific concepts used in research follow necessarily from the cultural axioms and core concepts. Finally, the empirical side of research is viewed within the relativistic framework as a convergence of the theoretical perspective and the empirical reality, as the investigator constructs the data on the basis of both his theoretical approach and the actual nature of the phenomena under study.

Table 1.3. Comparison of relativistic and non-relativistic approaches to the construction of theories of child development.

Discourse level	Non-relativistic	Relativistic
(1) Cultural axioms	Not included	Included Example: 'In culture X at time t, children are considered equal to adults as independent persons.' (EQUALITY)
(2) Core concepts in theoretical accounts of developmental psychology	Absolute status given to the core concepts. Example: 'Child–adult interaction *is* a bi-directional interchange of equal interaction partners.' Concept: BI-DIRECTIONALITY	Conditions of applicability of the core concepts of a theory are specified. Example: 'given the cultural axiom (1. above) in culture X at time t, child–adult interaction is *considered to be* bi-directional interchange of interaction partners, who are *believed* to be equal.' Concept: BI-DIRECTIONALITY
(3) Specific concepts used in research	Absolute status given to the particular concepts ('variables') that are construed as 'essence' of the phenomenon under consideration. Example: 'variables' of 'Mother's effect on child' and 'Child's effect on mother' in studies of child–mother interaction	Specific concepts used in research depend on the cultural axioms *and* core theoretical concepts that are based on the former. These specific concepts ('variables') have no relevance outside the context of higher-level abstractions from which they evolve
(4) Discourse about the empirical data in the coure of research	Absolute 'objective' status ascribed to the data. The data are assumed to represent the phenomena on which they are based in an objective way, so that data are 'collected' instead of 'constructed'. Example: 'measures' of 'variables' prove X, Y, or Z	The 'data' result from an active construction effort by the scientist, which is based *both* on the phenomena under study *and* on cultural and theoretical axioms, together with their specification in the construction of 'variables'

CHAPTER 2

Basic assumptions underlying psychological research

Any effort to construct a relativistic theory of developmental psychology is embedded in a wider network of cultural and scientific knowledge. That knowledge base which includes information about phenomena, and about the ways by which further knowledge about them can be obtained, is based on some axiomatic (core) ideas. Those premises are accepted by investigators since they are either explicitly considered to be true, or are followed implicitly as their truthfulness is felt to be beyond doubt. In this chapter a number of such basic assumptions used in psychology are analyzed. The aim of the analysis is to make explicit the assumptions that lie on the foundation of much empirical research in psychology as a whole, and in child psychology in particular.

2.1 Person/environment separation and relationships

Psychology usually separates its object—persons and their psychological phenomena—from their surrounding environments. This has been accepted practice since the discipline gained its independent status (see Super and Harkness, 1981). The separation of the target (foreground, object) from its context (background) is perceptually a necessary step in the research process. It delineates the phenomena under study from others and allows investigators to concentrate on some, rather than all, of their aspects.

The person/environment separation in psychological research can be accomplished in different ways. It depends on the particular strategy used (whtat) kind of information about the object of research becomes available to the investigator as the result of the study. There are two ways in which that differentiation is accomplished. First, it may take the form of *exclusive separation*—the phenomena are separated from their contexts, and the latter

16

are eliminated from any further consideration as irrelevant. This 'purified' phenomenon is further studied as if it were independent of its context. Some of the principal analyses of phenomena in child psychology follow this strategy. Many psychologists have made efforts to separate cognitive development from its social counterpart. As a result, cognitive development is often explained as a process that is independent of the social environments within which children's thinking actually occurs. Causal explanations for congitive development are found within that development itself, excluding the possibility that social experience participates in that process (see Valsiner, 1984a).

The second way whereby the separation of phenomenon from its context can occur takes the form of *inclusive separation*; the target is differentiated from its context, but the latter is retained in the subsequent analysis since it is considered to be interdependent with the former. Although the emphasis in research is on the object phenomenon, the relevance of its context is recognized in the investigation.

These two ways in which psychological phenomena can be studied closely parallel the distinction between open and closed systems (Bertalanffy, 1950), or between context-free and context-bound phenomena. The closed systems are systems that do not depend for their existence upon exchange relationships with their environments, and in which any change in the system inevitably leads towards structural breakdown of the system. In contrast, open systems are dependent upon exchange relationships with their environments and their structural organization is maintained, or enhanced, by these relationships. If closed systems can be conceptualized as context-free, then open systems by definition are context-dependent. Biological, psychological, and social systems are open. It is the open and not the closed systems that are capable of development. This important feature of developmental phenomena, their open systems nature, leads to the necessity that all developmental research should be systemic and ecological; it has to study the target object interdependently with its environment.

The development of open systems is characterized by the principle of equifinality—similar outcomes of development can result from developmental processes that can be vastly different from one another. It is in principle impossible to predict the outcomes of the development of an open system from the starting state of that system—because the system's interdependence with its environment and the possibility of different developmental trajectories keep the developing system open to adaptive changes most of the time. It is evident that because of the open system nature of development it is not possible to conceptualize development as taking place along a fixed, unilinear trajectory. Instead, multiple trajectories of development can be expected theoretically and sought in empirical studies, even if the sets of these trajectories occur within a certain relatively common range. Unilinearity of development can be observed only at an abstract level—as it characterizes a family of different developmental trajectories—and not at the level of particular forms of developing systems (see Werner, 1957).

Some examples will help to clarify the distinction between the exclusive and inclusive separation types. Consider the widespread issue of the 'nature' and 'nurture' in human psychology. The controversy about these two abstract causal agents has been a constant theme in psychologists' discourse (Pastore, 1949; Teigen, 1984). Historically it has emerged from the duality of thinking about God-given *natura* and this-lifely experience in the philosophies of the Middle Ages and Renaissance. The separation of these two agents is very much alive in contemporary psychology, irrespective of whether the 'nature–nurture controversy' is a 'hot topic' or a 'dead issue' in psychological disputes of the time. For example, a personality psychologist who builds his/her study of human personality on the strong belief that personality traits are stable, and potentially genetically programmed psychological entities, can use his measures to separate the 'true' personality traits from the 'noisy' everyday environmental settings where his subjects live. The data based on personality measures separate the particular material provided by the subjects (e.g. responses to questionnaires, or projective techniques) from their life environments, and eliminate any information about the latter by the mere exclusion of those from the issues covered. Others, who believe in the environmental conditioning of personality may undertake a similar effort, only in the reverse. The environments can be measured in ways that exclude from consideration persons' actions within them, or their self-reports. In this case, the environment has become the object of investigation, and it has been separated from its context, i.e. the person's actions and subjective self-reports about him/herself.

The 'weak' version of the exclusive separation of the phenomena from their contexts is also often used. It would treat both the person and his/her environment as two separate, independently measurable phenomena. Both the persons' self-reports and their environments can be studied by separate sets of measures—following the belief that 'nature' and 'nurture' both affect the personality. The aim of such a study may be to measure the extent of that influence, using an additive model that treats personality as the sum of 'trait' and 'environment' effects. Such an approach still uses the exclusive separation of person and environment, while trying to reveal their mutually parallel effects on the same targets.

An investigator who starts from the premise of context-boundedness of human personality would study human personality through inclusive separation of the phenomenon and its environment. Whereas the domain of the target (person) and its background (environment) is differentiated, she attempts to preserve the intrinsic connections between the target and its environment, which can be studied directly if the investigator analyzes the process of person–environment interaction. For such researchers personality is not a simple sum of person's and environment's characteristics, or their formal (extrinsic) correlation, but the functioning of a person–environment system where both constituents of the system are intrinsically related to each other, i.e. are interdependent. The person cannot function without an environment, and the environment of the person would not be the same if the person were eliminated from it. An investigation of their relationships might not be fruitfully done through the use of linear models (Thorngate, 1986), and the axiom of additive elementarism (see 2.4) is inapplicable.

What, then, can substitute the time-honored canons of basic theoretical psychology, that originate in classical physics? Instead of an emphasis on organism–environment co-relations (i.e. formal, extrinsic relationships between the two), investigation of the interdependence (intrinsic) relationships can be carried out. The notion of interdependence follows directly from the open-system view of the world—once the state of the organism and its change depends on exchange processes with its environment, the two are interdependent. The organism cannot function without its environment, and the environment requires the existence of the organism as part of its cycle of existence.

2.2 Static/dynamic aspects of the phenomena

In the first chapter I mentioned the paradox of developmental psychology; that research on issues of *change* is often performed with the the help of methods that are designed to reveal *static* features of the issues studied. A psychologist interested in a certain psychological phenomenon makes a decision (often an implicit one) about the inclusion/exclusion of the dynamic side of the phenomenon in the study. For example, a decision to use some standardized personality test which has high test-retest reliability is a step towards elimination of the dynamic nature of personality from a psychologist's theoretical view of the phenomenon. Aggregation of measures over time may further grant the stability of the meassures, by reducing the role of dynamic aspects of personality in the aggregate. Underneath these practical aspects of research are hidden theoretical assumptions. As a practical step is taken to overlook the dynamic aspect of the phenomena studied, the elimination of that aspect in the investigator's thinking has taken place.

In contrast, a theoretical interest in change and development makes it possible to retain information about observable dynamics in the phenomenon. This perspective is based on the idea that the phenomenon changes over time. In order to observe the phenomenon, the investigator needs to follow its changes over time, retaining the original sequence of the observed changes in the process of analysis. Different states of the phenomenon in that sequence are not considered to be independent of one another. Instead, it is axiomatically accepted that a previous state of the phenomenon leads intrinsically to the subsequent states. The temporal order of the observed state sequence serves as data for learning about the processes of change.

Any aggregation of the constituent states over the sequence into a total frequency count of states is geared towards goals that are diametrically opposite to the study of change. For example, consider a hypothetical sequence of behavioral states in the development of some phenomenon: A→B→C→A→B→C→X, where X constitutes an outcome (final state) of the developmental process in question. A simple aggregation of the frequencies of the behavioral states observed before the outcome would eliminate any information about the developmental sequence from consideration. Thus, the behavioral states A, B, and C are found to occur with equal frequency (2) in that sequence. This information includes no knowledge about the temporal relationships between the states—from the frequency count that was made it is impossible to retrieve whether A changed into B or vice versa, etc. Frequency counts are ways to construct data that do not afford knowledge about the dynamic, developmental aspect of the phenomenon. In contrast, a data construction strategy that retains the temporal sequence (e.g. a strategy that decomposes our example into: 'the sequence A→B→C→ occurred twice before the outcome X was obtained') present in the phenomenon is sensitive to the dynamic aspect of the phenomenon and may provide information about developmental issues.

If the study of change and development is the goal of an investigation, the researchers have to establish the domain of the phenomena in which the change is both expected and studied. An effort to study every possible aspect of a developing child at the same time may lead to an unlimited emphasis on the dynamic side of the phenomena in ways similar to Heraclitus' claim that one cannot step into the same river twice. Since every developmental process has its static outer limits, set by the context of the developing organism and the organism's own state, research on the dynamic aspect of further development of the organism may explicitly consider these (temporary) static constraints as a basis on which new development takes place. For instance, some intermediate outcome of development may serve as the static basis. A psychologist may study 8-year-olds' further cognitive development starting from the static basis of diagnosing that the children involved have already reached the stage of concrete operations. Or, likewise, the children's further cognitive progress (the dynamic, developmental aspect) may be studied on the basis of knowledge about the relatively stable state of the children's environment (e.g. the organization of their school environment: curriculum, discipline, etc.)

The selection of some stable aspects of the organism and its environment as the background, relative to which development is studied, does not deny the dynamic nature of the selected static background. It is a theoretical device that helps the investigator to avoid absolute dynamic relativism in empirical studies, where it is counterproductive. As long as the research interests are concentrated on a particular developmental issue, it can be studied by considering some related issues stable for the purpose of anchoring the developmental study in some more stable framework. A good example here is the relationship between development of child with that of culture (Valsiner, 1983a). Obviously, cultural change takes place on a different time scale from that of the developing child—what in child develops in the course of some years, the culture may have needed centuries to develop (e.g. child's development of writing skills and cultures' development of the same skills in history). Thus, if an investigator is interested in the empirical study of child development, the cultural environment in which the development takes place can be considered stable (i.e. unlikely to change at a pace comparable to child's development) for practical purposes of research. However, that assumption of practical stability of the culture is only a heuristic device that helps the investigator to study the particular child development issues.

To summarize: it is usually accepted in psychology that issues under study (including issues of development) must reveal their stable facet if they are to be scientifically interesting. That basic assumption determines the range of issues that can be addressed, how these issues are addressed, as well as the range of possible findings that become accepted as valid psychological data. The use of this assumption necessarily guides the investigator towards addressing non-developmental research questions. For developmental psychologists, the following of this assumption may be highly counterproductive.

2.3 Intra-class uniformity versus variability

Similarly to the static assumption underlying psychological research, the assumption of intra-class uniformity as the static basis for treatment of inter-individual differences is often traceable in psychology. The first reaction of an empirical psychologist to impending knowledge about observed variability in the data from a group/class of subjects is to try to eliminate it from further theoretical consideration. This is an effort similar to reduction of intra-individual change (variability) to the 'true' static depiction of the individual. It is applied synchronically to groups (classes) of individuals—inter-individual variability within a class is often considered 'erroneous' and is eliminated by averaging or prototyping (Valsiner, 1984b) that results in depiction of the modal case within the class as the representative of the whole class.

There are three ways in which the problems of variability are conceptualized in psychology. Historically the first of those has been to eliminate it from theoretical consideration. One way in which this can be accomplished is through studying psychological phenomena in which case the differences between individuals can be a priori considered to be minimal and inessential. Classical physics has provided thought models for that approach, which have been dominant in research on perception and psychophysics. It can also be illustrated through the example of the work of an anatomist. An anatomist who studies the basic structure of the body of representatives of a certain species—humans, for example—legitimizes his lack of interest in individual differences between members of the species by arguing that the *basic* anatomy of every person is the same as that of every other person. The anatomist is certainly aware of substantial differences in many aspects (e.g. height, weight, etc) of different bodies, but quite rightly argues that anthropometric inter-individual differences are irrelevant to his study in basic anatomical aspects which are shared by all members of the species. This way of dealing with inter-individual differences is based on the choice of those aspects of phenomena that are invariable across individual organisms. The choice, however, is made on theoretical rather than empirical grounds—an investigator starts his research by assuming that the inter-individual differences in the phenomenon studied either are absent (i.e. sufficiently minimal) or constitute an 'error' that obscures the actual 'true' picture of the inter-individually invariant phenomenon.

There are certainly many situations where the assumption of sufficiently minimal inter-individual variability cannot be accepted. Again, the rejection of the assumption can be both axiomatic or inductive. An investigator may opt for making the issue of inter-individual variability the object of investigation, a priori accept that this variability is not 'error' that obscures some invariant 'truth', but a representation of many individually 'true' states of affairs. On the empirical side of the study inter-individual variability also can easily be observed. This strategy of dealing with variability has given rise to the discipline of differential psychology, which from its very inception has been directly related to societal demands. For example, Binet's invention of mental tests was based on a direct practical need of the French educational system to classify and select schoolchildren to fit subsamples of them into different institutional niches in the system. Francis Galton's pioneering efforts in anthropometric and psychometric measurements in Victorian England were cast in his utopian framework of eugenics, to which he attributed societal and religious functions (Buss, 1979; Galton, 1904). Likewise, the proliferation of psychological testing methods during World War I was based on the needs of societal institutions in the selection of some individuals out of bigger populations. That interest was primarily pragmatic and practical, and led to no theoretical breakthroughs that could have explained how inter-individual differences come into being.

It can be argued that differential psychology has actually not considered variability in psychological phenomena at all, although this statement may seen counter-intuitive and contrary to the claims of differential psychologists themselves. What differential psychology has accomplished is to accept the fact of existence of inter-individual variability *within populations*, but at the same time it has attempted to eliminate variability *within individuals* from its scope of interest (e.g. Bem and Allen, 1974; Bem and Funder, 1978). Instead of considering every individual in a population (class) to be similar to every other individual, differential psychology has recognized that there are stable differences between the 'true' state of affairs in its psychological phenomena (e.g. intelligence, personality, character, temperament). Any instability observed within an individual over time is an obstacle on the road towards empirical discovery of these 'true' states of the particular individual. The ideal for differential psychology has seemed to be to discover the extent and nature of stable differences between individuals in a population, by assuming that any instability within the particular individuals is due to 'error' or 'noise' due to unaccountable and irrelevant causes. It becomes evident from this description that differential psychology's acceptance and study of inter-individual variability within populations is antithetical to the study of development of the individuals in that population, over time. The individuals are supposed to remain the same over their life course, although different individuals differ from others in a population by specifiable qualitative characteristics (e.g. individual-specific personality traits) and quantitative degrees of these characteristics (e.g. quantified 'amounts' of certain personality characteristics).

The third strategy for dealing with variability (of both kinds: between and within individuals) is practically absent in contemporary psychology, although some calls for its legitimacy have been voiced thus far (Valsiner, 1984b; van Geert, 1983, 1984). It involves the idea that *generality is evidenced in variability, rather than in uniformity, of behavior and thinking*. Variability is not a source of 'error' in the case of complex phenomena in psychology, but an indicator of psychological processes that can generate a variety of psychological outcomes, the function of which is both to adapt the organism to the environment and to accommodate the environment to the organism. In others terms—observable uniformity in an organism's behavior over time (self-consistency in behavior), or similarity in behavior between organisms (populational consistency), are special cases of either psychological (in the individual's case) or evolutionary/sociological (in the case of a species, or a society) processes that generate intra- or inter-individual variability in general. Uniformity in outcomes that results from these processes is a special case of the production of variability. It is the case where the variability produced is narrowed down to very few, or even one particular, outcome. Sometimes such produced uniformity may be adaptive (depending on the environmental conditions of the organism(s), but at other times it can be detrimental to the goals of adaptation. On the other hand, an organism's (or population's) variable nature may enhance its chance for adaptation when environmental conditions change. Processes that are capable of generating variable outcomes in populations or organisms thus can have adaptive advantages over others which can produce only uniformity of outcomes.

The implicit, culturally axiomatic nature of how variability is treated is particularly influential in the more applied areas of psychology in general, and child psychology in particular. Some of the ways of handling variability in child psychology lead necessarily to non-developmental research efforts.

Others may guide an investigator towards the study of developmental processes that consistently generate inconsistencies in the organisms' behavior over time, and which may therefore facilitate their adaptation process.

2.4 Additive elementarism versus structural wholism

The world that surrounds us can be perceived in different ways. From one perspective it can be viewed as the sum of independent elements. In contrast, it can also appear to us as a system consisting of interdependent constituent parts that are united in some structural whole. The disagreement between these two—'atomistic' and 'wholistic' world views—has been evident since the beginning of ancient Greek philosophy. The basic assumption of *additive elementarism* is the model of the world in which the latter is thought of in terms of classes of independent things which, if combined by simple summation, make up more complex things. In contrast, the assumption of *structural wholism* leads its bearer to think of the world in terms of the whole that consists of interdependent parts, which are necessary for the functioning of the whole. The latter position is illustrated by Paul Weiss, one of the originators of the systems approach in contemporary biology:

> A living system is no more adequately characterized by an inventory of its material constituents, such as molecules, than the life of a city is described by the list of names and numbers in a telephone book. Only by virtue of their ordered interactions do molecules become partners in the living process; in other words, through their behaviour. And since this involves vast numbers of disparate compounds, all living phenomena consist of *group behaviour*, which offers aspects not evident in the members of the group when observed singly. (Weiss, 1969, p. 8).

In the history of Western science, the assumptions of additive elementarism and structural wholism have existed in parallel since the beginning of the seventeenth century, when Francis Bacon explicitly formulated the canons of the scientific method on the basics of the former. In contrast, the development of the alternative scientific method on the basis of the structural-wholistic assumption began almost two hundred years later, and was wrought by the scientific endeavors of *Naturphilosophie*. Ordinarily, representatives of that school of thought have been characterized by value-laden descriptors that considered them 'romanticists' who were by the implication of that term quite far from the 'exactness' ideal of Baconian accumulation of facts. This popular and poetic image of *Naturphilosophen* is biased in the direction of presenting them as 'soft' or non-rigorous thinkers and researchers. There is little substance behind such labelling efforts. Although it is true that the *Naturphilosophen* included some prominent poet-scientists (e.g. Johann Wolfgang Goethe) who may be more widely known in their culture for their literary role, there were also a number of representatives of the so-called 'hard' science who adhered to the ideas of that school (e.g. Hans Christian Oersted, the discoverer of electromagnetism). In contrast, scientists from the Baconian school of thought were often involved in the mystical extension of their science (e.g. astronomers were also astrologers, chemists were also involved in alchemy), thus the distinction between science and mystery was not strict in the past centuries, neither for Baconians nor for *Naturphilosophen*. Natural philosophers relied on some aspects of Immanuel Kant's multi-faceted contribution to knowledge. It was on the foundation of Kantian ideas that *Naturphilosophie* began to build up a new, non-Baconian, scientific method, as Williams (1973, p. 17) has summarized:

> Kant and *Naturphilosophie* did produce a scientific method peculiar to *Naturphilosophie* and of obvious importance to the historian of nineteenth-century science. But there was a final effect that deserves mention. Kant, and more particularly the *Naturphilosophen*, attempted to substitute a new cosmic metaphor. The world of the eighteenth-century *philosophie* was a machine; the *Naturphilosophen* insisted it was an organism. Its laws were laws of development; its basic theoretical paradigm was field theory in which connections between parts were as important as the parts themselves.

In psychology, the two alternative scientific methods have guided the thinking of investigators in different directions. The Baconian method has dominated psychology—especially in its non-developmental aspects. It has also had a profound effect on child psychology. In contrast, traditions of Gestalt psychology have promoted the wholistic perspective on psychological phenomena. These two perspectives are investigators' alternative methodological assumptions on which their research is built. Needless to add, the issue of choice between these assumptions acquires particular relevance in the study of child development. The perspective of structural wholism is undoubtedly better suited for the study of development, granted that the systemic whole gets adequately and validly analyzed. The Baconian additive elementarism, in contrast, reduces that whole to the sum of its elements, which may suit for the purpose of a non-developmental description of phenomena, but which is not capable of capturing the processes by which development is made possible. Such additive elementarism of the Baconian scientific method was not a pure import from the 'hard' physical sciences, as it is sometimes assumed by psychologists. Instead, it constituted an effort to free facts from their theological-dogmatic contexts. W. Stanley Jevons has understood the revolutionary role that Bacon's philosophy played at his time:

> Francis Bacon spread abroad the notion that to advance science we must begin by accumulating facts, and then draw from them, by a process of digestion, successive laws of higher and higher generality. In protesting against the false method of the scholastic logicians, he exaggerated a partially true philosophy, until it became as false as that which preceded it. His notion of scientific method was a kind of scientific bookeeping. Facts were to be indiscriminately gathered from every source, and posted in a ledger, from which would emerge in time a balance of truth. It is difficult to imagine a less likely way of arriving at great

discoveries. The greater the array of facts, the less is the probability that they will by any routine system of classification disclose the laws of nature they embody. Exhaustive classification in all possible orders is out of the question, because the possible orders are practically infinite in number. (Jevons, 1873, pp. 576–577).

This description of the nature of the Baconian scientific method would apply quite adequately to the state of affairs in contemporary child psychology. An ever-increasing number of facts is accumulated without explicit and systematic concern about the assumptions on which that kind of data construction is based, and efforts towards abstracting 'laws' of child development from these masses of data either fail explicitly, or use some hidden theoretical framework to make sense selectively of some of the existing facts. Since, as Jevons noted, the set of possible orders into which the large databank can be imperfectly fitted at some level of approximation is practically infinite, many competing common-sense based 'theories' can gain some support from some of the data (see Cairns and Valsiner, 1984). The Baconian ideology of the 'scientific method', as it is applied to developmental phenomena, leads inevitably to increasing theoretical confusion. Fashionable commonsense ideas of the given time are often used as 'theories' in psychology. The progress of science cannot be based on the mass accumulation of facts, but is wrought by careful coordination of the investigators' theoretical activities with their empirical observations, where the former influences the latter and that, in its turn, corrects the former.

As an example of how additive elementarism has guided an area of psychological research away from addressing developmental issues, consider approaches to the study of children's intelligence; the psychometric and the Piagetian. The traditional psychometric approach has utilized the additive elementarism of Baconian heritage *par excellence*. A child's intelligence is measured by counting the *sum* of test items that the child has answered 'correctly' (from the psychologist's perspective). Inter-individual differences in intelligence are conceptualized in a quantitative-additive fashion, and the psychological processes that were actually used by children to give their answers (both 'right' and 'wrong') to the test items are left out of consideration. Furthermore, the development of intelligence of a particular child over time is viewed as quantitative gain – a developing child's IQ may be shown to increase as a sign of increase in intelligence. The concept of intelligence in this framework of thought becomes an ideal substance that is assumed to be present in the child's mind, and the amount of which may change as the child grows. In its explanatory function, such conceptualization of intelligence bears remarkable similarity to explanations in other domains of human cognition (see Horton, 1967).

In contrast, Piaget's view of intelligence as a process of adaptation emphasizes the connection between the developing child and his environment, where the activity of the child results in the construction of the child's cognitive development through series of equilibrations and re-equilibrations (Piaget, 1977). The child's cognitive processes undergo a series of qualitative transformations, and once these transformations are accomplished afford the child new ways of thinking. Intelligence in Piaget's thinking is no longer a 'substance' that is measured by summing up 'correct' answers on a test, but a cognitive system that organizes the child's interaction with the environment.

Another example of the successful use of the structural-wholistic perspective comes from neuropsychology. In the case of patients with brain lesions the systemic functions of the whole brain is hard to overlook in the clinical research process. The lesion constitutes a static trauma to a particular area in the brain, but the whole structure of the brain is set to work towards attempting to overcome the adverse effects of the lesion. Luria (see Luria and Artemieva, 1970) has emphasized the systemtic functioning of the brain in the context of suggesting 'syndrome analysis' as the basic scientific research strategy for neuropsychology:

> The neuropsychological investigation is based on the assumption that any psychic activity constitutes a complex functional system that depends on the joint work of a whole complex of brain (and foremost—cortical) zones, and that every part of the brain carries its own, highly specific function that guarantees the factor which is important for the flow of complex forms of psychological activity. It can be thought, following that assumption, that damage to every part of the brain that eliminates that factor results in the immediate *primary defect*, which, in its turn, leads to a number of secondary or *systemic deficiencies*, which disturb the normal functioning of those psychological activities, for which that factor is necessary. (Luria and Artemieva, 1970, p. 106)

According to Luria, the neuropsychological 'syndrome analysis' involves the comparison of changes in the work of the brain that has been damaged in certain specific locations, while the whole organism continues to cope with the tasks that the brain system has to mediate. Localized brain damage alters certain functions directly, others by proxy, while leaving many of the functions intact. An investigator who compares the impaired functions with the frame of intact ones analyzes the psychological 'syndrome' structure of the brain lesion. Likewise, the idea of such systemic analysis can be directly applied to child development. For example, a new action emerges among the whole repertoire of a child's actions. This action immediately reorganizes the child's behavior—the new action becomes used in a particular situation, and its presence facilitates the development of some other actions, while leaving others the way they were. In 'syndrome analysis', the issue of dynamic change in the phenomena is viewed in the context of its static aspects, relative to which change is observed.

The investigator's choice between additive elementarism and structural wholism can be accomplished on different grounds. As long as the choice is based on the person's ideological preferences it is possible to evidence efforts to study developmental phenomena on the basis of the elementaristic assumption. However, if the developmental nature of the phenomena is considered to be the basis of choice between these two axiomatic assumptions, then the selection of additive elementarism as one's foundation for empirical research is unproductive given the investigator's goals. Development is a characteristic of structured biological, social, and psychological phenomena that depend upon environments for their emergence, maintenance, change, and reproduction. Development is possible in the case of open systems, and the structural-wholistic assumption is therefore the only viable choice for an investigator who is truly interested in developmental research. Within the realm of different structural-wholistic models of development, of course, a wide variety of concrete ways of description and explanation can be constructed. However, the understanding that it is theoretically impossible to study development when the additive atomism assumption is accepted has only rarely been recognized in much of contemporary child psychology.

2.5 Maximization or satisficing

Psychological research is often based on the assumption that the organisms tend to maximize their gains whenever it is possible, and minimize their losses. Quite often, subects in laboratory experiments are expected to demonstrate their maximal performance, triggered simply by the instruction of an experimenter. This assumption seems to be mediated by traditions of economic thought, which have developed within the Western industrialized cultures in conjunction with economic activities and the Protestant work ethic (Weber, 1930).

The idea of competitive comparison is closely intertwined with the economic thinking about maximization of action results. Positive value attributed to achievement is evident in psychologists' jargon used in talking about their data. For example, statements like 'Boys were found to *do better* on test X than girls', or 'Women *were found to be better* than men in Y' illustrate the implicitly coded cultural value of 'winning' in a 'competition' when different groups of subjects (or individual subjects) are compared with one another.

The axiom of maximization is often applied in a value-laden manner to different aspects of subjects' performance in psychological experiments. For example, in animal experimentation an active organism (e.g. a rat who solves a Skinnerian box task by a series of trials and errors) may be considered to 'do better' than a seemingly passive organism (e.g. an 'insightful' rat who solves the problem by trying once), given that the former 'tries harder' than the latter. This *maximization of effort* seems to be considered a prerequisite for success—in full accordance with the cultural value attached to the Protestant work ethic. Likewise, *maximization of outcomes* often gains positive connotational valence in psychology. The cultural-societal background of the maximization assumption is quite extensively studied by historians and sociologists (e.g. Tawney, 1926; Weber, 1930).

An alternative assumption to the 'maximization'-based world view emerges from the work of Herbert Simon, and takes the form of *satisficing*. Instead of maximizing the outcomes of one's decisions under conditions of incomplete information, an actor may opt for finding a course of action that is 'good enough'—or, in other terms, set up the goal of satisficing for oneself (Simon, 1957, pp. 204–205). The conceptual difference between satisficing and maximizing is directly related to the assumption about the nature of the problem that the acting organism is trying to solve. Maximizing is possible where the problem is finite. This is the case when the set of its conditions, possible outcomes, and potentially usable courses of action is fixed (so that the organism can calculate the maximally useful strategy of action), and when all the information about the task is available to the problem solver. However, these conditions are only rarely true about problem-solving processes: usually the task situation is changeable over time. Partially because of the dynamic nature of the task, it is only rarely that the problem solver has access to all the aspects of the task situation. Furthermore, many tasks performed in life take place under time constraints that render a thorough analysis of the whole situation impossible. It is under these conditions of reality that satisficing becomes a more adequate assumption to accept about organisms than maximizing can be. Or, in other terms, maximizing is a special (boundary) case of satisficing—a case when an organism considers only 'the best' solution to a problem 'good enough'. This may be the case in those domains of life where competition is a legitimate aspect of the task, so that for some of the competitors winning is considered to be the only satisfactory solution in the task. In other domains of life, however, competition plays only a small role, and the range of solutions that are perceived to be sufficient can be wide. In fact, the majority of exchange processes between organisms and their environments are based on the regulation of the organism's state in ways that maintain it sufficiently above the conditions of the minimal threshold of necessity.

It becomes evident that psychology's frequent acceptance of the assumption of maximization in the efforts and outcomes of the behaviour of subjects (animals or humans) may be unwarranted. For example, some studies in child psychology may point to the finding that mothers are better at taking care of infants than fathers. This finding follows from the emphasis on maximization—it is implicitly assumed that both categories of subjects (mothers and fathers) are trying their best to 'win' over the other in competition that is judged by the investigator. This picture of parents' child-minding efforts built around the idea of competition, biases the discourse in psychology in ways that need not be warranted. Alternatively, mothers and fathers need not be in competition with each other (as an individual father and mother, or as the class of mothers against the class of fathers), but may play *complementary* and *supportive* roles. The mother may indeed be 'better' than the father in the care of an infant, by merely taking greater responsibility for the task, but the father can take over that task and perform it in ways that are good enough. Both the mother's and the father's ways of giving care to the infant are sufficient (although these ways are undoubtedly different). Thus, the comparison between the mother and the father along the lines of the maximization assumption can seriously bias child psychology's knowledge base about parenting. In fact, the question of mechanisms of parenting (shared by both mothers and fathers, but implemented in different ways) is replaced by the question of outcomes (parental behaviour) viewed in the context of implied mother—father 'competition' or rivalry.

Obviously there may exist some psychological phenomena to which the assumption of maximization fits well. However, the application of that assumption to almost all phenomena in psychology, and without considering the nature of the phenomena in the first place, leads psychology into a conceptual dead-end where only a careful theoretical analysis can free pscy-hologists' empirical inclinations.

As in the case with other basic assumptions described in this chapter, the acceptance of one of the assumptions instead of the other, explicitly or implicitly, determines the kind of information that empirical research in the discipline can obtain about the given phenomena. It determines where and how psychologists try to find lawfulness in their empirical data, and where they fail to find it.

2.6 Conceptualization of lawfulness

Dissatisfaction with the 'law-less' nature of psychology surfaces in psychol-ogists' thinking from time to time. It usually proceeds as follows: psychology has not revealed any fundamental laws of behaviour or thinking, its knowl-edge base contains a poorly ordered multitude of empirical facts, common-sensical concepts, and mediocre predictions of a statistical kind. Quite often, this unhappy picture is followed by a more positive note of reference to the 'infancy' of the discipline (with a reference to the underlying assumption that the science which is now in its infancy will some day 'grow up'). Sometimes, the standard explanation along the lines 'we do not have enough data about X' is used as an apology for the shallowness of much of the scientific thinking in psychology.

Lack of data is always the case in any scientific venture, the aim of which is the acquisition of new information and the arrival at new understanding. However, by mere accumulation of data, laws of psychology cannot be revealed. These laws need to be actively constructed by scientists. That construction of laws is based on the empirical data on the one hand, and on the assumptions about what the 'law' is and how to construct it, on the other. The scientific endeavor is always based on the interaction of the scientist's mind with his activities by which the empirical phenomenology of the particular branch of science is explored.

Kurt Lewin was one of the few theoretically minded psychologists of the past who worried about the lack of theoretical analysis of what is lawful in psychology. His analysis of the theoretical traditions of psychology led him to outline the implicit differences in what is considered lawful in psychology. Following the traditions stemming from mediaeval physics (which, in its turn, originated in Aristotle's philosophy), psychology was seen by Lewin to follow the lead of physics in determining what 'lawful' means. Lewin (1931, p. 144) remarked:

> For Aristotle those things are lawful, conceptually intelligible, which occur *without exception*. Also, and this he emphasizes particularly, those are lawful which occur *frequently*. Excluded from the class of the conceptually intelligible as 'mere chance' are those things that occur only *once*, individual events as such. Actually since the behavior of a thing is determined by its essential nature, and this essential nature is exactly the abstractly defined class (that is, the sum total of the common characteristics of a whole group of objects), it follows that each event, as a particular event, is chance, undetermined.

Contemporary child psychology has continued along the Aristotelian lines in its conceptualization of lawfulness. Abstractly defined classes of individual subjects are often believed to be explained by the abstract essences that are used as the classification bases. Lewin's example (1931, p. 153) illustrates that operation of thought:

> The fact that three-year-old children are quite often negative is considered evidence that negativism is inherent in the nature of the three-year-olds, and the concept of a negativistic age or stage is then regarded as an explanation (though perhaps not a complete one) for the appearance of negativism in a given particular case! . . .
> The classificatory character of its concepts and the emphasis on frequency are indicated methodologically by the commanding significance of statistics in contemporary psychology. The statistical procedure, at least in its commonest application in psychology, is the most striking expression of this Aristotelian mode of thinking. In order to exhibit the common features of a given group of facts, the *average* is calculated. This average acquires a representative value, and is used to characterize (as 'mental age') the properties of 'the' two-year-old.

The use of 'essences' of classes to establish the meaning of lawfulness in psychology has perhaps been the most widespread application, but by no means is it the only possible one. Lewin himself emphasized the need to transcend that Aristotelian notion through conceptualizing the relationships of a person and the environment in terms of field theory. His suggestion (see also Lewin, 1933, 1939) involves the recognition of lawfulness in the *single cases* of person–environment relationships, thus dissociating the concept of lawfulness from the idea of recurrence of the phenomena. Such treatment of lawfulness is inherently related to the structural-wholistic assumption (2.4), as well as to the notion of systemic causality (see 2.7). The lawfulness of individual persons' psychological phenomena has been claimed by various psychologists over time (see Franck, 1982; Grossman, 1986 for overview). From the perspective of developmental psychology, the assumption of lawfulness has to proceed one step further and include the *newly emerging particular instances* of phenomena that result from the process of development of the given child.

2.7 Assumptions of causality

The issue of what is lawful in psychology is closely connected with the conceptualization of causality in investigators' minds. Causality has been one of the most fiercely debated issues in the history of philosophy since the times of ancient Greece. The types of causality outlined by Aristotle have been intermittently used by people both in everyday life and science. Several causes can function in parallel, at the same time. Aristotle outlines the *material* cause as being that out of which a thing comes to be and which persists . . . e.g the bronze of the statue, the silver of the bowl.' (*Physica*, book II, 194:25). His treatment of the *formal* cause linked the outcome that is being caused to the essence of the class to which the outcome belongs. The *efficient* cause referred to 'the primary source of the change or coming to rest; e.g. the man who gave advice is a cause, the father is the cause of the child, and generally what makes of what is made and what causes change of what is changed' (*Physica*, book II, 194:30). Finally, Aristotle emphasizes the *purpose* as the cause—acting 'for the sake of' something is considered the cause of that thing (Hardie and Gaye, 1930).

Aristotle's conceptualization of the four different senses in which cause is thought of constitutes an effort to analyze causality into its constituents. However, he is not blind to the relationships between causes, and to the issue of presence versus absence of the causes:

> Some things cause each other reciprocally, e.g. hard work causes fitness and *vice versa*, but again not in the same way, but one as end, the other as the origin of change. Further the same thing is the cause of contrary results. For that which by its presence brings about one result is sometimes blamed for bringing about the contrary by its absence. Thus we ascribe the wreck of a ship to the absence of the pilot whose presence was the cause of its safety. (*Physica*, book II, 195:10, quoted via Hardie and Gaye, 1930).

Different conceptualizations of causality that scientists adhere to serve as basic assumptions in their research. Like other basic assumptions outlined in this chapter, conceptualization of causality determines what kinds of empirical data are derived from reality in the course of scientific research. For example, a neuropsychologist may elect to use Aristotle's notion of the material cause as *the* meaning of cause in his empirical research. A cognitive psychologist studying similar phenomena may stick to defining causality in terms of Aristotle's formal cause. A positivist may solve the difficulty with defining causality by denying its existence at all. All these scientists, when narrowing down the meaning of causality to fit their respective inclinations, would easily deny the relevance of reciprocal causality in their research. As a result, their research activities would not result in empirical data that could retain information about reciprocal relationships present within the phenomenon under study.

The scientific meanings of causality are also dependent on the semantics of the ordinary language terms that are used in discourse (von Glasersfeld, 1974). Brown and Fish (1983) have demonstrated that causality is implied by verbs that point towards either the subject or object in ordinary-language sentences. The implicit causality embedded in the semantic structure of language serves as the basis for building more explicit cognitive models of casuality attributions.

In most general terms, scientists' basic assumptions about causality are of two kinds. Causality is considered to be either *elementaristic* or *systemic*. In the first case, a certain causal factor A is considered to cause an outcome B, under all circumstances. In the second case, the outcome (B) is considered to be a result of interaction of parts of the causal system A (that includes parts a1, a2, a3, etc.). When the assumption of elementaristic causality guides the investigator's thinking, explanation of an outcome is considered sufficient when the particular causal agent is specified. For example, a child's perform-ance in mathematics at school can be attributed to the child's 'intelligence' is general, or 'Q-factor' in particular. Such an approach refrains from considering the interaction of the specified causal factor with other similar factors, or external conditions, and it implicitly accepts the assumption of elementaristic causality. Explanations through reference to a psychological term that serves as an explanatory principle (see Bateson, 1972—Metalogue: What is instinct?) are widespread in psychology.

In the history of occidental sciences, the canons of elementaristic causality can be traced back to David Hume. Hume (in *A Treatise on Human Nature*, first published in 1738, here cited in a concentrated form via Hume, 1854, pp. 221–223) outlines the following rules that have influenced scientists' discourse about causality since his time.

(1) The cause and effect must be contiguous in space and time.
(2) The cause must be prior to the effect.
(3) There must be a constant union betwixt the cause and effect.
(4) The same cause always produces the same effect, and the same effect never arises but from the same cause.
(5) Where several different objects produce the same effect, it must be by means of some quality which we discover to be common amongst them.
(6) The difference in the effects of two resembling objects must proceed from that particular in which they differ.
(7) When any object increases or diminishes with the increases or diminution of its cause, it is to be regarded as a compounded effect, derived from

the union of several different effects which arise from the several difference parts of the cause. The absence or presence of one part of the cause is here supposed to be always attended with the absence or presence of a proportionable part of the effect. This constant conjunction sufficiently proves that the one part is the cause of the other.

(8) An object which exists for any time in its full perfection without any effect is not the sole cause of that effect, but requires to be assisted by some other principle, which may forward its influence and operation.

It is evident that Hume's conceptualization of causality involves a basically static view of the world, where independent objects are constantly intertwined with one another in space and time ('constant conjunction'). The same cause always produces the same effect, and the latter can only result from the particular constant cause—which is immutable and would give rise to the same effect at every time it occurs. Discussing the issue of constant cause–effect relationship, Hume (1854), p. 222) comments:

> The same cause always produces the same effect, and the same effect never arises but from the same cause. This principle we derive from experience, and is the source of most of our philosophical reasonings. For when by any clear experiment we have discovered the causes or effects of any phenomenon, we immediately extend our observation to every phenomenon of the same kind, without waiting for the constant repetition, from which the first idea of this relation is derived.

This quote illustrates the acceptance of the ideas of *homogeneous* classes by Hume—not only are cause-effect relationships constant, but once they are established in the case of some cases (through 'any clear experiment'), that finding can be extended to *all* cases of the given class (kind). Furthermore, Hume's conceptualization of causality involves additive elementarism (as described in 2.4), if we consider his Rule 7. Both the cause and the effect are separable into their parts (elements), so that if some of the cause-elements are subtracted from the cause, the 'proportionable' extent of effect is likewise altered. The contemporary thinking about decomposition of outcomes of some study into an additive conglomerate of their 'causes' (as exemplified by the use of regression and analysis of variance methodology) follows faithfully the guidelines established by Hume, who, however, was aware of the limits of applicability of that idea. He cautioned against overly wide extension of Rule 7 (Hume, 1854, pp. 222–223):

> We must, however, beware not to draw such a conclusion [i.e. that absence or presence of a part of cause relates directly to absence or presence of the proportionable part of effect] from a few experiments. A certain degree of heat gives pleasure; but it does not follow, that if you augment it beyond a certain degree, the pleasure will likewise augment; for we find that it degenerates into pain.

In contrast to the atomistic and static world view inherent in Hume's thinking about causality, the conceptualization of *systemic* causality emphasizes the functional relationships between different parts of the causal system (Weiss, 1978). These relationships give rise to different outcomes. Thinking in terms of systemic causality has developed in conjunction with those areas of science where the objects of investigation are sufficiently complex to render element-aristic notions of causality a priori inadequate—ecology (see Hutchinson, 1948), medicine (see Kuipers, 1984; Kuipers and Kassirer, 1984), economics and psychology (Bandura, 1983; Maruyama, 1963; Simon and Rescher, 1966).

Systemic causality can be either *circular* or *linear* in its form. In the biological world, the overwhelming majority of causal mechanisms are circular or cylic—i.e. a series of biological or biochemical processes is organized in such a way as to form a closed circle of mutual transitions, the byproducts of which lead to certain outcomes. In the case of such a cyclical arrangement of the relationships of the parts of the causal system (see Figure 2.1), it is not possible to attribute causality for the outcomes (X, Y, Z) of the system to any one (or few) of its parts (A, B, C, D, E) separately from the others. It is the whole cyclically arranged system that causes the outcomes, and not any single components of the system.

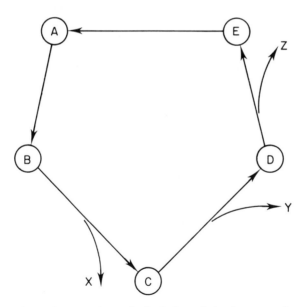

Figure 2.1. A schematic depiction of circular systemic
causality

The linear form of systematic causality involves a sequence of factors (A, B, C, D) that are parts of the causal system, which lead to a certain direct outcome (X), or to Y that illustrates the case where the outcome is a byproduct of the system:

$$A \rightarrow B \rightarrow C \rightarrow D \rightarrow \text{outcome X}$$
$$\downarrow$$
$$\text{outcome Y}$$

In the case of linear systemic causality, it is obviously possible for an investigator to limit the analysis of causality to the immediate predecessors of the outcomes (D for X, C for Y), and thus reduce the sequentially organized causal system to an emphasis is one of its constituents that is temporally the closest to the outcome. Many common-sense treatments of causality involve such reduction. Consider a hypothetical example of a person who explains her/his misbehavior under the influence of alcohol only through the effect of that substance. She eliminates certain factors in the chain of interrelated causal events that preceded the actual alcohol intake (e.g. frustration at home → need for company → meeting friends in the street → their suggestion for having a drink→ . . .) from her causal analysis. Only the immediate antecedent (drinking) is considered to be the cause of the outcome (misbehaviour) in this reduction of the actual causal system to an elementaristic model of causality. The beginning part of the causal chain is dropped from consideration, and only the proximal (antecedent) event in the chain is attributed the status of the cause. This example need not illustrate the general rule in reduction of causality from its systemic-linear nature to an elementaristic attribution. In fact, any particular, even in a sequence of the causal structure leading to an outcome, may be separated from its context and attributed the status of 'the cause'. Sometimes investigators subscribe to the cognitive explanation of an outcome of a long causal sequence of events through selecting an event close to the beginning of the sequence. The most vivid example of such reduction of linear causal system to elementarist causality can be found in psychonalytic explanation of adults' pscychological problems by pointing to some events that took place in early childhood. Causal inference from problems in infancy in those of adulthood is thus made, bypassing all the events of later childhood and adolescence that are the intermediate predecessors of the adult's psychological states.

Both the elementaristic and systemic causality as described here are context-free in their nature. The functioning of the causes and causal systems described thus far excludes reference to any contextual conditions that are either necessary or constrain the transition from causes to outcomes. The difference between *context-free* and *context-bound* conceptualizations of causality leads to the distribution of *direct* and *catalyzed* causality. The first of these two, as mentioned, is context-free: when that cognitive model is applied by a researcher to the research materials no stipulation about external circumstances of its applicability is required. The second model—called here catalyzed causality—involves such external conditions which themselves do not participate in the causal process, but their presence is necessary for allowing the causal system to function. Both elementaristic and systemic causality models can be catalyzed. For example, in order to let an elementaristic causal connection A→X become actual, an additional catalytic condition C is necessary:

$$A \rightarrow X$$

Likewise, the systemic-circular model of causality may be catalyzed:

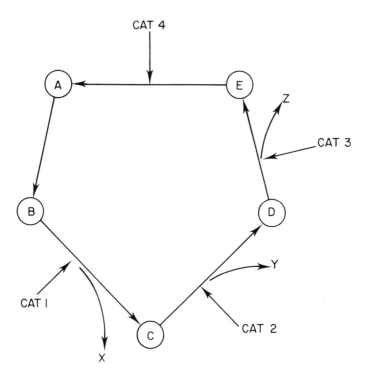

Figure 2.2. A schematic depiction of the catalyzed version of circular systemic causality ('cat' = catalyzing agent)

The notion of catalyzed causality introduces the role of the context which is necessary for the cause→effect relationships to be present. The catalyzing agents themselves do not produce the effects, and are not direct parts of the causal system. Their presence, however, is necessary for the outcome to emerge as the result of the work of the causal system. An example of catalyzed causality can be seen in the thinking of cancer researchers, who use the distinction between carcinogens (causes that produce cancer) and co-carcinogens (agents that do not produce the disease by themselves, but whose presence enables carcinogens to cause tumors). In psychology, it is part of the stock of basic knowledge of experimenters who condition animals in learning experiments, that the success of their conditioning efforts depends upon some 'incentive conditions'—circumstances of the setting and of the state of the animal—without which the animal's learning cannot be demonstrated.

Different perspectives on conceptualizing causality constitute the basic assumptions that lay the foundation for investigators' research efforts. Once a certain view of causality is accepted—implicitly or explicitly—it determines the outer range of possible interpretations that the investigator may devise by the end of his empirical study.

In sciences that are influenced by positivist thought, the issue of causality may be resolved through the denial of its existence, and through its replacement by the measurement of formal relationships between variables. However, the common-sense interest in the meaning of the data, conceptualized in terms of some form of causality, remains implicitly present in the thinking of the majority of psychologists (see Valsiner, 1986). The basic assumptions about causality constitute cognitive models that guide our thinking about psychological phenomena, both in psychology and in our everyday life.

2.8 Scientific background of basic assumptions in psychology: common sense and classical physics

It has been demonstrated by many scientists that psychology has taken over its axioms from the 'hard science' of classical physics. As was shown above, psychology's concepts of lawfulness originate in Aristotle's metaphysics, which has produced a discrepancy in the discipline between pscyhological phenomena and psychology's knowledge base. Lewin (1931) advocated the replacement of Aristotelian physics with another classical-physical basis for psychology's thought models—that of Galileian physics. Haslerud (1979) and Brandt (1973) have likewise pointed to the classical-mechanics roots of psychology.

Without doubt the majority of psychology's models of thought originate in classical physics. However, there seems to have been a powerful social choice-mechanism operational in the coining of psychology's models—the common-sense thinking of the laypersons who served as consumers of psychology's applied efforts in society. Ways of thinking *which resemble the style of physics* (which, obviously, has been considered a science with considerable social prestige in Western industrializing societies) *and which follow the content of common-sense ideas* (which are shared by laypersons within the culture) about human beings, their thinking and behaviour, and the ways in which different events (conflicts, personnel selection, etc.) can be managed, found their way to becoming accepted as the basic assumptions underlying psychological research. The limiting role of common-sense thinking in selective acceptance of physics-based thought models in psychology has been demonstrated by Smedslund (1978, 1980) and Harré

(1981). Harré conceptualizes psychological theories as social talk, which constitutes one of the many kinds of discourse forms in a society. His analysis of the content of some examples of contemporary theorizing in experimental social psychology leads him to characterize psychological talk in quite direct terms (Harré, 1981, pp. 219–220):

> In looking at psychological theories *as* talk, we are free to consider them as one among several possible contributions to the interpretation of what is going on, and to examine them for their display of 'interests' and the uses of rhetorics to further those interests. It may be that a psychologist chooses a rhetoric because that is what he thinks is demanded of him by his professional colleagues and by the expressive demands of his social circle. By talking and writing in a certain way, he publicly displays himself as 'rational' and presents himself as a 'scientist'. In a similar way, a [British] Trade Unionist may adopt a rhetoric for making television appearances which he would never use in everyday life, displaying himself as serious, committed, a mere servant of his Executive Committee, and so on.

The acceptance of ideas from classical physics into psychology has taken place under the mediation of the common sense of psychologists and the social expectations placed upon psychologists by laypersons in society. The common sense—shared by psychologists and laypersons—contains a set of basic assumptions that are axiomatically and usually implicitly considered to hold true for psychological phenomena. The particular assumptions outlined above—separation of person from environment, emphasis on static aspects of phenomena over their dynamic side, assuming homogeneity within populations and individuals, tendency towards an additive elementarism in viewing psychological phenomena, considering psychology's subjects to be 'maximizers' rather than 'satisficers', feeling secure in the lawfulness of 'big numbers', and electing to look for some (rather than other) kinds of causality in the phenomena—all of them guide a psychologist's and layperson's efforts to make sense of psychological phenomena. In the situation where psychology lacks an emphasis towards 'self-analysis' of the set of basic assumptions on which much of its empirical activity is based, no breakthrough in the basic knowledge can take place. Instead, the discipline is limited to the uncontrolled and implicit following of the fads and fashions in the society, where different basic assumptions may sometimes gain dominance in laypersons' minds, only to lose it after a while. Psychology's 'recurrent structure' of general approaches to its phenomena (Buss, 1978; Flanagan, 1981) resonates with the fluctuations in the implicit social representations (see Moscovici, 1984) in the culture, and follows the latter.

2.9 Cultural nature of the basic assumptions: can psychology become a culture-free science?

All of psychology's basic assumptions that were outlined above are products of cultural history—as long as it is understood that all human psychological phenomena are products of social relationships. These assumptions constitute social representations, or cultural cognitive folk models, that function as socially constructed cognitive devices to help individual persons in their thinking. As social representations, these models undergo change in unison with historical changes in the culture. These latter changes may be relatively conservative, in comparison with political and social events in societies, which sometimes may take place in a very short historical time interval. A study of the history of the culture(s) within which a particular scientific discipline has emerged can enlighten our understanding of the background of the basic assumptions that have served as the foundation for the discipline. For example, the Puritan cultural innovation in seventeenth-century England and Pietiṣt religious movements in Germany (e.g. see Merton, 1936) set the stage for the development of what is widely known as 'the scientific method'—first in astronomy and physics, and later in other disciplines. The separation of the secular science from religion was itself embedded in the Puritan religious belief system, that made such differentiation available to the generations of scientists who received their primary socialization under the novel social environments. In contrast, the alterative scientific method based on the idea of systemic analysis of phenomena emerged in the social context of *Naturphilosophie* as that school of thought was triggered by social events in continental European cultures in the second half of the eighteenth century. Both of the two scientific methods are cultural-historical inventions, which is further exemplified by the almost religious fervent which is characteristic of proponents of either of the two when they sometimes set out to deny the other the social status of being labelled 'scientific'.

It is evident that different cultures around the world have different histories, which give rise to different social representations about psychological phenomena and to the ways of their investigation. The cultural-historical nature of psychology's basic assumptions leads to the crucial issue of how psychology's 'scientific method' may be a product of only some cultures' histories, so that it may have limited applicability to psychological phenomena of *Homo sapiens* as a species, i.e. across cultures all around the world. The basic assumptions accepted within psychology in Western industrialized countries have a paradoxical effect on the discipline's knowledge base. On the one hand, these assumptions delimit the ways in which psychology's subject matter is studied. That narrows down the otherwise unmanageable multitude of approaches to the few that 'make sense'. On the other hand, these assumptions serve as the basis for our inability to explain many psychological phenomena that are evident in cultural conditions which differ from ours. The basic assumptions connect psychologists' scientific and extrascientific thinking—as persons within the given culture, psychologists are devoted to its mores that they have learned to honor from childhood. At the same time—as scientists their belief in these mores should not blind them to their relativity. Kingsley Davis, in his analysis of the sociological background of the supposedly science-based 'mental hygiene' movement in the USA in the 1930s, reached a conclusion that:

> Mental hygiene hides its adherence behind a scientific façade, but the ethical premises reveal themselves on every hand, partly through a blindness to scientifically relevant facts. It cannot combine the prestige of science with the prestige of the mores, for science and the mores unavoidably conflict at some point, and the point where they most readily conflict is precisely where 'mental' (i.e. social) phenomena are concerned. We can say, in other words, that devotion to the mores entails an emotional faith in illusion. Devotion to science, on the other hand, when social illusion constitutes the subject matter of that science, entails the sceptial attitude of an investigator rather than of the believer toward the illusion. (Davis, 1938, p. 65).

Since psychology as science is inevitably embedded in the framework of 'illusions' which cultural history has developed as basic assumptions in relating to the world, it cannot solve the problem of cultural guidance of the science, neither by denial of its cultural relativity (e.g. as exemplified in the positivistic and physicalist traditions in the discipline), nor through replacement of its scientific goals by the devout following of some cultural ideals (e.g. as exemplified in different versions of the 'humanistic psychology'). A possible way to overcome the difficulty created by the implicit cultural-historical nature of the basic assumptions is the relativistic perspective. That perspective entails simultaneous analysis of the psychology of the subject and of the investigator, relating the psychological data obtained from the former to the web of conceptualizations used by the latter. Or, in other terms, the investigator is expected to reveal the hidden basic assumptions of his/her empirical research, and relate those assumptions to the research materials in that research. No empirical research result in psychology has absolute truth value on its own. The only truth value psychological data possess is explicitly relative to the set of theoretical assumptions in the investigator's thinking. For example, a certain finding by a German child psychologist studying Samoan children does not characterize Samoan children in the absolute sense as a piece of knowledge in the ever-accumulating databank, but provides information about these children relative to the particular set of assumptions that this particular psychologist used in his/her study. Since different psychologists use different, and quite often implicit, assumptions, then it is not surprising that different psychologists have produced different and mutually non-complementary data, although they may start their investigation from the same set of research materials. If the traditional way in dealing with the conceptual issue in psychology has been to expect the 'data to speak for themselves' (relationship INVESTIGATOR (==) DATA), then the present framework includes the investigator's relationship to one's own conceptual background in the inferential process (relationship: (INVESTIGATOR (==) ASSUMPTIONS) (==) DATA).

The suggested relativistic approach replaces the investigators' emphasis on *similarity in likeness* (e.g. efforts to find similar results in the same psychological experiments in different cultures) by an emphasis on *similarity in diversity*. The former is a special case of the latter. If psychological processes are viewed as context-dependent generative mechanisms of action and cognition, then it is unlikely that they generate similar outcomes over time (although they themselves may remain the same). Therefore, it is unlikely that two investigators, who start from the same basic assumptions and who study highly similar subjects, end up with similar results. Such dissimilarity in their results (which are outcomes of the work of some psychological processes in the subjects) does not necessitate the positing of dissimilar psychological processes that stand 'behind' the 'data'. Different outcomes can be produced by the same psychological process, as well as similar outcomes by different processes. We can learn about that background of the 'data' only when we make the investigators' implicit assumptions explicit.

Furthermore, if two investigators start from mutually irreconcilable basic assumptions, then their empirical research results remain largely separate from each other. For instance, if one researcher views a phenomenon through the perspective of elementaristic causality, and the other through the prism of systemic causality, then the empirical findings of these investigators will necessarily differ from each other. Knowledge of the epistemological background of that difference may help us to understand the ways in which otherwise similar investigators (e.g. psychologists) may arrive at vastly different empirical results, that are derived from the same psychological phenomenon. A relativistic perspective accomplishes a task that can help to clarify *why* psychology has resulted in many different perspectives and empirical data, rather than accomplishes the impossible task of reducing that variability to some narrow, singularly 'true' perspective.

2.10 Summary: basic assumptions in psychology and the study of development

This chapter made explicit a number of social representations on which psychology has been built and which are products of cultural history. These representations—called basic assumptions in the chapter—form the axiomatic basis of psychology's knowledge structure. A number of these assumptions are antithetical to the study of developmental phenomena, and are therefore better avoided by developmental psychologists. First, the exclusive separation of the person from environment which has been widely used in non-developmental psychology makes it impossible to study developmental processes because the latter are open-systems phenomena. Development is possible only in the case of open systems, where the developing organism is intertwined with its environment and changes it in the process of development. This feature of development calls for inclusive separation of organism and environment, as was outlined in the chapter.

Secondly, the non-developmental traditions in psychology have emphasized the static aspect of psychological phenomena, and have eliminated their dynamic side from consideration. This practice has beeen based on the basic assumption of the higher relevance of the 'being' (ontological) side of phenomena over their 'becoming' or changing aspects. The inappropriateness of this basic assumption for developmental research was outlined—developmental processes cannot be studied via methods that eliminate the change in phenomena from consideration through an emphasis on 'true' measures of the static being.

Other basic assumptions likewise direct psychological research in directions of thinking that are antithetical to the study of developmental processes. Psychological phenomena are often viewed from the perspective of additive elementarism that eliminates the systemic relationships between different parts of an organism and environment from consideration. Usually, this approach coincides with the application of the cognitive model of elementaristic causality in the research process. Lawfulness is often considered from the standpoint of recurrence of specimens of phenomena that belong to the same class. This approach to psychological laws eliminates from the research process both the variability within a class, and dynamic changes in the particular phenomena from one to another instance of occurrence. The actions and thinking of human beings are often considered to work towards maximization of certain outcomes of their actions and thoughts, while minimizing others. This implicit cognitive model may be inadequate even for a few areas of non-developmental psychology, and may be a gross misrepresentation of developing organisms which may function on the basis of satisficing—solving particular issues encountered in their development in ways that are good enough, rather than resulting in maximum benefit of any sort. Developmental processes are characterized by high redundancy in potential routes of change, and complementarity in the functions of different factors that canalize development, rather than by highly 'economic' and 'cost-saving' strategies. Development in its reality is wasteful, whereas the majority of cognitive models on which psychological research on development is based include the assumption of rational economy of the process.

The brief analysis of the culture-bound axiomatic basis of much of psychology in chapter 2 served two functions. It clarified the 'blind spots' of psychological theory in general, and its conceptual difficulties when it deals with developmental issues in particular. Secondly, it outlined the notion of a relativistic science of psychology, where the empirical data are located at the intersection of the investigator's axiomatic bases and the psychological reality, and where empirical results are meaningful only relative to the investigator's assumptions. The latter, of course, have to be made explicit in every case. The next chapter will deal with a number of major theoretical frameworks that exist in developmental psychology. The basic assumptions utilized in these theories will be analyzed, and the links of these theories to the one outlined in this book will be demonstrated.

Theories of development and general methodology in psychology

The basic cultural-cognitive axioms that have shaped human thought and the science of psychology have created a situation where very few empirically oriented investigators study developmental processes. Indeed even fewer psychologists have tried to deal with the theoretical issues of development. The purpose of this chapter is to analyze those attempts which have been made at theoretical explanation of development that serve as the historical predecessors of the present theory.

3.1 Frames of reference in psychology

Any theoretical or empirical stance in developmental psychology is embedded in a reference frame of thought, which in its turn comes from investigators' cultural backgrounds. These reference frames guide investigators' thinking towards some (rather than other) theoretical and empirical research issues and strategies. Different studies of child development have been conducted within different reference frames. Very often it is the difference of these frames that makes it impossible to relate different studies, or that makes certain kinds of data irrelevant for some theories.

3.1.1 The intra-individual frame of reference

This reference frame treats all issues of an individual's psychological organization as results of some processes (or their interaction) *within* the individual person. The majority of personality theories are phrased within the intra-individual reference frame. As an example, consider Freud's reconstruction of personality using the concepts of id, ego and superego. All these three components of personality are located within the person, and their functional relationships determine how the person exists as a personality. The personality is decontextualized, and explained fully in terms of its intrinsic organization.

In developmental psychology, any theoretical approach that explains development either by reference to elementaristic traits or systemic mechanisms which are supposed to locate strictly inside the organism uses the intra-individual reference frame. Very often psychologists who use this reference frame model their thinking along the lines of traditional genetics, posit the existence of psychological analogues of genes that are supposed to cause temporal unfolding of predetermined developmental sequences of phenomena. For example, the widespread acceptance of Piaget's stage-account of cognitive development without a simultaneous emphasis on his theory of equilibration is built on such predeterministic ideology. Children are considered to progress through the predetermined sequence of stages *because* that is believed to be the normative sequence of development. Tautological explanations (e.g. 'John, who is 14 years old, can use formal operations *because* he is at the formal-operational stage') are rampant in such use of Piaget's stage-account. The 'stage' is treated as a concept that supposedly explains the phenomena described by it. Such 'black box' explanations (see Bateson, 1972, pp. 39–40) serve the function of stopping researchers accomplishing the task of disentangling the contents of the 'black box'.

Invariably all maturational accounts of individual organisms' development make use of the intra-individual frame of reference. The use of that framework may be adequate in some domains of developmental biology (e.g. explanation of metamorphosis in insects), but its extension to other species whose ontogenetic existence depends more evenly on both genetic and environmental factors factors can be unwarranted. Even in modern genetics a number of issues (e.g. the principles of the formation of the tertial structure of protein—see Stent, 1981) cannot be explained by straightforward pointing to its genetic code as its intrinsic cause. The ideas of probabilistic epigenesis (Gottlieb, 1976) which constitute an interactive perspective on development are gradually becoming more widely acceptable in developmental biology. The intra-individual frame of reference is of limited use in the explanation of development, since development is a central characteristic of open systems—the definition of which involves an emphasis on organism–environment relationships. To explain open-systems phenomena by attributing causality into the system and failing to mention interdependence with environment equals eliminating the open-systems nature of the phenomena.

3.1.2 The inter-individual frame of reference

This frame of reference is by far the most widely used reference framework in psychology at large. It involves comparison of an individual organism (or samples of organisms) with other individuals (samples), in order to determine the standing of these subjects relative to one another. For example, any comparison of two (or more) persons with one another, resulting in statements like 'Jimmy is better than Johnny and Mary in reading and writing, but worse than the other kids in arithmetic', involves thinking within the inter-individual frame of reference. A quick introspective scanning of our everyday-life activities and thinking may reveal that this frame of reference is very often used, particularly on occasions where inter-individual competition is required, and emphasized. An emphasis on competition between individuals necessarily results in taking into account differences between those individuals. In that emphasis, the inter-individual frame of reference differs cardinally from the intra-individual one which disregards inter-individual variability. In contrast the inter-individual frame of reference promotes the search for differences between individuals in the causal mechanisms underlying their acting and thinking, or at least in the quantitatively variable outcomes produced by qualitatively similar mechanisms that are shared by individuals in a population.

The inter-individual reference frame is also used to compare groups of persons. In this case, groups (samples) serve as the basis for reconstructing the modal or average individual—the prototype for the whole sample (Valsiner, 1984b). For example, a comparison of two samples of subjects—e.g. boys and girls—on some measure that leads to a statement about a difference (or lack of it) between the samples uses this frame of reference. In psychological research literature, we often come across statements like 'the experimental group was *found to do better* than the control group' in an experiment. In these comparisons, both samples—boys and girls, and the experimental and the control group—are dealt with as if they were individuals, who are compared with each other. This is similar to a comparison between Johnny and Jimmy, where a parent of one of them may arrive at a statement, 'Jimmy does better than Johnny in X, Y, or Z'.

In non-developmental psychology, the inter-individual frame of reference has guided the *normative* ('populometric', or 'parametric'—as these terms were used in Raymond B. Cattell, 1944) tradition of psychological measurement. In the case of that reference frame, the environmental context in which the individuals function is excluded from consideration as a part of the particular issue. This feature of the inter-individual frame is similar to the intra-individual reference frame—both explain their phenomena without including their context in the explanation. For example, finding out that Jimmy's IQ score is 115 can lead a psychologist to the comparison of Jimmy with the average for a population (100), and to relative statements such as that 'Jimmy has above-average IQ'. However, Jimmy's particular environmental context in the process of testing his IQ—the test materials, Jimmy's conceptualization of the tasks involved, his motivation to pass the test at the level of his maximum performance at the testing time, etc.—all these aspects are fully and irreversibly eliminated from the psychologist's information base about Jimmy's 'intelligence'. The inter-individual frame of reference leads to decontextualized knowledge, which in its turn leads to attribution-based explanation of the psychological phenomena in question (see Valsiner, 1984a, for further analysis of that aspect). As outlined in chapter 2, psychology's theoretical mainstream emphasizes decontextualization of individual psychological phenomena. From that perspective, the use of the inter-individual frame of reference is very natural. However, its effect on the advancement of psychological knowledge may divert psychologists from theoretical explanations of the issues which the empirical data represent. This danger was nicely described by Cattell (1944, p. 300):

> If individuals can be given a score simply from putting them in rank order—and people can be put in rank order for anything under the sun—there is very little incentive to find the exact nature of the thing with respect to which they are being put in rank order. The facility with which IQ or percentile scores can be used in educational and placement problems has apparently obscured interest, for example, in the problem of the nature of intelligence at different age levels . . . while the readiness with which interests can be ranked . . . seems to have made it superfluous to ask 'What is interest?'.

The use of the inter-individual reference frame in developmental psychology has led the discipline away from the study of developmental processes (see McCall, 1977). This frame of reference is the one in which the use of statistical methods and their epistemological basis fits in most with the scientific goals of the discipline. The emphasis on the use of statistical methods leads developmental investigators *de facto* into the realm of non-developmental empirical questions. The use of correlational techniques applied to longitudinal data from some sample of developing organisms is aimed at detecting inter-age *stability* in the *relative standing* of the individuals within the sample, and does not reveal any information about either the individuals' development, or the development of the sample as a group. McCall has provided an illuminating figurative description of this problem:

> Relying solely on an individual difference approach to establish the validity of infant tests or to learn about mental development is rather like concentrating on predicting a 10-foot height difference in mature giant sequoia trees from the size of seedlings while completely ignoring the issue of how all the trees eventually grow to be over 300 feet tall. (McCall, 1977, p. 338).

Both the intra-individual and inter-individual reference frames, aided by the use of statistical methods, are unfit for the tasks of developmental psychology because of their axiomatic background of decontextualization of phenomena. The inter-individual reference frame cannot capture the generative and creative aspects of development. *Generativity* (as it is defined by Sandor Brent) implies that 'each structure in a developmental series is not merely the predecessor in time but is an active agent in the process by which its successors come into being' (Brent, 1984, p. 156). An inter-individual comparison of children at a certain developmental level does not afford explanation of how the given psychological phenomenon that a particular child demonstrates has developed from (and with the help of) its predecessors. A teacher who compares Johnny with other children in the class and labels him as 'the most difficult child in the class' has shed no light on the developmental question of how Johnny has developed to be 'difficult'.

In a similar vein, the inter-individual reference frame is unsuitable for explaining the *creativity* of development. Brent (1984, p. 156) defines creativity as the process 'by which new forms and new information can be acquired or produced', which 'integrate with a previously existing generative process'. Continuing our hypothetical example—the teacher who has labelled Johnny 'difficult' on the grounds of comparing him with other children in the class has no way of explaining how Johnny might in the future either become a delinquent, or improve and cease to be 'difficult'. From inter-individual comparisons, no *individual* prediction that is based on explanatory theories dealing with the functioning of the individual, can follow (see Allport, 1942). The inter-individual frame of reference may attempt to predict constancy of the relative positioning of individuals in a sample over time, but is insensitive to the functioning of a causal system that generates change in these relative positions of the individual in the group.

3.1.3 The individual-ecological frame of reference

The individual–ecological frame of reference considers an individual person (or a social group—a 'collective' individual) as it acts upon its environment to solve some problem, created at the given time by the given structure of the environment and by the individual's goals. The person's (or group's) actions are viewed in the context of problem-solving situations that emerge in interaction with the environment. Questions asked about these actions concentrate on the issue of *how* (in what ways) a person solves the given problem. Whether she is 'better' or 'worse' at that than other persons are, is unimportant.

The individual–ecological reference frame includes the context of action in its sphere of study. This makes that frame of reference suitable for developmental research. The individual–ecological reference frame is most notably present in Piaget's developmental theory (see 3.2). It is also evident in a number of other research directions of microgenetic kinds (Anzai and Simon, 1979; Duncker, 1945; Köhler, 1925; Werner, 1937, 1957). This frame of reference emphasizes the individual's confrontation with life tasks through which individuals become participants in their own development (see Lerner and Busch-Rossnagel, 1981). However, the individual–ecological frame excludes the purposeful actions of other organisms around the person, who may set up task situations for her with different socially defined end goals in mind. In order to take the social and purposeful organization of individuals' task environments into account, a fourth frame of reference is outlined.

3.1.4 The individual-socioecological frame of reference

The individual–socioecological frame of reference differs from the individual-ecological frame by the presence of *assistance from another individual* (or individuals, groups, etc.) in the process of individual–environment trans-action. Within this reference frame, an individual's actions and thinking to solve a problem that has emerged in the person–environment transaction, is not a solitary, but a social event. A person who is confronted with a problem may ask for help from somebody else, who may be more experienced in solving that kind of a problem. For example, for quite a long time in ontogeny, a child depends upon others who help him to acquire culturally appropriate and successful ways of solving problems in his world. Help can also be sought even from another person who has less experience with the given problem, but who, by being related to the problem solver, can be used as a 'social other' whose presence helps the problem solver to deal with the problem. An example of the latter case is a young mother with a 2-year-old child, whose husband has deserted her. The child, and the mother's feeling of responsibility towards him, may help her to cope with the psychologically traumatic event.

In any species where parent–offspring contact is relatively long and where the adult organisms carry out the task of teaching (explicitly, or by example) their young some important survival skills, the application of the individual–socioecological frame of reference in psychological research is warranted. In developmental psychology, the use of that reference frame is exemplified by Vygotsky's theoretical contributions to the discipline. Child development takes place not only within structured task settings that the child masters in action and thinking, but these settings are purposefully set up to aid the child in the process of development and to guide him towards becoming an adult who has constructed an internalized knowledge base in the course of growing up within a culture, that is sufficient for life within that (and perhaps some other) cultures.

3.1.5 Independence and mixing of reference frames in psychology

It should be admitted that these four reference frames occur in an unevenly distributed fashion across different domains of psychology. Some of these references frames are more usual in some areas than in others. For example, the intra-individual reference frame is usually applied in psychodynamically oriented settings of research and clinical practice, where the goal is to treat the psychological issues of individual clients. The inter-individual reference system is that which the majority of psychologists of quantitative inclination continue to use. It is the most suited framework for solving applied problems that involve the selection of some individuals from a population for a particular task, relatively quickly, on a large scale if necessary, and without much worry about the causality of the phenomena used in the inter-individual comparisons. Only some areas in psychology—particularly in the cognitive domain—have adopted the individual–ecological reference frame. The individual–socioecological frame of reference is rare in contemporary psychology, although the renewed interest in Vygotsky's psychological heritage may perhaps lead more investigators to adopt it. It is adequate for many problems in developmental psychology, where psychological phenomena undergo changes that are guided by 'social others'. For example, a psychological analysis of children's accidents and their prevention may benefit from the latter reference frame (Gärling and Valsiner, 1985).

In accordance with the uneven presence of these reference frames in psychological research traditions, methods of inductive inference in psychology have been invented, mostly to fit the inter-individual frame. It is within this frame that statistical methodology has been put to extensive use—sometimes up to the point where its use becomes a goal in itself for some psychologists' research games! The application of statistical methodology in research conducted within the intra-individual reference frame is also possible, although rare (see A. L. Baldwin, 1940, 1942, 1946; Kelly, 1955). In contrast, the two ecologically oriented reference frames exclude the use of traditional statistical methodology from the research process since their basic assumptions and those of the statistical world view do not match one another (see chapter 5 for a discussion on existing formal methods of modelling development of systems).

It is necessary to stress here that whichever of the four reference systems is adopted depends on the psychologist's general perspective. The scientific value of adopting any of the four is determined by the adequacy of the reference frame to the phenomena under study and the investigator's goals. There is, of course, always the possibility that any of the four frames of reference can be combined with others. In psychology, the inter-individual and intra-individual reference frames have traditionally been linked together. The majority of empirical studies in psychology are conducted within the inter-individual frame of reference, but interpreted within the intra-individual frame. This switching of frames is often unwarranted (see Valsiner, 1986). Likewise, makers of the computerized control systems bear in mind not only the task that the new program must perform, but also depend heavily on the structure of the hardware (intra-individual reference frame) and, in addition, consider the new program's chances of success within the inter-individual reference frame of the competitive market place. In a similar vein, parents of children, who teach the children new skills (that the children develop within their individual–socioecological reference frameworks), are eager to find out from a psychologist 'how my child is doing' in comparison with other children in the given age group. The parents also hope that knowledge and skills that they have helped their children to develop, will be used by the children individually in situations where parental presence and guidance are not available (within the individual–ecological contexts). Educating children for facing different life situations in their future illustrates the combination of the individual–socioecological and individual–ecological frames.

The possibility of combining the four reference frames does not make it a desirable strategy for psychologists to mix them in their research and practice. Although every psychological phenomenon can be simultaneously considered within each of these frames, different research goals of psychologists may make it necessary to consider them separately. A conscious and explicit decision by a psychologist not to use a particular frame of reference on theoretical grounds (despite the fact that its use is possible in practice) may help to reach the particular scientific goals that the psychologist has. The four frames of reference, although combinable, provide science with distinctly different kinds of knowledge, each of which may have its place somewhere in the knowledge structure of psychology.

The two ecological reference frames are at the centre of attention of the research program of the studies of children's action development that is described in this book. Other developmental theories have used these ecological reference frames in the past. The theoretical perspective represented in this book is an attempt to integrate a few of the older, well-known but often incompletely understood, theories in psychology. In order to make the roots of the present theory directly available to the reader, a short overview of theories of the past that constitute the basis of the present one is necessary. All these theories implicitly made use of either the individual–ecological or individual–socioecological reference frames. All of them were dissociated by their authors from the use of intra- or inter-individual frames on theoretical grounds.

The theoretical perspective described in this book is based on the developmental thinking of Jean Piaget, James Mark Baldwin, Heinz Werner, and Lev Vygotsky. It also borrows heavily from the field-theoretical thinking of Kurt Lewin. As will be obvious from the short analysis that follows, all these thinkers developed their theories in an interdependent way. For example, Piaget was strongly influenced by Baldwin, and Vygotsky by Baldwin, Piaget, Werner, and Lewin. All of these thinkers attempted to explain child development along the traditions of systemic thinking of *Naturphilosophie*, as they pondered about different ways in which to explain organism–environment relationships and their deveopment.

3.2 Piaget's theory of development

Piaget's theory of development which is embedded in his genetic epistemology (Piaget, 1972) is one of the precursors of the theoretical framework outlined in this book. Since Piaget's contribution to epistemology is multi-faceted and often reduced to its least developmental aspect (that of his stage theory), it is necessary in this context to analyze the way in which Piaget's theoretical position relates to that outlined here.

In most general terms, Piaget's emphasis on *dynamic structuralism* that involves the subject's *active interaction* with the changing environment in the *process of equilibration* which leads to *restructured knowledge* serves as the main theoretical linkage of his theory to the one presented here.

3.2.1 Dynamic structuralism

Piaget's dynamic structuralism has been an implicit part of his thinking since his earliest writings, thus antedating by far the social fashion for structuralist thought in France after World War II (see Kurzweil, 1980, for an overview of the French structuralist movement). It was, however, the case that the social discourse in France about structuralism motivated Piaget to make *his* kind of structuralist thinking explicit (Piaget, 1970b).

Historically Piaget follows the lead of his predecessors in Gestalt psychology and biology in his refusal to reduce the phenomena of the world into their constituent elements that are void of structural wholeness. In this emphasis, Piaget's roots are in the *Naturphilsophie* of the nineteenth century, mediated via the thinking of J. M. Baldwin and E. Claparede. His conceptualization of 'structure' involves three key ideas: *wholeness, transformation*, and *self-regulation* (Piaget, 1970b, p. 5). The last two ideas are crucial in making Piaget's brand of structuralism developmental in its nature. Structures (in the natural world, as well as in action and thinking) are wholes which are constantly being transformed from one state to another via self-regulatory processes taking place at the intersection of the organism and its environment. Piaget's emphasis on transformation as an operation which transforms one state of a structure into another has been largely left without further elaboration (see Vuyk, 1981, p. 55). The concept of 'self-regulation' entails self-maintenance and 'closure' by the structure. In parallel with the distinction of open and closed systems, Piaget introduced his notion of open versus closed structures (Piaget, 1970b, pp. 14–16 and 44–51. He described closed structures as closed systems:

> the transformations inherent in a structure never lead beyond the system but always engender elements that belong to it and preserve its laws. Again an example will help to clarify: In adding or subtracting any two whole numbers, another whole number is obtained, and one which satisfies the laws of the 'additive group' of whole numbes. It is in this sense that a structure is 'closed', a notion perfectly compatible with the structure's being considered a substructure of a larger one; but in being treated as a substructure, a structure does not lose its own boundaries; the larger structure does not 'annex' the substructure; if anything we have a confederation, so that the laws of the substructure are not

altered but conserved and the intervening change is an enrichment rather than an impoverishment. (Piaget, 1970b, p. 14).

The 'conserved' nature of the closed structure involves the presence of 'perfect' regulations within these structures, which are possible in the case of decontextualized systems (a 'substructure' functions in 'confederation' with a larger structure, in ways that do not alter the former's laws of functioning). From the perspective of the present theoretical system, the paradox in Piaget's developmental theory is embedded in the conjunction of his emphasis on organisms's active role in interaction with the environment on the one hand, and the preferred status alotted in his epistemology to context-free logico-mathematical structures, on the other. This paradoxical nature of Piaget's theory seems to be a historical outgrowth from the efforts evident in the occidental sciences to separate the ideal logical forms of thinking from the complexity of culturally devised and changeable meanings (e.g. Boole, 1854).

Piaget does not deny the existence of other structures, which (in parallel with open systems) he calls 'open structures':

> there is, of course, an immense class of structures which are not strictly logical or mathematical, that is, whose transformations unfold in time: linguistic structures, sociological structures, psychological structures, and so on. Such transformations are governed by laws ('regulations' in the cybernetic sense of the word) which are not in the strict sense 'operations', because they are not entirely reversible (in the sense in which multiplication is reversible by division or addition by subtraction). Transformation laws of this kind depend upon the interplay of anticipation and correction (feedback). (Piaget, 1970b, pp. 15–16).

Although Piaget recognizes the existence of a wide variety of 'open structures', he nevertheless follows his implicit assumption that developmentally such structures are directed towards reduction of their openness. Vuyk has traced the background of this assumption:

> Though Piaget came to agree with Bertalanffy that every structures of [the open] type is open to the environment with interactions between the two, he did add an important restriction. According to Piaget the system always strives for closure. This is due to the fact that an open system *is threatened* by the environment: lack of food, sex, cognitive stimulation, etc. Therefore the organism tries to extend its mastery of the environment, biologically by, for example, the extension of its territory, and cognitively by extending its knowledge of the environment. . . . If the organism could succeed in closing the system this would mean a restriction of the organism's action to a circumscribed field in such a way *that the exchanges would guarantee the conservation of the system*. Seen in this way the closure of the system is no more than a limit that is never attained. (Vuyk, 1981, p. 57; italics mine—J.V.)

Vuyk's analysis of Piaget's axiomatic background brings out the conservative stance that the 'open' structures assume in respect to potential change: these structures are 'threatened' by their environments and tend towards a

state where restricted interdependence with the environments makes it possible for those structures to restrict them to self-conservation. In the case of
'open structures' Piaget introduced the notion of *cyclic order* which in many
ways parallels the issues of systemic causality (discussed in 2.7). Piaget's cyclic
order expresses both the stable (conserved) structure and simultaneously it
'represents an opening to the environment as a source of ailment' (Piaget,
1971b, p. 156).

Piaget's cyclic closure of a structure involves a set of 'dynamic elements'
(A, B, C, . . . Z) of the structure and a corresponding set of 'energetic
elements' (A', B', C', . . . Z') that are necessary for the maintenance of the
former. The cyclic closure of the system is organized by system–environment
interaction, as is evident in a schematic description provided by Piaget
(1971b, p. 156):

$$(A \times A') \to (B \times B') \to (C \times C') \to \dots$$
$$\dots \to (Z \times Z') \to (A \times A') \to \text{etc.}$$

At step, 1, A interacts with A' and results in B. The next step involves
the interaction of B with B' which results in C, and so on, until the interaction
of Z with Z' closes the cycle as it results in A. The cycle maintains itself
through the transformations . . . A to Z to A . . . etc., due to the interaction
with the environment, whereas at the same time the system itself stays in
a 'steady state'. Piaget's explanation of the closure of the open structure
interdependently with the environment illustrates how complex structures can
be maintained, but does not yet offer an explanation for their development.
Development is integrated into this descriptive system when the whole
process cycle (A . . . Z . . . A) assimilates new input information into its
structure with a simultaneous accommodation of the structure to the incoming
information.

3.2.2 Equilibration and re-equilibration as mechanisms of development

Development in Piaget's theoretical system is explained through the process
of equilibration and re-equilibration. For Piaget, equilibration involves the
process that is aimed at elimination of disequilibrium by either a return to a
previously present state, or by a progression to a qualitatively new
equilibrium:

> We can observe a process (hence the term 'equilibration') leading from certain
> states of equilibrium to others, qualitatively different, and passing through
> multiple 'nonbalances' and reequilibrations. Thus the problems to be solved
> involve various forms of equilibrium, the reasons for nonbalance, and above
> all the causal mechanisms, or methods, of equilibrations and reequilibrations.
> It is especially important to stress from the very beginning the fact that, in
> certain cases, the reequilibrations merely form returns to previous equilibriums;
> however, those that are fundamental for development consist, on the contrary,
> in the formations not only of new equilibriums but also in general of better

equilibriums. We can, therefore, speak of 'increasing equilibrations,' and raise the question of self-organization. (Piaget, 1977, pp. 3–4).

This quote from Piaget reflects the bifurcational nature of his understanding of the process of equilibration. Under some conditions, a disequilibrium situation is resolved by a return to a previous (or similar to previous) equilibrium state, but under other circumstances the process of equilibration can lead to the establishment of a new equilibrium state. The qualitative 'break' between the return to the previous state and advancement to a new state captures the qualitative nature of development. The process of 'progressing equilibration' (compare also Vuyk's (1981, p. 68) term 'improving equilibration' for Piaget's 'equilibration majorante'—see Inhelder, Garcia, and Voneche, 1976, pp. 39–42; Piaget, 1977, part 6) constitutes the theoretical explanation that captures the open-ended nature of development.

Piaget views equilibration as existing in three forms. At the beginning of subject–object interaction there is the equilibration between the assimilation of action schemes and their accommodation of the objects of action. The second form of equilibration involves mutual relationships between schemes. Finally, Piaget (1977, pp. 8–9) outlines the importance of the progressive equilibrium between differentiation and integration of the organism—involving relations of the schemes to the totality that includes them as its constituents.

3.2.3 Complementary processes in development: assimilation and accommodation

Piaget's developmental theory is built on the role that assimilation and accommodation *interdependently* play in the organism's *process of adaptation* to its environment. As soon as the environment changes, the adaptation process begins as well. Since the environments of living systems are in constant flux, the process of adaptation cannot end as long as the organisms are alive. In the case of humans adaptation involves also purposeful action upon environment with the goal of reaching a new state of the organism itself.

Assimilation and accommodation 'are not two separate functions but the two functional poles, set in opposition to each other, of any adaptation' (Piaget, 1971b, p. 173). There is no assimilation (integration of new elements to an existing scheme or schema) without its corresponding accommodation (the change of the scheme/schema to fit the conditions of the environment). The interdependence (rather than independent coexistence) of assimilation and accommodation constitutes the mechanism of adaptation, so when these concepts are used to explain development it is it that interdependence that must be explicitly outlined (see Figure 3.1)

The assimilation/accommodation relationship is one of Piaget's concepts

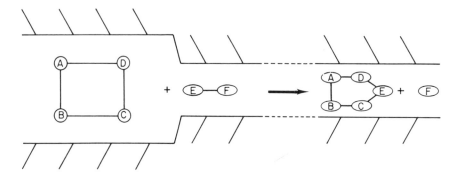

Figure 3.1. A schematic depiction of the interdependence of assimilation and accommodation in Piaget's equilibration theory. The original structure ABCD that exists in the 'wide area' of the environment receives an input from the environment in the form of structure EF, while moving into the 'narrow area' of the environment. Element E from the input structure is assimilated into the original structure, at the same time as the new structure accommodates to the environment (by shrinking its size), and the form of the components of all of the structural units. (The latter change is depicted in the form of transformation of the circles into ellipses in the scheme)

that has been consistently misrepresented in many didactic efforts to teach beginning psychology students about Piaget. Very often, the two concepts are presented in textbooks as if they were separate adaptation mechanisms, which are applicable independently from each other. That basic misunderstanding of Piaget's central concepts involved in adaptation continues beyond the teaching contexts, and has triggered Piaget himself to emphasize the gravity of that misunderstanding (Piaget, 1970a, 1971b).

3.2.4 Piaget and non-equilibrium thermodynamics in explanation of development

The bifurcational idea of the process of development has been influential in contempoary physical and biological sciences over recent decades (see Bohm, 1980; Pattee, 1973; Polanyi, 1958; Prigogine, 1973, 1976b; Weiss, 1969). It has revolutionized scientific thinking in these sciences. In psychology, however, this idea has been largely overlooked, despite its availability (London, 1949; London and Thorngate, 1981).

There exists, however, a difference between Piaget's conceptualization of development in terms of equilibration and that of contemporary non-equilibrium thermodynamics (Prigogine, 1976a, 1982). Differently from Piaget, the latter perspective emphasizes the role of *increasing disequilibration* in the development of new structures. This process of the development of new structures through amplification of fluctuations in biological systems has been described by Prigogine and Nicolis (1971, p. 113):

a new structure or organization . . . is always the result of an instability. It originates in a fluctuation, i.e., in a fundamentally stochastic element. A fluctuation is usually followed by a response that brings the system back to the original state and which is a perfectly deterministic process. It is only at the point of formation of a new structure that fluctuations are amplified, reach a macroscopic level, and finally stabilize to a new regime representative of the structure arising beyond instability. Once this effect is allowed by the boundary conditions imposed on the system, it will happen with probability one, provided the fluctuation is created initially by some mechamism.

The difference in emphasis (Piaget—on the tendency towards equilibrium; Prigogine and Nicolis—towards increased disequilibrium) parallels the contrast outlined above (3.2.1) between Piaget's conceptualization of the tendency towards the closure of open structures and the theory of open systems. In both cases Piaget's thinking is based on the idea that structures strive towards greater stability (equilibrium) and independence on the environment (closure), even if he accepts that they can never practically achieve those end states. Both the open-systems perspective of Bertalanffy (1950, 1960, 1981) and the theoretical framework of contemporary non-equilibrium thermodynamics emphasize the opposite. The development of new structures is possible once an old structure is moved far from its previous equilibrium, and the interdependence of the system and its environment is the inseparable aspect of the life of the system. At first glance the distinction between these axiomatic positions may look like the old cognitive problem that one encounters in the case of a half-filled glass of water—is the glass half-full or half-empty? However, the theoretical repercussions of the differences between Piaget and open-systems approaches at that highly abstract level are considerable, and worth explication.

To summarize, both in contemporary biological and physical sciences, and in Piaget's theory of psychological development, the process of emergence of new structures (biological or cognitive) involves the overcoming of some disequilibrium state in the organism's relationship with the environment. This overcoming takes either the form of restoration of the previous state of affairs, or, if the disequilibrium is beyond a certain threshold condition, of the development of a qualitatively new state. Such bifurcational nature of development is an important aspect that the theoretical system of this author borrows from Piaget and the contemporary thermodynamic thinking, leaving aside disagreements between them. Piaget's dynamic structuralism leads to the consideration of how novel action structures develop when a child is acting upon structurally organized environments, and under structured efforts by the caregivers to guide that transaction. Piaget's developmental theory of equilibration served as one of the bases of the present theoretical system since it was aimed to overcome the static nature of the majority of structuralist accounts of the world on the one hand, and the unstructured nature of most of the dynamic perspectives in psychology on the other.

Piaget was not the first theoretician in psychology who attempted to integrate the obvious interdependence of the structural and functional sides of psychological phenomena. His link with James Mark Baldwin's thinking is important in that respect.

3.3 J. M. Baldwin's epistemology for psychology

Baldwin's contribution to the theoretical side of understanding development is based on the natural-philsophical and dialectical thought of the nineteenth century. It antedates Piaget's theoretical system in its emphasis on the active-constructive role of the developing child in his/her environment, and in the use of the concepts of assimilation and accommodation to explain how the development proceeds (Wozniak, 1982). Likewise, Baldwin's emphasis on the dialectical person–society relationships is a forerunner to the dialectical perspective that was later developed by Vygotsky in the framework of the cultural-historical school of thought in psychology (see 3.5).

A number of theoretical points that Baldwin introduced into psychology are of relevance from the perspective of the present theory. These include: (a) an emphasis on organism–environment relationships, and his emphasis on the interactionist perspective in thinking about the evolutionary process; (b) the role of the self–other relationships in ontogenetic socialization; and (c) his concerns about how to construct research methodology for psychology such that it could not violate the nature of psychological phenomena.

3.3.1 Baldwin's conceptualization of development

Baldwin's emerging dialectical philosophical viewpoint made it possible for him to overcome the heredity-environment dualism in thinking and replace it with an interactionist perspective that views these two working together (e.g. Baldwin, 1902, pp. 76–77; see also Baldwin, 1930). Baldwin's interactionist perspective led him to be one of the forebears of the feedback principle that he first described while reporting his empirical observations on the development of voluntary movements in his infant daughter (Baldwin, 1892). The feedback principle, extended both to ontogeny and phylogeny, made it possible for Baldwin to introduce the concept of 'circular reaction' and to let that concept play an important role in his theory of 'organic selection':

> There is a characteristic antithesis between movements always. Healthy, overflowing, favorable, outreaching, expansive, vital effects are associated with pleasure; and the contrary, the withdrawing, depressive, contractive, decreasing, vital effects are associated with pain. This is exactly the state of things which a theory of the selection of movements from overproduced movements requires, i.e., that increased vitality, represented by pleasure, should give excess movements, from which new adaptations are selected; and that decreased vitality represented by pain should to the reverse—draw off energy and suppress movements.
> If, therefore, we say that here is a type of reaction which all vitality shows,

we may give it a general descriptive name, i.e., the 'Circular Reaction,' in that its significance for evolution is that it is not a random response in movement to all stimulations alike, but that it distinguishes in its very form and amount between stimulations which are vitally good and those that are vitally bad, tending to retain the good stimulations and to draw away from and so suppress the bad. *The term 'circular' is used to emphasize the way such a reaction tends to keep itself going, over and over, by reproducing the conditions of its own stimulation. It represents habit, since it tends to keep up old movements; but it secures new adaptations, since it provides for the overproduction of movement-variations for the operation of selection.* This kind of selection, since it requires the direct cooperation of the organism itself, I have called 'Organic Selection.' It might be called 'motor' or even 'psychic' selection, since the part of consciousness, in the form of pleasure and pain, and later on experience generally, intelligence, etc. is so prominent. (Baldwin, 1896, p. 304, italics mine - J.V.)

It is not surprising that Baldwin could bring into the thinking about evolution the psychological factors that serve as criteria in the individual's selective retention of its actions in the environment. Baldwin was first and foremost a psychologist whose primary interest was turned towards the question of understanding how ontogeny is organized (see Baldwin, 1930, pp. 6–7). By applying the idea of selection from species to individual organisms, and emphasizing the meaningful basis (pleasure/pain distinction at first, intelligence subsequently) of the circular reactions between human beings and their environments, Baldwin paved the way to the application of the variational mode of thinking in psychology. That perspective itself, though, remained rare in the decades that followed, and stays such at the present time (see Valsiner, 1984b). Baldwin's ideas are directly relevant to the theoretical system developed in this book (see Chapter 4, especially section 4.3.1).

3.3.2 Child development through relationships with others

Baldwin's emphasis on the social nature of individual-psychological phenomena can be viewed as a historical predecessor to Vygotsky's cultural-historical thinking. For example,

Man is not a person who stands up in his isolated majesty, meanness, passion, or humility, and sees, hits, worships, fights, or overcomes, another man, who does the opposite things to him, each preserving his isolated majesty, meanness, passion, humility, all the while, so that he can be considered a 'unit' for the compounding processes of social speculation. On the contrary, *a man is a social outcome rather than a social unit*. He is always, in his greatest part, also some one else. Social acts of his—that is, acts that may not prove anti-social—are his *because they are society's first*; otherwise he would not have learned them nor have had any tendency to do them. (Baldwin, 1902, p. 96).

The point about the primacy of society over individual in ontogeny is the forerunner of Vygotsky's concept of internalization of higher psychological functions (see 3.5.1). Baldwin's thinking includes conceptualization of the individual person's inevitable dependence upon the society in his development. Individual persons differ from one another, but all of them have developed in the web of their society, and in this sense they all are dependent upon their culture. Baldwin's thinking about the individual–society relationship is similar to the concept of 'independent dependence' that is outlined below (see 4.1.3)

3.3.3 Baldwin on methodology

After spending some energy on organization of psychology laboratories in different American universities, Baldwin's own thinking about the role that the newly developing application of the experimental methodology in psychology took an innovative turn in the beginning of this century. This happened in conjunction with his thinking about the 'genetic logic' (Baldwin, 1906). Baldwin's philosophical elaboration of issues of the logic of development led him to postulating two basic axioms of developmental science:

> *First.* The first or negative postulate: *the logic of genesis is not expressed in convertible propositions.* Genetically, A == (that is, *becomes* . . .) B; but it does not follow that B == (becomes. . .). A.
> *Second.* The second or positive postulate: that series of events only is truly genetic which cannot be constructed before it has happened, and which cannot be exhausted by reading backwards after it has happened. (Baldwin, 1906, p. 21).

These 'postulates of method' constitute the foundation for Baldwin's rejection of the traditional scientific method. In his autobiographical retrospect, Baldwin explained the reasons why developmental psychology needs to overcome traditional methodology (Baldwin, 1930, pp. 7–8)

> The Spencerian or quantitative method, brought over into psychology from the exact sciences, physics and chemistry, must be disgarded; for its ideal consisted in reducing the more complex to the more simple, the whole to its parts, the later-evolved to the earlier-existent, *thus denying or eliminating just the factor which constituted or revealed what was truly genetic.* Newer modes of manifestation cannot be stated in atomic terms without doing violence to the more synthetic modes which observation reveals. The qualities of flower and fruit, for example, cannot be accounted for, much less predicted, from the chemical formulas of processes going on in the tissue of the fruit tree.
> A method is therefore called for which will take account of this something left 'over and above' the quantitative, something which presents new phases as the genetic progression advances. This something reveals itself in a series of qualitative aspects . . . (italics mine – J.V.)

Baldwin's emphasis on analyzing the *series* of *qualitative transformations* of the developing phenomena was a predecessor to Vygotsky's work towards developing non-reductionist and qualitative methodology for psychology. Baldwin was perhaps the first developmental psychologist to understand that the canons of the scientific method that fit the study of static aspects of phenomena are counterproductive for the study of their dynamic aspects.

Furthermore, Baldwin's thinking reflects the beginnings of the individual–sociolecological perspective on the course of human development. These aspects of Baldwin's contribution constitute the deep historical roots of the present theoretical system.

3.4 Heinz Werner's conceptualization of development

Piaget's emphasis on differentiation and integration as processes which result from the joint activity of assimilation and accommodation is paralleled by Werner's efforts to conceptualize the direction and pathways of development.

Development can be expected to involve some general direction, which may be hidden in a great variety of particular developmental processes of individual organisms. Werner (1957, p. 126) has outlined the general principle of development (which he termed 'orthogenetic') that specifies the direction of development:

> Developmental psychology postulates one regulative principle of development; it is an orthogenetic principle which states that wherever development occurs it proceeds from a state of relative globality and lack of differentiation to a state of increasing differentiation, articulation, and hierarchic integration.

Werner considered his 'orthogenetic principle' to be a 'heuristic definition' that itself would not be subject to empirical testing, but would rather serve as an axiomatic basis for the work of developmental psychologists. The roots of this principle are deeply embedded in the knowledge base of biological sciences, particularly in embryology, where similar theoretical ideas have guided the discipline ever since Karl Ernst von Baer introduced them in 1820s and 1830s (Raikov, 1961).

Werner's emphasis on differentiation includes the notion of 'hierarchic integration' as the given quote illustrates. Differentiation involves both the quantitative aspect of development (greater separation of different parts of the organisms from one another and their higher specialization) and the qualitative development of new (hierarchical) relationships between different parts of the organism.

Werner's 'orthogenetic principle' does not preclude equifinality in development. As a 'formal regulative principle' it was not meant to predict particular development courses in their specificity (Werner, 1957, p. 130). It does not contradict the existence of multiple routes within developmental processes:

> The orthogenetic law, by its very nature, is an expression of unilinearity of development. But . . . the ideal unilinear sequence signified by the universal law does not conflict with the multiplicity of actual developmental forms . . . coexistence of unilinearity and multiplicity of individual developments must be recognized for psychological just as it is for biological evolution. In regard to human behaviour in particular, this polarity opens the way for a developmental study of behavior not only in terms of universal sequence, but also in terms of individual variations, that is, in terms of growth viewed as a branching-out process of specialization and aberration. (Werner, 1957, p. 137).

The multiplicity of trajectories of individuals' development can be highly complex in their oganization. Contemporary research in developmental biology of organisms whose structural (cellular) development takes place in shorter time frames than in the case of human children has revealed great complexity of ongoing developmental changes in simple organisms (Lewin, 1984). In the domain of children's motor development, Trettien (1900) has demonstrated that different infants progress through different sequences of motor skill attainment: some progress from stationary position to bipedal locomotion via the crawling/creeping intermediate state, but others bypass that state and begin walking independently after getting up from their sitting position. Werner's 'orthogenetic principle' does not contradict such multilinearity of development, as it is formulated at the highly abstract level, as Werner himself pointed out. The multiplicity of developmental routes to the same end state is one of the characteristics of the open systems (Bertalanffy, 1950). Werner's 'orthogenetic principle' is applicable only to open systems (since closed systems are incapable of development, i.e. differentiation and hierarchical integration).

Werner's contribution to the study of development is relevant in the context of this book in two respects. First, his 'orthogenetic principle', when interpreted as allowing for different developmental courses that lead to similar outcomes, constitutes the basis of the explanation of ontogenetic development of children's action structures. Secondly, his emphasis on hierarchical reorganization of differentiating organisms makes it possible to conceptualize the emergency of qualitatively new parts of developing structures. It is largely (but not exclusively) that idea that links with Vygotsky's emphasis on the 'cultural' development of children. Werner's earlier work served as a direct source for Vygotsky's thinking of child development.

3.5 Vygotsky's cultural-historical approach

Vygotsky's approach is based on the organismic-dialectical philosophical traditions of the nineteenth century of which marxist philosophy was a part. His theoretical approach was advanced under the societal conditions that called for application of marxist philosophy to biological and social sciences, without prescribing the exact ways in which these sciences were to accomplish that task. Thorough analyses of Vygotsky's theory can be found in a number of sources (Davydov and Radzikhovskii, 1980, 1981; Kozulin, 1984: Van der Veer, 1984; Van Ijzendoorn and Van der Veer, 1984; Wertsch, 1981, 1985). However, the increasingly widening interest in Vygotsky's thinking largely bypasses the theoretical ideas developed by that interesting 'social natural philosopher'—using here a label that adequately characterizes Vygotsky's way of thinking. Many of Vygotsky's ideas that emerged in close connection with his contemporary international psychology have been dissociated from their intellectual contexts in the presently available English-language translations. The abbreviated and modified nature of the majority of translations has served as a serious barrier that has complicated the appreciation of Vygotsky's ideas in all of their elegance.

The central issue in Vygotsky's theoretical thinking is the *development of qualitatively novel ('higher') psychological functions in the history of cultures and ontogeny of children in the process of organisms' (i.e. culture, or child) goal-directed acting upon their environments*. In child development, the developing child and the cultural environment of the child are intrinsically related. The cultural environment is organized by active members of the culture who belong to the generations older than the child. That environment itself guides the child towards the personal (but socially assisted) invention of culture. Furthermore, the 'social others' of the child may assist in child development directly, by becoming involved in the instruction (Russian: 'obuchenie') process.

The theoretical framework in which the children's relationships with their environments (and with other human beings) is cast has been called by Vygotsky 'zona blizaishego razvitia' in a figurative way. That concept has been translated into English usually as 'Zone of Proximal Development' (abbreviated as ZPD, see Rogoff and Wertsch, 1984; Vygotsky, 1962, 1978), or alternatively as 'zone of potential development' (see Vygotsky, 1963).

The basic theoretical feature of the ZPD concept for Vygotsky was the interdependence of the process of child development and the socially provided resources of that development. That interdependence was conceptualized by Vygotsky in structural-dynamic terms, following the lead of his contemporary Gestalt psychology. Vygotsky gave credit to Koffka (see Vygotsky, 1960, pp. 440–441) in overcoming both the preformationist and environmentalist perspectives on the relationship of the learning and instruction. The preformationist (hereditary determinist) view on the issue reduced the relationship to the dominance of the biological development of the organism. The child was considered to be ready for instruction when the processes (that were to be the object of instruction) were ready in their mature form. Vygotsky characterized this perspective in terms of 'instruction drags after development, the development always is ahead of instruction' (Vygostky, 1960, p. 439). Indeed, when causality for child development is fully attributed to maturational (genetically predetermined) course, then thinking about the role of instruction in that development would be viewed as superfluous by definition. The opposite of the maturationist view—the environmentalist perspective on child development—performed a similar (but opposite) extreme reduction of the issue to one of its sides. For an extreme environmentalist (of Watsonian, or Pavlovian kinds), instruction (teaching) is equated with child development, and the child's contribution to it is reduced drastically. In this case, as Vygotsky figuratively remarked, 'development follows instruction, like shadow follows the object of which it is a shadow' (Vygotsky, 1960, p. 440).

In contrast, Koffka's view of learning and instruction emphasized the interdependence of the two processes, linking development to the general influence of instruction that makes it possible for the organism to transfer what is learned in one setting into another. Vygotsky, however, proceeded in his thinking beyond Koffka—by asking the question of at which developmental stage of the emergency of some new psychological function would instruction be most appropriate? That question was answered by him by locating the most appropriate time for linking instruction with learning at the time when new functions are *beginning* to emerge, but have not unfolded yet. Likewise, the instruction would have no effect on learning if the novel psychological function is beyond the current biological capacity of the organism. It is within the range between the 'already begun, but not yet developed' and 'fully developed' state of a function in child development. Vygotsky stated:

> the crucial characteristic of instruction is the fact, that instruction creates the zone of proximal development, i.e. elicits in the child, promotes, and brings to movement a number of internal developmental processes, which at the present time are available for the child only in the sphere of relations with the people around and in joint action with peers, but which later, undergoing internal course of development, become then the internal property of the child himself. (Vygotsky, 1960, p. 450).

However, according to Vygotsky, ZPD can also be constructed without the direct efforts at instruction on behalf of adults. It can be constructed by simple organization of the child's environment, for example. Vygotsky's discussions of child development at the preschool age illustrates that case:

> The experience of child-rearing in the family shows that a child, who is surrounded by books, on the sixth year of life acquires reading without any teaching. The experiences of kindergartens shows that learning to read has its place in a preschool institution. One of the important moments which is important for the definition of the linkages of the programme, consists of what could be called embryonal instruction or pre-teaching . . . (Vygotsky, 1956, p. 437).

Finally, the developing child can construct the ZPD for himself in the process of play. Vygotsky viewed the crucial role of children's play in the construction of their future development through ZPD:

> the play creates the zone of proximal development of the child. In the play the child is always above his average age, above his usual everyday behavior; in play he is as if head-high above himself. The play contains in a condensed way, like in the focus of a magnifying glass, all tendencies of development; in play the child tries as if to accomplish a jump above the level of his ordinary behavior. (Vygotsky, 1966. p. 74).

It becomes clear that Vygotsky's concept of ZPD served for him as a theoretical construct that made it possible to view the child–environment relations in the context of the individual–sociological frame of reference (as it is defined in this book). More empirical aspects of the ZPD concept will be discussed in chapter 4 (see 4.3.5). Besides that concept, two other general aspects of Vygotsky's theory are relevant in the present context: (1) the role of internalization in human development; and (2) the emphasis on the meaning as the unit of analysis of higher psychological functions.

3.5.1 The process of internalization

Observations of children's development give ample evidence about psychological phenomena that first emerge in child–adult interaction and are subsequently carried over to the sphere of the intra-individual psychological functions of the child. Such transition of phenomena from person– environment relationships to the inner psychological organization of the person is labelled internalization. For developmental psychology it is the process of internalization that needs to be described and explained.

In contemporary presentations of Vygotsky's ideas to the international readership (e.g. in Vygotsky, 1978), the issues of internalization are given adequate attention as a central idea which constitutes the backbone of Vygotsky's thinking. The intellectual and cultural history of the idea is well outlined by Wertsch and Stone (1984).

Vygotsky's emphasis on internalization (interiorization) is another issue in which he relied constructively on the world psychology of his times. Its roots are embedded in the thinking of Janet, Baldwin, Stern, and Piaget. At the same time, the idea of internalization borrowed from other psychologists was considered by Vygotsky to develop further Marx's basic idea of human psuchology as a system of social relationships. He conceptualized internalization as 'set of social relationships, transposed inside and having become functions of personality and the forms of its structure' (Vygotsky, 1960, pp. 198–199). In disagreement with Piaget's concept of egocentric speech, Vygotsky formulated his major principle of development:

> The actual course of the process of development of the child's thinking takes place not in the direction going from the individual to the socialized state, but starting from the social and proceeding to the individual—such is the main result of both theoretical as well as experimental investigation of the problem that interests us. (Vygotsky, 1956, p. 89).

Vygotsky's indebtedness to Janet in formulating the general law of internalization in human psychological development is clearly evident in his writings. For example:

> The history of the development of signs brings us, however, to a far more general law that directs the development of behaviour. Janet calls it the fundamental law in psychology. The essence of that law is that the child in the process of development begins to apply to himself the very same forms of behaviour which others applied to him prior to that. The child himself acquires the social forms of behaviour and transposes those onto himself. In application

to the domain of our interest, we could say that the truthfulness of that law is nowhere as evident as in the use of signs. The sign originally is always a means of social contact, means of influence upon others, and only subsequently finds itself in the role of a means for influencing oneself. (Vygotsky, 1960, p. 192).

The idea that words develop from being originally commands for others into means of regulating one's own self (see also Vygotsky, 1960, p. 194) is one of the cornerstones of Vygotsky's explanation of the ontogeny of speech and thinking. The issues of speech and thinking are but a special topic within the general domain of children's cultural development. In more general terms, Vygotsky formulated the 'general genetic law' of cultural development:

We could formulate the general genetic law of cultural development in the following way: every function in the cultural development of the child comes onto the stage twice, in two respects; first—in the social, later—in the psychological, first in relations between people as an interpsychological category, afterwards within the child as an intrapsychological category. . . .

All higher pscyhological functions are internalized relationships of the social kind, and constitute the social structure of personality. Their composition, genetic structure, ways of functioning—in one word—all their nature is social. Even when they have become psychological processes, their nature remains quasi-social. The human being who is alone also retains the functions of interaction. (Vygotsky, 1960, pp. 197–198).

The closeness of this general perspective to that of Baldwin (see 3.3.2) is quite evident in this quote. In its generality, Vygotsky's 'general law' is similar to Werner's 'orthogenetic principle'. Vygotsky's thinking about internalization resulted from his constructive development of ideas that had occurred previously in the work of Janet, Baldwin, Piaget, Bühler, Kretschmer, and Marx. Vygotsky did not invent the idea of internalization anew. Instead, he integrated different existing viewpoints creatively into a new general principle.

The idea of internalization of social experience was analyzed by Vygotsky in different empirical contexts. Consider his example of the process of development of indicatory 'gesture' in the child's mind:

When the mother comes to the aid of the child and comprehends his/her movement as an indicator, the situation changes in an essential way. The indicatory gesture becomes a gesture for others. In response to the child's unsuccessful grasping movement, a response emerges not on the part of the object, but on the part of another human. Thus, other people introduce the primary sense into this unsuccessful grasping movement. And only afterward, owing to the fact they have already connected the unsuccessful grasping movement with the whole objective situation, do children themselves begin to use the movement as an indication. The functions of the movement itself have undergone a change here; from a movement directed toward an object it has become a movement directed towards another human being. The grasping is converted into an indication. Thanks to this, the movement is reduced and abbreviated, and the form of the indicatory gesture is elaborated. We can now say that it is a gesture for oneself. However, his movement does not become a gesture for oneself except by first being an indication, i.e., functioning objectively as an indication and gesture for others, being comprehended and understood by surrounding people as an indicator. Thus, the child is the last to become conscious of his/her gesture. Its significance and functions first are created by the objective situation and then by the people surrounding the child. The indicatory gesture initially relies on a movement to point to what others understand and only later becomes an indicator for the child. (Reproduced with permission from Vygotsky, 1981, p. 161; original: Vygotsky, 1960, p. 196).

This example illustrates the dependence of the particular internalization process on the context of the child's relationship to the environment, which is regulated (by the adult caregiver's responding to child's effort, and later gesture) by the social others surrounding the child. Only some parts of this process take place under conditions of immediate interaction of the child with the adult. Once the gesture had already begun its relocation in the inside direction, the presence of interaction may perform only a supportive function in the internalization process. It is then the cultural structure of child's environment that serves as the field which sets up external limits for the child's acting and—eventually—to the direction of what becomes internalized.

3.5.2 The function of meaning

The meaning of signs in a culture can arise from the multitude of particular and idiosyncratic uses of the signs in social communication. It is at this point of theorizing that Vygotsky's emphasis (following Paulhan, 1928) on the difference between 'meaning' and 'sense' may be worthwhile mentioning. Vygotsky states:

The sense of a word . . . is the sum of all the psychological events aroused in our consciousness by the word. It is a dynamic, fluid, complex whole, which has several zones of unequal stability. Meaning is only one of the zones of sense, the most stable and precise zone. A word acquires its sense from the context in which it appears in different contexts, it changes its sense. Meaning remains stable throughout the changes of sense. (Vygotsky, 1962, p. 146).

The developing child is from the very beginning embedded in the context of meanings, as these are defined within the culture (e.g. meaning of child-bearing, indigenous understanding of conception and pregnancy—see Monberg, 1975; meaning of abilities of children at different ages—see Harkness and Super, 1983). In the immediate social environment of a developing child in any culture, these meanings guide child development through providing a framework for parental understanding of child-rearing goals and methods, as well as via creating a basis for organization of children's everyday environments. In addition, these meanings help the parents to interpret the development of their children. These cultural meanings constitute the context of child development with which any behavioral events in children's lives are interdependent.

On the other hand, the *personal sense* of a sign develops in the course of the individual child's ontogeny, and with assistance from the social environment. However, although the development of sense is aided by that environment, it is not determined by it. This constrained indeterminacy in the children's sense development guarantees the open-ended nature of cultural change, which is wrought by individuals' transactions with their cultural environments. New meanings can emerge in the culture as a result of convergence of personal senses of different individuals. Meaning, thus, is not a pre-given and immutable ideal entity, but a byproduct of social transaction that is used to regulate the person–environment relationships once it emerges. Meanings are thus dynamic—they emerge, develop, and dissipate in their cultural contexts, interdependently with changes in the personal sense of the members of the culture. On the other hand, cultural meanings themselves are constantly undergoing change, part of which is due to the innovations that children introduce into their (and their parents') senses during their development. The children's environments are structured by the cultural–historical meanings that which they include. These meanings are coded into objects and events of the particular child's environment through the actions of the people who surround the child and on the basis of their personalized senses derived from the meanings. Within such culturally structured (meaningful) and personalized ('sense-ful') environments developing children invent (or re-invent, by imitation) novel ways of acting and thinking, out of which only those that end up being accepted by the child *and* his social environment might be retained. Baldwin's 'circular reactions' (see 3.3) in the actions of the developing child are embedded in their culturally structured environments that (rather than the child's 'pleasure' or 'pain') guide the process of child development. That guidance, however, is accomplished within the total structure of the life environment of the developing child, rather than in only some of its aspects. A theoretical system that describes that guidance has, therefore, to be akin to a field theory.

3.6 Kurt Lewin's field theory

Kurt Lewin, 'is recognized as a great psychologist, but the nature of his greatness seems not to be clearly understood' (Henle, 1978, p. 237). Lewin's theoretical perspective developed within the web of Gestalt psychology on the one hand, and on the basis of his own personal experiences during the World War I on the other (see Lewin, 1917). His interest in overcoming the person-versus-environment dualism in psychology led him to propose new ways for psychology to view the lawfulness of psychological phenomena (see 2.6 above). Lewin's major concern was with the improvement of the scientific nature of the psychological theories of his time, which were hopelessly built onto culture-specific implicit assumptions. In this sense the state of affairs in theorizing in psychology has not changed since Lewin's times (see Benigni and Valsiner, 1985).

Lewin's theoretical system went through different stages in its development. After starting from the issues of connection between action, will, and emotion (see, for example, an overview by Zeigarnik, 1981), his interests proceeded towards finding adequate qualitative-structural formalisms to describe the structure and events in the 'psychological space' (Lewin, 1933, 1935a, 1938). After his topological and vector concepts were introduced, Lewin turned again to the issues of how these concepts can capture the dynamic aspect of the person–environment system, investigating a number of issues pertaining to children (Barker, Dembo, and Lewin, 1941; Lewin, 1939, 1942) or adults (Lewin, 1948, 1951; Lewin, Lippitt and White, 1939). Two aspects of Lewin's theoretical heritage contribute to the foundation of the present theory: (1) qualitative-structural analysis of the person–environment fields; (2) the emphasis on the dynamic nature of the field, and the description of how the field is transformed.

3.6.1 The structure of the person–environment field

Lewin's theory may be best understood in the framework of thinking of contemporary empirically minded psychologists as a metatheory (Henle, 1978). Lewin himself has noted the metatheoretical nature of his field theory:

> Field theory . . . can hardly be called correct or incorrect in the same way as a theory in the usual sense of the term. *Field theory is probably best characterized as a method:* namely, a method of *analyzing causal relations and of building scientific constructs.* This method of analyzing causal relations can be expressed in the form of certain general statements about the 'nature' of the conditions of change. (Lewin, 1943a, p. 294)

Lewin's widely known general formula (Behavior = function of Person and the Environment) constitutes the core of his field theory. The interpretations of that formula have sometimes overlooked the *interdependent rather than co-relational* nature of the link between the Person and the Environment. For Lewin, the intrinsic (rather than formal-statistical) nature of the conjunction between P and E was of central theoretical importance. He explained:

> In this formula for behaviour, the state of the person (P) and that of his environment (E) are not independent of each other. How a child sees a given physical setting (for instance, whether the frozen pond looks dangerous to him or not) depends upon the developmental state and the character of that child and upon his ideology. The worlds in which the newborn, the one-year-old child, and the ten-year-old child live are different even in identical physical or social surroundings. This holds also for the same child when it is hungry or satiated, full of energy or fatigued. In other words, $E = F(P)$. The reverse is also true: the state of the person depends upon his environment, $P = F(E)$. The state of the person after encouragement is different from that after discour-

agement, that is an area of sympathy or security from that in an area of tension, that in a democratic group atmosphere from that in an autocratic atmosphere. . . .

In summary, one can say that behavior and development depend upon the state of the person and his environment, $B = F(P,E)$. In this equation the person (P) and his environment (E) have to be viewed as variables which are mutually dependent upon each other. In other words, to understand or to predict behavior, the person and his environment have to be considered as *one* constellation of interdependent factors. (Reproduced with permission from Lewin, 1951, pp. 239–240).

Lewin's analysis of the person–environment field led him to the introduction of the concepts of 'barrier', 'boundary', 'boundary zone' to characterize the structure of the field. It also facilitated the description of the field in terms of its demand character ('valence') and of different 'forces' that reflect the person's locomotions in the process of restructuring of the field. Although Lewin was careful not to extend his field notions to include absolutely every aspect of P–E relationships in the past, present, and future, he still included the 'psychological past' and 'psychological future' alongside the 'psychological present' in the field in those cases when these concepts· can be exactly determined (e.g. see Lewin, 1943a; Lewin, Lippitt, and Escalona, 1940, p. 36).

Lewin's goal of building up psychology's formal-theoretical system that could represent science of the Galilean kind (see Lewin, 1931) led him to juggle with different areas of mathematics that could, in principle, provide the formal basis for that new psychology (e.g. Lewin, 1936a, 1938). These formalizations of basic organismic thinking of Lewin's are less important in the context of the present book than is the emphasis on the *structured nature of person–environment relationships* and his efforts to analyze these relationships in ways that retain it, rather than eliminate it for the sake of the traditions of psychological methodology. Lewin's insistence on building a psychology that would resemble Galilean physics was largely a theoretical endeavour where the ideal psychological 'laws' would follow the closed-systems axioms of classical physics, rather than the open-systems basic assumptions of organismic phenomena that are capable of development. The paradoxalical nature of Lewin's theorizing is somewhat similar to that in Piaget's. Lewin, like Piaget, has the ideal of developing psychological theory along the Galilean lines of closed systems, abstracting general formal laws from complex reality. In practice, though, Lewin's descriptions are close-to-reality structural maps of the life space and its 'forces', that remain far from the Galilean ideal of the analogue of 'frictionless spaces' for psychology. Lewin's use of formalisms in his field-theoretical descriptions was more reality-bound than mathematical (see London, 1944; Sorokin, 1956). Nevertheless, or perhaps because of that, Lewin's field descriptions of psychological phenomena provide a picture of thorough understanding of the complexities involved in them, which no other theoretical system in psychology after Lewin has managed to do.

3.6.2 The field dynamics and Lewin's conceptualization of development

The dynamic nature of the field structure is the idea that is inseparable from Lewin's concept of the field. However, Lewin's (and his students') empirical interests concentrated largely on issues that required microgenetic rather than ontogenetic perspectives, even when Lewin studied children or wrote about them. Thus, among the problems studied empirically by investigators in the 'Lewin group' were issues of the effect of unfinished activity on memory (Zeigarnik, 1927), change in the aspiration levels under conditions of failure (Hoppe, 1930), relationships of frustration and regression in children (Barker, Dembo, and Lewin, 1941), prospects for cultural reconstruction in postwar Germany (Lewin, 1943b, 1943c), culture change in general (Lewin, 1948), adolescent (Lewin, 1939) and marital conflicts (Lewin, 1948). Lewin's interest in the dynamics of social groups (Lewin, Lippitt and White, 1939; Lewin, 1951) bears marks of a similar microgenetic emphasis. Although he occasionally talked about ontogeny (in the context of the transformation of the psychological field over time), Lewin never studied it over any considerable length of time.

Lewin comes close to dealing with issues of development from two perspectives. His efforts to reformulate the concept of learning from the position of field theory necessarily involved some explanation of development (Lewin, 1942). In this context, Lewin emphasizes the change of meanings in the cognitive structure of the field, once the field has undergone transformation:

> Learning, as a change in cognitive structure, has to deal with practically every field of behaviour. Whenever we speak of a change in meaning, a change of such cognitive structure has occurred. New connections or separations, differentiations or dedifferentiations of psychological areas have taken place. The 'meaning' of an event in psychology may be said to be known if its psychological position and its psychological direction are determined. In Mark Twain's *Life on the Mississippi*, the passengers on the boat enjoy the 'scenery,' but for the pilot the U-shape of the two hills, which a passenger admires, means a signal to turn sharply, and the beautiful waves in the middle of the river mean dangerous rocks. The psychological connection of these 'stimuli' with actions has changed, and therefore the meaning has changed. (Lewin, 1942, pp. 228–229)

Lewin's more explicit effort to conceptualize development is present in the monograph on frustration and regression in children (Barker, Dembo, and Lewin, 1941). He emphasizes the widening of the child's space of free movement in ontogeny. In his description of the developmental processes in general Lewin follows largely the line of thought shared by Werner and the Gestalt tradition of emphasizing differentiation and integration as the basic characteristic of development (Barker, Dembo, and Lewin, 1941, pp. 18–20). For Lewin, of course, it is the person–environment field ('life space') that becomes gradually more differentiated and integrated as the child develops. The child becomes increasingly more able to organize parts of his physical and social environments as means to reach some end. The growing child tries increasingly to organize the environment so that the satisfaction of his needs is not left to chance.

To summarize, Lewin's theoretical emphasis was developmental (dynamic) mostly in respect to the changes in the field structure over shorter periods of time. This emphasis can be summarized by the term 'microgenetic' which, in accordance with its narrower German original term ('Aktualgenese'—see Draguns, 1984) has been used in psychology in a very specific sense in the context of perceptogenesis. However, the English term may be fruitfully used to denote any restructuring of a psychological structure in the course of a limited period of time. Lewin's field-theoretical thinking emphasized the dynamic, microgenetic aspect of psychological process. However, Lewin's thinking was not outrightly developmental in its nature. For example, he was not much interested in the developmental question of how children's life spaces develop over longer time periods, although he recognized the question as one of scientific importance, and provided some general ideas about it from the position of his field theory.

3.7 Summary: frames of reference and theories in developmental psychology

Chapter 3 outlined an analysis of reference frameworks in psychology into which any theoretical or empirical study inevitably is mapped. It also provided a brief review of the theoretical background of the theoretical approach of the present book.

First, the four-fold classification of psychology's approaches according to their 'reference frames' makes it possible to set different theoretical systems in psychology up in their appropriate contexts of ideas. Thus, the predominant *inter-individual* frame of reference, supported by statistical methodology, is shown to be adequate for only some research questions in psychology, but not for all. Likewise the use of the *intra-individual* reference frame overlooks the important characteristic of psychological phenomena—their open-systems nature. In contrast, the two ecologically oriented reference frames—the *individual–ecological* and *individual–socioecological*—are appropriate for the study of developmental phenomena. The theoretical perspective outlined in the present book belongs into the individual-socioecological frame of reference.

The present theoretical framework is not without its predecessors. In that context, the contributions of Jean Piaget, James Mark Baldwin, Lev Vygotsky, Heinz Werner, and Kurt Lewin were analyzed in chapter 3. Different aspects of the thinking of these theorists constitute direct origins of the present system: Piaget's ideas of the co-action of assimilation and accommodation, Baldwin's 'circular reaction', Vygotsky's thesis of the internalization of external functions, and Werner's reiteration of the laws of development of nineteenth-century *Naturphilosophie* that are subsumed under the label of 'orthogenetic principle'. Finally, Lewin's emphasis on the lawfulness of every individual case, and his efforts to provide structural-dynamic descriptions of some psychological cases, has enriched the perspective of the author. In chapter 4, the theoretical system for explaining the canalization of children's actions towards their culturally acceptable form is provided. It borrows different aspects from the traditions introduced by the theorists whose work was outlined in chapter 3. However, its synthesis of the concepts and its emphasis on the bounded (constrained) nature of psychological development provides a novel theoretical perspective for developmental research. It also leads to some general epistemological issues which are only briefly mentioned in this book, since they largely remain beyond what this book is meant to accomplish.

CHAPTER 4

The theoretical system

The theoretical system presented here constitutes an attempt to conceptualize two aspects of the development of children's actions and thinking in culturally organized environments. The first aspect involves the dynamics of children's acting and thinking in settings where they are confronted with the necessity to accomplish some tasks—that they themselves elect to perform, or which are set up for them by other people. Much of such task-oriented acting by children takes place in socially regulated ways—on the one hand, children try to reach solutions to problems that they are faced with, but on the other, their efforts are guided and redirected by others. Such interdependence of children's actions with those of other people determines the wide variability of the form of their (nominally 'same') actions (see 2.1 on the open-systems nature of psychological phenomena). Furthermore, the child's actions are embedded in constantly changing environments. As the child progresses towards a goal (or replaces one goal with another), the whole task-field is restructured *at each step* of the child's or adults' acting in the setting. It seems appropriate to use the label *microgenetic* to describe this context-bound, dynamic, and interpersonally assisted nature of children's actions in their everyday environments (see Draguns, 1984, for the history of that term in English-language psychological literature).

The second aspect of our present theoretical endeavor is *ontogenetic*. It involves efforts to explain the process of children's individual development within their changing environments. Although the present theoretical system may be adequate for any period of ontogeny—from birth to death—it is selectively applied in the present book to childhood years in general, and issues of children's actions at mealtime during their second year of life in particular (see chapters 6 and 7).

In this chapter, the theoretical system that constitutes the core of the author's approach to developmental psychology is outlined. It is based on an intermediate position in the epistemological question of deterministic

75

versus indeterministic accounts of development. The present standpoint eliminates the usual exclusively disjunctive view of the determinism/indetermi-
nism issue, and replaces it by a conjunctive axiom. Thus, developmental
process is at the same time both determinstic and indeterministic. In order
to avoid getting lost in any kind of pseudo-dialectical verbiage that can easily
follow the acceptance of this axiom, it is necessary to explain the perspectives
from which these two views are united in the same whole. The process of
development is considered deterministic in the sense that it is always guided
by some set of constraints (in psychology: external and physical, or internal
and cognitive or emotional) that organize the development in some (rather
than other) future direction. However, the *exact* future state (i.e. within the
general direction provided by constraints) of the developing organism is
necessarily indeterministic (unpredictable in any exact ways from some
previous state). A closer analysis of the basic assumptions of the theory
would clarify the rationale for solving the determinism/indeterminism issue
by seeing them as united within the whole of a developing organism.

4.1 Basic assumptions of the theory

In the most general terms the present endevor may be classified as belonging
to the category of 'dynamic interactionism'—a term that is quite fuzzy in its
meaning if left without further explanation. In terms of the four reference
frames in psychology (see 3.1) this theory makes use of the *individual-
socioecological* frame of reference. The theory is an effort to integrate the
theoretical perspectives of Lewin, Vygotsky, and Piaget in psychology with
some basic notions from evolutionary biology (Waddington's idea of canalization) and contemporary non-equilibrium thermodynamics. The dynamic
interactionism of the present theory is explicitly structuralistic—it emphasizes
the obvious fact that both the developing child and his environment are
structurally organized. That structured nature of the child and his environment is not static and immutable, but is dynamically transformed both micro-
genetically (as the child and/or his caregivers act within the environment) and
ontogenetically (as the child develops in transaction with the environment). A
number of basic notions on which this theory is built must be made explicit
before the theory is outlined in detail.

4.1.1 The structure of child's actions within environment

From the time of conception onwards the developing organism—embryo,
fetus, and neonate—goes through a series of structural-anatomical transformations which provide the basis for all the behavior that can be observed in
the newborn. The structural organization of newborn's anatomy and physio-
logical functioning set constraints on the range of behaviors that the baby
displays. These constraints likewise determine the boundaries of the set of

new behaviors that the baby can learn at the given time under social circumstances that promote their acquisition (see 3.5). Only a limited subset of what the baby can learn at the time ends up being acquired by him, and the newly acquired capabilities widen the set of potentially learnable skills at the next period of development. By actualizing some of the potentially learnable skills at a given time, the child actively participates in the construction of his future potential development. However, that participation is always constrained by the child's physical, emotional, and cognitive constraints that are structurally organized at any time in development. For example, the increase in infants' body weight beyond the capacity of their muscle strength in the middle of their first year of life may lead to the disappearance of the newborn 'walking reflex' in the usual environmental conditions (Thelen, 1983). However, such a 'regress' is not to be the case for long—the developing cognitive capacities and haptic exploration lead the infants to progress further from quadrupedal to bipedal mode of locomotion. That progress is made available by the neurophysiological system of coordination of the muscles of the body that participate in bipedal locomotion. Once an infant masters walking independently, his quick access to different areas in his environment is facilitated, which in its turn leads to further psychological development by the new encounters with the environment made available to the child by the new skill.

The child's current psychological organization determines in which ways the child can act. Thus, a 2-year-old who is beginning to use verbal commands to control his own behavior is engaged in limiting the latter via the help of the former. Or an adolescent may use her emotional involvement with a referent group or person to abandon some rational ways of thinking, and acting. The connection between emotions, cognition, and action *within* the person's psychology and behavior constitutes a system in which different components are connected in complex qualitative ways. That system cannot be reduced to the sum of its parts. Any reduction of such systemic complexity to a conglomerate of 'quantitative measures' of each of the supposed components would eliminate the systemic nature of the person's functioning from consideration at the outset of the psychological study. No linear equation with the factors of 'action', 'emotion', and 'cognition' neatly displayed in it makes it possible to explain the structural organization of the whole that exists due to the interaction of these three as its parts. Furthermore, much of psychologists' research habit also involves the replacement of the original object of investigation by another—mostly the move from the study of individual cases to samples of such cases. Thus, a psychological study of a sample of 'difficult adolescents' that involves the measurement of the three interconnected aspects—emotions, cognition, and actions—by administering to each adolescent in the sample some independent quantitative measurement techniques from each of these three domains would eliminate the systemic organization of the adolescents' individual persons from consideration. Such research replaces the original phenomenon (i.e. systemic connection of emotion—cognition—action within each particular adolescent) by another, artificially constructed phenomenon (e.g. formal relations between quantitative measures of action, emotion, and cognition *within the sample*, with the intention of generalizing the findings to some general population). For understanding how *samples* of adolescents are organized, such replacement of the intra-systemic (intra-individual) analysis of the phenomenon by an inter-systemic (inter-individual) research question can be of value for sociology of adolescence. However, in the process of such research efforts the original structured (systemic) nature of the original *psychological* phenomenon is irreversibly lost (Valsiner, 1984b, 1986). It can be retained only if the investigator proves that research results based on samples (and generalized to some population) can be applied to individuals in the population as well. The latter is possible only under the assumption that every individual in the population is qualitatively similar to every other individual. On the basis of the principle of equifinalty applicable in the case of open systems in biology (and psychology), that assumption is unwarranted. In the realm of biological organisms and human personalities, development takes place in a multitude of ways. In the case of each, the developing organism is qualitatively structured, and advances further in development as its structural organization becomes intertwined with its life environment. The latter, as we see next, is also a structured entity.

4.1.2 The structured nature of child's environment: the precursor for development

The newborn child inherits not only its biological (genetic) background, but also the structural organization of the environment into which it is born (West and King, 1985). The child's behavior is interdependent with the possibilities that the environment provides, and the latter is structurally organized all through ontogeny. As the newborn develops, its actions begin to reorganize the structure of the environment. Likewise, the people around the child purposefully rearrange the structure of the child's environment so that it can eliminate dangers (e.g. taking away dangerous objects) and promote socially relevant goals (e.g. the integration of young children into the family's subsistence activities and their participation in social rituals). It is the people in the child's environment who guide the child's development in accordance with their personal goals and on the basis of their interpretations of cultural expectations (cf. Newson, 1974; Newson and Newson, 1968, 1975, 1976).

Thus, we can advance a general *principle of the structured nature of environment*: at all times in the course of life, the child's environment provides a structured framework in which development takes place. During development that framework undergoes a number of transformations. In one extreme, some of these are wrought by the actions of the developing child. On the other side, some transformations are due to factors in the environment that are beyond the child's control. However, the majority of transformations are controlled simultaneously both by the child and the environment itself (including other persons who may reorganize the environment for the child). Whatever are the roles of the child, other people, and environmental factors in transforming the environment—the latter is never in a random or unstructured organizational state.

The principle of the structured nature of children's environments was formulated in its extensive form first by the Russian psychologist Mikhail Basov, whose considerable contribution to developmental psychology has been almost fully unnoticed (despite its international avilability— (see Basow, 1929; also in Valsiner, 1987). Basov emphasized the relational nature of the concept of environment—it is always definable as 'environment of X', rather than 'environment' in any absolute sense:

> the coordinated factors in the case of the concept of environment are the organism, and some portion of the rest of its world—that part of it which is in certain relationships with the given organism. . . . No single organism, including man, is related to the whole world in such a way that is obligatory for considering the whole world its environment. Every organism has its limits in establishing relations with its world; for some organisms that limit is very small, for others imperceivably large. Starting from that, it can be said that the segment of reality in connection with which the given organism practically exists, constitutes its environment. (Basov, 1931, pp. 69–70).

Basov addressed the question of the nature of organization of the environment, recognizing the implications that different possible answers to that question carry with it. Accepting that the whole world is characterized by interdependence of parts within their whole, Basov addressed the issue at the level of particular environments of people:

> Let us consider that question [of the nature of environment] only as it appears in the case of humans. Consequently, here we talk about the environment of some specific individual who lives at a specific time, belongs to a particular human society and social class, etc. What is the environment of such X like in its structure? Is it some kind of a wholistic system in which phenomena are related to one another, or is it a simple sum, a conglomerate, of their mechanical grouping? This question is very important because, in accordance with one or the other view on the structure of human environment our practical relation to it would vary. If the environment is a set of separate factors that are totally unrelated to one another, then our relation to it is determined. Every factor will in this case be evaluated in itself—today one, tomorrow another—and after such account of all the separate factors ends we have accounted for all the environment, so that nothing is left over. If the environment is a wholistically organized system of phenomena, then, obviously, our practical relation with it must take that into account. The separation of independent elements in that case will not give the same result as in the first condition, since the organized whole is always larger than the sum of its elements, and—its most important

aspect is that quality is something else than a simple conglomerate of elements. (Basov, 1931, p. 73).

The influence of Gestalt psychology's emphasis—about the primacy of the whole over the sum of its parts—on Basov's thinking about human environments is obvious in this quote. Differently from those Gestalt psychologists of his time who came closest to addressing developmental issues (e.g. Koffka), Basov emphasized the Gestalt-like nature of both the organism's actions and the environments in which these actions take place. The question—posed in the quote above—of the nature of particular environments of developing humans was largely rhetorical as Basov asked it—his theoretical background made it possible to answer it only in the structuralist direction:

> elements of environment do not exist separately from one another, but in a mutual relationship and in the unity of the whole. While examining one of the relations [in that whole], we drag behind it a long chain of relations that do not exist without one anther. This is because all these phenomena emerge from some shared origin and therefore are related to one another by cause-conse- quent relationships. And since it is so, it means that these relations can be ordered in a hierarchical way. (Basov, 1931, pp. 74–75).

The principle of hierarchical organization—the core of Heinz Werner's 'onto- genetic principle' that applies to *organisms*—was applied to their *environments* by Basov. His emphasis upon the inequality between different parts of the environment from the standpoint of the environment as a whole (albeit that of a particular individual) renders all efforts towards quantitative measurement of children's environments largely groundless. The assumption of the structured nature of children's environment is important since it reveals the inadequacy of solely quantitative empirical research methods. As a rule, these methods reduce the structure of children's environments to quantitative indices of different kinds. Furthermore, these methods are usually applied within the inter-individual frame of reference that does not produce data on actual child–environment transaction.

4.1.3 Organism–environment relations: their 'independeht dependence'

As was emphasized above, *both* the developing organism and its environment are organized in a structural way. Both constitute structures of physical, psychological, and cultural kinds. All of the life of the organism takes place within its environment—thus, the structural nature of the organism's behavior has to related to the structure of the environment in some way.

The nature of that relationship becomes particularly complicated in the case of human ontogeny, where children gradually come to act in ways that go beyond the immediately available environmental conditions. They learn to change their environment, often pursuing some longer—or shorter-term objective, and thus participate in their own further development. Often, the direction in which child development is perceived to move is characterized as a transition from 'dependence' to 'independence'. Such a description, however, overlooks the basic interdependence of the child and the environment.

Instead of thinking of the concepts of 'dependence' and 'independence' as opposites, it is possible to see them as characteristics that are embedded in the same whole. In the case of the organism–environment system as that whole, the interdependence of these concepts can be helpful in explaining how children develop in ways that are simultaneously dependent and independent of the environment. For example, child development can be described as proceeding through different states of 'independent dependence' (rather than into 'independence'). This alternative concept (Valsiner, 1984a) illustrates the difference between the common-sense and scientific terminology quite well. From the perspective of common sense, a child (or an adult) who behaves or thinks 'on his own' and is not seen to be influenced by others, is considered to be 'independent' in our everyday discourse. However, from the perspective of developmental sciences (that rely on the axiom that only open systems are capable of development), the child can never be 'independent' from his environment. In the present context, we can think of an 'independent' (in our common sense) child as actually being 'independently dependent'—if we look at the child's immediate action, it seems to be unconstrained by any factors, and any efforts to introduce constraints may be actively blocked (e.g. a 2-year-old showing a temper-tantrum in a public place). However, if we consider the phenomenon more carefully it becomes evident that the seemingly 'independent' action has emerged in the context of the child's dependence upon its environment and social interaction partners. The latter may facilitate the emergence of the notion of 'independence' as part of the child's emerging cognitive system. Consider an observation of a mother and her 3.5-month-old daughter interacting. The mother tries to get the infant to pull herself up from the back first to sitting, and then to the standing position. She manages to get the infant to hold on to a ring, and pulls the child up to stand, commenting: 'You are a big girl! You did it all by yourself!' It was obvious that the task described could be accomplished only by the mother–infant joint efforts, where the mother played the leading role. Nevertheless, after the task was accomplished, she discounted her own role in it and attributed the responsibility fully to the child's action—all by *herself!* This, of course, happened when the observer (who shared the mother's cultural background) was present, and thus the other's verbal comment obviously played a communicative role in her showing herself and her daughter to the observer from the *culturally expected angle* of doing one's best for the baby whose early independence is promoted. On the one hand, the mother's verbal commentary about the child's behavior constitutes early exposure of the child to the use of language in making self-attributions in situations where the child depends on cooperation for accomplishing some task. On the other, the mother demonstrated her own 'independent dependence' by sending the message to the observer that was prescribed by her own background socialization.

The concept of 'independent dependence' was introduced in a context (Valsiner, 1984c) of efforts to make sense of curious features of human personality: many people claim that their thoughts and actions are completely 'independent', whereas in actuality they may—*on their own initiative*—follow the rules that somebody else has set up for their acting and thinking. Child-rearing ideologies often put an emphasis on developing 'independent dependence' of children to their culture as an important educational goal. Thus, the explicit emphasis on 'conscious discipline' that is evident in the pedagogical writings of the well-known Soviet educationalist Anton Makarenko illustrates the social context of that general goal. According to him, the model Soviet citizen.

> is expected not only to appreciate to what end and why it is necessry for him to carry out this or that command, but also actively to endeavour to carry it out to the very best of his ability. Yet that is still not everything. Our citizens are expected to do their duty at any moment of their lives without waiting for instructions or orders, they are expected to be ready to take the initiative and be possessed of creative will. It is hoped at the same time that they will only do what is really useful and necessary for our society and our country and that in this work they will not be deterred by any difficulties and obstacles. . . . In respect of our common enemies it is demanded of every individual that he resolutely obstruct their activities and be constantly vigilant whatever unpleasantnesses and dangers might ensue. (Kumarin, 1976, p. 246)

Such statement of the goal of arriving at 'conscious discipline' as a result of education matches educational and child socialization goals in principle in any culture, although the particulars of how the socialized person is expected to act obviously vary. In a way, the common-sense concept of 'independence' can be viewed as the successful result of cultural socialization within Western industrialized cultures. That concept has been socialized in conjunction with Protestant religious belief systems. That belief itself is an example of independent dependence—individuals are socialized within the culture (case of dependence) to believe that they are independent of their environment and 'free' to act in any way (idea of independence). The belief in one's independence is thus dependent on the culture within which one is socialized. The process of socialization, however, necessarily involves cooperation of different persons—of both the socializers and the socialized. James Mark Baldwin described this process, that illustrates the point made here fairly well:

> The growth of human personality has been found to be pre-eminently a matter of social suggestion. The material from which the child draws is found in the store of accomplished activities, forms, patterns, organizations, etc. which society already possesses. These serve as ready stimulating agencies, loadstones

so to speak, to his dawning energies, to draw him ever on in his career of growth into the safe, sound, useful network of personal acquisitions and social relationships which the slow progress of the race has set in permanent form. All this he owes, at any rate in the first instance, to society. (Baldwin, 1902, p. 75).

In the present context, the meaning of 'independent dependence' is defined in ways that include organism–environment relationships. In terms of the *boundaries that define the range of possibilities* of behavior, any organism is fully *dependent* on both its own structure and on that of the environment. At the same time, *within* the boundaries of the set of possibilities an organism may (but need not always) have the opportunity of choice between different ways of behaving, or of constructing new ways of acting which are possible given the particular coupling of the organism and the environment.

The concept of 'independent dependence' is closely linked with the ecological approach in psychology where the person–environment interdependence is turned into the object of investigation (Valsiner and Benigni, 1986). The structures of the person and the environment specify the dependence of the person on the environment, and that dependence makes it possible for the person to act independently (but within limits) upon the environment in an effort to restructure it. When the environment is transformed, its relationship with the person is changed, and this change guides the person's development. Further elaboration of the multiplicity of courses of development requires the adoption of some spatial-dynamic metaphoric image that can be used to describe the organism–environment relationship and its development. Waddington's metaphor of the 'epigenetic landscape' and his concept of 'canalization' may prove to be useful to that end.

4.1.4 Development by canalization

The notion of canalization was introduced to developmental biology by Waddington (1942, 1966, 1968, 1970) who used it in discussing genotype–phenotype relationships. The term 'canalization' describes an epigenetic mechanism that leads to definite outcomes: 'The main thesis is that developmental reactions, *as they occur in organisms submitted to natural selection*, are in general canalized. That is to say, they are adjusted so as to bring about one definite end-result regardless of minor variations in conditions during the course of the reaction' (Waddington, 1942, p. 563).

Waddington's concept of 'chreod', or buffered developmental pathway, illustrates the notion of the structured nature of the organism and its environment. According to Waddington's formulation, the genome's interaction with environment results in conditions which define the set of further possible pathways of change (cf. Waddington, 1966, pp. 109–111). The 'chreods' (or in other terms 'necessary pathways') are structurally organized on the plane of an 'epigenetic landscape' (see Figure 4.1).

84

The developmental pathways are constructed to possess self-stabilizing characteristics that restrain the variation of the organism–environment system as it changes over time (Waddington, 1970, pp. 185–186). By restraining the further development of the organism the chreods mediate the process of development via *canalization* (gradual guidance and direction). The notion of canalization is of theoretical importance for developmental biology and psychology since it illustrates the bounded character of developmental processes. Development is canalized in the direction of the organism's adult state by a system of constraints that leave the *particular* individual organism's developmental route largely indeterminate (and therefore adaptable to unexpected changes in the environment) in the sense of *exact* prediction of its future. However, the *principal direction* of development in general terms is predictable from constraints that constitute the canalizing system.

Waddington's concept of canalization cannot be carried over from its original context to the present one without some modifications. Two important changes are necessary. First, the set of constraints that are present in human socialization are not present in a static form during the whole period of childhood (e.g. like the 'valleys' on Waddington's epigenetic landscape). Instead, the particular constraints are set up by the relationships within the CAREGIVER(S) ⟷ (CHILD ⟷ ENVIRONMENT) system. The

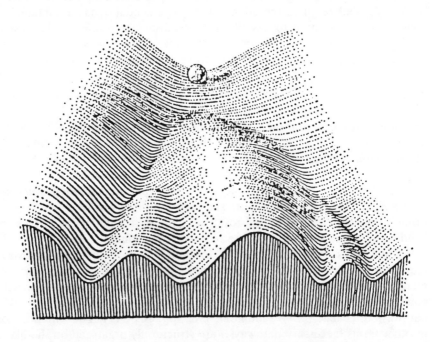

Figure 4.1. An example of the 'epigenetic landscape'

constraint structure is not 'just there' for the child to develop by, but is made up by purposefully acting participants who take the child's current developmental state into account in one or another way. Secondly, the child itself can actively constrain its own development—in the immediate (short) term or by feed-forward preparation of constraints a longer term ahead. In either case, the child participates actively in its own development by altering its constraining structure. Canalization as the general mechanism of children's action and cognitive development is a gradual process where earlier child–environment structures guide the child's subsequent development in the direction of new structures, which in their turn canalize the child's progress further.

4.1.5 Meaningfulness of person and environment

As Vygotsky began to realize in the course of his venture into psychology, human being are constructors of meanings and personal senses (see 3.5.2). A human child is born not only into a physically structured environment (like the offspring of all species), but also into one that is meaningfully organized. Places, objects within places, and different actions that can be performed with objects either have culturally specified meanings for people, or develop them in accordance with the culture's folk model of meanings at the given time (Holy and Stuchlik, 1981).

The inevitability of the development of meaningfulness of environments stems from the human use of signs in controlling their environments and themselves (Vygotsky, 1978; Vygotsky and Luria, 1930). The adults and older children either have developed their own personal understanding of the world around them (system of personal senses), or are on their way to estabishing such system. In contrast, the newborn is at the very beginning of that developmental course. His advance along these lines involves strong reliance on the personal senses of people around him in the form of intersubjectivity (Trevarthen, 1977, 1979a, 1979b, 1982). In the context of intersubjective processes of child–others interaction, the child constructs his own personal sense system under the guidance of other people: parents and other adult relatives, older siblings, peers, and even younger siblings. The developing child is a co-constructor of the cultural meaning system, since he is a target of his caregivers' purposeful and culturally organized actions. However, the child's input into the cultural meaning system is mediated by the personal sense systems of his caregivers. The cultural meanings are not transmitted from society to child's parents and from them to the child in an immutable form. Instead, each participant in this social communication process is a co-constructor of the cultural meanings. Thus, the parents develop their personal sense system on the basis of *their* interpretation of cultural rules and expectancies. The part of their personal sense systems that is relevant for child development involves their meaningful organization of the home environment (that will be shared by the children), and their thinking about child-rearing goals and practices. The multitude of different objects in adults' homes that are parts of their personal culture is noteworthy (see Czikszentmihaly and Rochberg-Halton, 1981). As the children develop, they act within such personalized environment of the parents, and acquire information about their meaningfulness by parental counter-actions to their actions. The children develop their versions of the cultural meaning system as a result of their social interaction with others. These versions are constructed by the children, and do not constitute a simple copy of the parents' sense systems. Children's versions build in innovative ways upon the structure of the culturally organized information that they experience in interaction with others and in their exploration of the man-made physical environment. The children grow up in meaningfully structured home environments that they inherit socially (by the mere fact of being born to *their* families), and which guide them towards construction of their own personal sense systems.

4.2 The possible and the actual in psychological phenomena

Traditional modes of thinking in psychology have been particularly ineffective in dealing with events that *could, but need not, happen*. This is the distinction between the *possible* and the *actual*. Conceptual traditions in psychology have offered many ways for describing and explaining what actually happens, while leaving largely unanalyzed its relationships with what is possible. In cognitive psychology, efforts to reconstruct knowledge about the person's possibilities frequently take the form of looking for 'competence' *in* the person, rather than in person–environment relationship. The need to examine these relationships is particularly important in developmental psychology. Development constitutes the process of transformation of what is possible at an earlier stage of organism's life, into what is actual at a later stage. The later stage in its turn provides the organism with new possibilities, some of which become actualized and serve as a basis for still further development.

Usually, it is the prediction of the actual future occurrence of psychological phenomena, rather than their possible occurrence, which has been attempted in psychology. Since the prior performance can be only a small (actualized) aspect of the total set of possibilities of an organism within a given environment, and since the realm of possibility may change over time, the prediction of subsequent performance is unlikely to be accurate. Furthermore, even if it happens to be adequate, it does not explain the processes by which the subsequent performance came into being. The explanation of psychological development through the prediction of future performance from some earlier performance without an analysis of the organism–environment interdependence that generates the performances is not feasible on epistemological grounds. Historically it originates in psychology's traditional emphasis on decontextualization of its phenomena, which has been the reason for much of psychology's inefficiency in explaining its phenomena.

In principle it may be impossible to get to know a child's competence on the basis of analyzing only his performance, if the latter is taken out of its environmental and temporal context. How, then, can the issue of the child's potentials be addressed? Here it is suggested that the competence can be studied by analyzing the actual performance as it relates to what is possible for the given child in the particular context. The latter is defined by a set of constraints (boundary conditions) that both the organism and its environment set up for their relationship at a given time. An approach based on understanding sets of constraints has been proposed in other areas of contemporary science. David Bohm explains its rationale viewed from the perspective of physics:

> What is needed in a relativistic theory is to give up altogether the notion that the world is constituted of basic objects or 'building blocks'. Rather, one has to view the world in terms of universal flux of events and processes. Thus . . . instead of thinking of a particle, one is to think of a 'world tube'.
>
> This world tube represents an infinitely complex process of a structure in movement and development which is centered in a region indicated by the boundaries of the tube. . . . One can perhaps illustrate what is meant here by considering the 'stream of consciousness'. This flux of awareness is not precisely definable, and yet it is evidently prior to the definable forms of thoughts and ideas which can be seen to form and dissolve in the flux, like ripples, waves, and vorticles in a flowing stream. As happens with such patterns of movement in a stream som ethoughts recur and persist in a more or less stable way, while others are evanescent. (Reproduced with permission from Bohm, 1980, pp. 9–11).

Bohm's idea of the 'world tube' is illustrated by schematic drawings in Figure 4.2

That figure illustrates how a constraint-oriented approach affords the study of possibility of events. The actual position of phenomena in either of the two worlds tubes A or B in Figure 4.2(a) can be located in any place within the 'tube' at the given time. Furthermore, over time the phenomenon may move to another location within the tube. There exists a wide variety of possible trajectories of the examples of the phenomenon within the 'world tube', *all of which inevitably come to the range specified by the boundaries of the 'tube'.* Communication between two processes ('world tubes' A and B in Figure 4.2(b) can be conceptualized as a connection that is set up between the 'tubes' with the help of constraints which channel the 'signal' process from 'tube' A to 'tube' B.

However, there is an important distinction between the physical and the biological worlds—the latter involves active participation by organisms in the construction of their development, whereas the former does not. This difference seems to be lost in Bohm's example. In nature and society, thelimits of what is possible develop together with the organism's active efforts

(a)

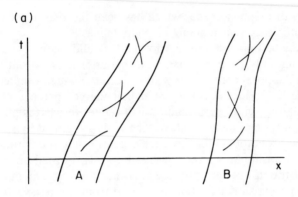

(b)

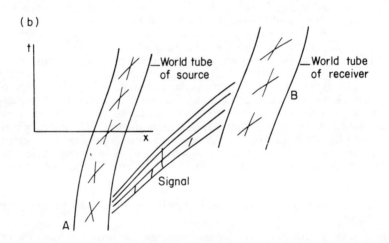

Figure 4.2. The world according to Bohm: description of processes as 'world tubes' (A), and the meaning of communication between two 'world tubes' (B). (Combined from Bohm, 1980: A, p. 10; B, p. 136, reproduced with permission)

to change its relationship with its environment. Organisms do not experience their environments passively, but construct (and reconstruct) both their environments and, through those, themselves (Baldwin, 1892; Lewontin, 1978, 1981). Thus, when a system, functioning within its current boundary conditions, develops into a qualitatively new state, *new* boundary conditions are set up for the further development of the system. These new constraints guide the system towards the possibility of developing into another new qualitative state, which in its turn would bring along a new set of constraints, and so on until the organism ceases to exist.

4.2.1 Constraints on the possibilities in child–environment relations: an illustrtion

When an infant begins to take an interest in objects, but before it can crawl, the set of objects that it can manipulate is limited by the impossibility to get to the objects outside the given location by the infant (organismic constraints), and by the availability of objects in the surroundings (environmental constraints). These two sets of constraints complement each other. While reaching for some of the objects in the immediate vicinity, the infant may exercise some motor skills that gradually assist and support locomotion. Once the infant has started to locomote (creep and crawl, and then walk independently), the previous constraints on its access to objects are changed, and replaced by others (e.g. parents' efforts to 'baby-proof' the home, taking dangerous objects away from the child's reach). The transition of the child into a new state in development has produced a qualitatively new set of constraints, which help the child to advance to the next state (with its novel constraints), and so on. For example, by the time a child is 3, the physical constraints that parents had used previously to prevent the child from getting into dangerous areas in the home, may no longer be necessary. The child by now has developed some internalized knowledge about the nature of these areas, and has internalized the physical 'barriers' that formerly constrained its access to these zones. Furthermore, the child can now be controlled by the caregivers through distal (verbal) means, which is a characteristic of another state of the child that renders the excesses of physical boundaries in the environment unnecessary for controlling the child's actions.

To summarize, the process of development is always limited by some boundary conditions (constraints) that are set up within the organism—environment relationships at any given time. These constraints define the set of what is possible in the organism–environment interaction, or (in terms often used in psychology) the *competence* of the organism *within* the given environmental conditions, and *at the given time*. Since biological and social phenomena are open systems, it is theoretically impossible, without eliminating the open nature of organisms, to talk about the competence of the *organism*, viewed independently from its environment. The term competence is applied here to the organism–environment relationships, although it may at first sound unusual because of its individual-directed connotation in everyday language. It refers to the circular relationship between the organism and its environment. Out of the set of possible forms of organism–environment relationships, the active organism actualizes some subset into its performance. By doing that, the organism actively participates in the construction of its further development. The organism's actions lead to its transformation into new states, with new sets of constraints that organize the possibilities for further development of the organism.

4.2.2 The concepts of constraint and boundary

Constraints delimit different areas of the field ('zones') and so canalize the development of an organism. In that sense the two concepts are related to each other: zones are specified by constraints, and constraints define zones

Webster's *Third New International Dictionary* (1981, p. 489) provides a set of meanings for the term 'constraint' that originates from a combination of the Latin verbs *'con'* + *'stringere'* (to draw tight). 'Constraint' is (1) the act or action of using force to prevent or condition an action; (2) the quality or state of being checked, restricted, or compelled to avoid or perform some action; (3) compulsion by circumstances, the force of necessity; (4) control over one's own feelings, behavior, or actions that is exercised either to feign or repress; and (5) the sense of being constrained, checked, or inhibited. These different meanings of the term, assembled into the dictionary, converge on the notion of control of action. The use of the term 'constraint' in science is rooted in the common language, where in the Western cultural meaning systems the emotional connotation of the term often includes an implicit reference to the control of actions against the actor's wishes or wellbeing. This negative connotation of the term in our common sense is not to be taken over when constraint is used in psychological discourse. Irrespective of whether the parents or children experience negative (or positive) emotions when child socialization through canalization by constraints takes place, the scientific use of the term constraint should remain neutral in its ideological connotations. Constraints are just a part of children's developmental setting as it is viewed from the present standpoint; they are neither negative nor positive in any sense. Their existence can be often proved by the subjects' active emotional protest actions observed in the real life. These actions should not divert the developmental psychologist from his task of explaining the process of child development in general. Rather, the constraints used in child socialization set the stage for the child's constructive further development—both in the possible 'negative' and 'positive' valued directions as these are judged by people who have vested personal interests in children's development within their culture.

The term 'constraint' has been used in similar neutral manner in other sciences. For example, Pattee has described its use in physics:

> In common language the concept of constraint is a kind of forceful confinement which limits our freedom. The same general concept may also hold in physical systems where the constraint is a fixed boundary, like the box which confines the molecules of a gas. . . . In other words, constraints are most easily explained as the invention of the physicist who sees a new way of looking at a problem which is much simpler or more useful than taking into account all degrees of freedom with equal detail. (Pattee, 1971, pp. 260–261)

> Constraints, unlike laws of nature, must be the consequence of what we call some form of material structure, such as molecules, membranes, typewriters,

or table tops, these structures may be static or time-dependent, but in either case it is important to realize that they are made up of matter which at all times obeys the fundamental laws of nature in addition to behaving as a constraint. (Pattee, 1972, p. 250).

It is easy to see that the physical definition of constraint covers only a narrow area of the semantic field of the term as it can be used in psychology. In the analysis of child development we may have examples of physical constraints in early childhood (playpens, safety latches, baby-gates) that indeed limit the degrees of freedom of the child's actions. However, once the child develops further, the physical constraints give way to internalized psychological phenomena (e.g. beliefs, rules of logic, social norms) that continue to serve the function of constraining the person's degrees of freedom of acting, feeling, and thinking. Many people are actively seeking ways to construct such constraints within themselves—often by establishing a set of external constraints initially, which are gradually transformed into a set of intra-personal psychological constraints. Psychology's conceptual knowhow that affords explanation of such phenomena is still largely underdeveloped. Very real phenomena—for instance, joining the army, or a religious cult, or aligning one's acting and thinking with the propagated ideas of a social institution—are only rarely described (Festinger, Riecken, and Schachter, 1956) and even less effectively explained. Fortunately, new ways of analyzing personality organization in relation to its control over the environment have recently been developed that may help to overcome this conceptual weakness of traditional psychology (see the concepts of secondary and primary control introduced by Rothbaum, Weisz, and Snyder, 1982).

The majority of psychological phenomena that are the results of socialization processes—norms of acting in different settings, moral beliefs, sociopolitical or religious convictions—constitute cases of internalized (cognitive and emotional) sets of constraints. These constraints cannot be studied by an analysis of the person's external environment, but require a combination of observation of his actions within an environmental setting, and his own thinking about these actions, as the database. Although in this book the concept of constraint is used mostly in ways that apply to physically or behaviorally verifiable limitations set upon the children's action, this more restricted empirical application of the term should not obscure its internalized nature in middle and later childhood and adolescence, as well as in adulthood. Constraints organize both inter-individual and intra-individual aspects of psychological processes. It is only in the early years of child development that they can be analyzed as basically external. In later years they become internalized from the children's external experience, and constructed by children internally in their minds. By basing the theory in the present book on the idea of constraints as the major canalizing device of child development, the way into the inevitable methodological difficulty of accessing the internal constraint system of a person is likewise opened. That difficulty may be as formidable as the history of specifying what 'schema' means has been in cognitive developmental psychology.

The theoretical framework in this book cannot be attributed any originality in adopting the idea of constraints as its basis. Lewin's field theory is historically the pioneering framework within which the concepts denoting constraints ('boundary', 'barrier') were introduced. It is interesting that Lewin did little to elaborate on the meanings of these terms, whereas his treatment of other concepts of the field theory is extensive (e.g. Lewin, 1936a, 1938). He defined the boundary of a psychological region as 'those points of a region for which there is no surrounding that lies entirely within the region' (Lewin, 1936a, p. 118). Bringing in more specific examples where boundaries are involved, Lewin had little difficulty in finding instances of domains within which the boundary concept is intuitively feasible. For example, Lewin illustrated his definition of boundary by analyzing how it structures the person's locomotion:

> In carrying out a locomotion the experience of crossing a boundary is often a clear one. This is for instance the case when one climbs over a fence or enters a strange house for the first time; or, to use an example of a quasi-social locomotion, if one is admitted to membership in a club by some special ceremony. Thereby the position of the boundary is quite accurately determined. However, there are cases in which one can establish with certainty that the locomotion has proceeded from one region into another one, although the crossing of the boundary does not become evident as a special event during locomotion. For instance, one can gradually pass from one circle into another. A path may lead from the mountains into lower hills and on to a plain, or from a great city through more and more open suburbs into the country and it may be impossible to describe definite boundaries between these regions. The same is true for all gradual transitions between two regions. For instance, it can happen in conversation that one is not even aware of a 'gradual transition.' That the person has passed the boundary can then be inferred only indirectly from the fact that he is in another region. In these cases it even remains doubtful how many boundaries and intermediate regions the locomotion has crossed. (Lewn, 1936a, p. 119)

Lewin's passing interest in the nature of different kinds of boundaries may be explained by his overwhelming use of the concepts of 'force' and 'locomotion' for the explanation of a person's transformation of the life space. For Lewin it was possible to be satisfied with a look at only those boundaries in a person's life space that could be described as strict and well-delineated, and which can be described by his use of topological diagrams which he and his disciples were always fond of drawing. In contrast, the present theoretical framework does not use the concept of 'force' in its explanatory terminology but concentrates on the canalizing role of different sets of zone boundaries instead. Therefore in the present context it is essential to analyze the concepts of boundary and zone in greater depth.

Lewin's suggestion for solving the problem of gradual boundaries in the life space was to describe them through the concept of 'boundary zone'—not as a one-dimensional but at least a two-dimensional region. According to the width of 'boundary zones' it is then possible to talk about more or less 'sharp' boundaries (Lewin, 1936a, p. 120). Through equating the 'width' of the 'boundary zone' with its 'unsharpness', Lewin created a convenient way for his descriptive topology to reduce fuzzy-looking boundary zones into their strict descriptions by Jordan curves (see Lewin, 1936a, p. 121, for the argument in favor of this transformation). However, his treatment of the issues of 'boundary zone' and 'sharpness of the boundary' remains confused because of his efforts to talk of the field structure and its dynamics at the same time, as can be seen in the following quote:

> Sharp psychological boundaries correspond best to mathematical boundaries. On the other hand not every boundary with pronounced depth implies an unsharp transition. An example from social psychology may serve as a demonstration. While the boundary between different economic classes is in general relatively unsharp and is characterized by a gradual transition, the boundary of some social groups such as an exclusive club is sharply defined. This means that for every person it is clearly determined whether or not he belongs to the group. Nevertheless the boundary of such a group can have the character of a boundary zone. In order to join the club for example it may be necessary to have one's name put on a waiting list in advance. Sometimes several such stages are prescribed. Therefore the existence of a boundary zone does not necessarily lessen the sharpness of the boundary, for the boundary zone itself may be a region which is clearly structured and sharply defined as to its boundaries. (Lewin, 1936a, pp. 121–122)

The first part of this quote describes the structure of field conditions (with fluid and sharp boundaries) in their static form. Both fuzzy (as in the case of social class boundaries) and strict (e.g. the example of the exclusive club) boundaries coexist within the same field. However, the second part of the quote refers to the microgenetic transformation of the person's field over time (e.g. the route by which a person can gradually maneuver himself to become a member of the club). The would-be member of the club gradually crosses the boundary, and viewed over time the boundary for him indeed constitutes a boundary zone that can be crossed only gradually. However, all through the period of *the given* person's movement to club membership, the strictness of the static nature of the boundary between the members and non-members of the group *remains the same for other persons*—both current members or outsiders. It is in this context that Basov's emphasis on treating environment as a relational concept (see 4.1.2) is worth reminding. The person who is in the process of joining the club changes the boundary of the club membership *for himself* while moving to become a member, but not for any other person (neither those who are already members, nor for those who remain non-members).

The mixing of structural-static and microgenetic perspectives in Lewin's thinking in the case of defining the nature of boundary zones may have contributed to the conceptual difficulties that Lewin had in defining the boundary concept in lieu of the existence of both strict and fuzzy boundaries in the field at the given time, and the change in the nature of these boundaries (e.g. fuzzy ones becoming strict, or vice versa) over time. Lewin used his concept of 'boundary' usually in cases where he provided analysis of phenomena from the perspective of their mostly static state of existence (e.g. Lewin, 1933, 1935a, 1935b, 1936a, 1936d). However, even in these cases he tended to fuse the structural description of the person–environment fields with the dynamic functioning of 'locomotion' and 'forces' in that field. For example, he described the individual as a *relatively* closed system, where 'how strongly the environment operates upon the individual will . . . be determined (apart from the structure and forces of the situation) by the functional *firmness of the boundaries* between individual and environment' (Lewin, 1933, p. 619). Similar emphasis on the use of his boundary concept is evident in his efforts to analyze the psychological issues of minority groups, especially when he tried to explain the tragic history of the sitatuion of Jews in Germany during and before the 1930s (Lewin, 1935b). As a new immigrant the United States, Lewin was obviously interested in understanding the organization of life in his new country, and again his use of the boundary concept served the purpose in his German–American comparison. Lewin argued that in the case of personality structure of Americans the most private regions are made inaccessible to others through excessively 'thick' boundaries, whereas the comparable boundary in the personality structure of Germans covers a 'zone' consisting of different, less 'thick' boundaries to be crossed by others in their becoming close to the person (see Lewin, 1936b, p. 283 and 284). Again, in these examples Lewin fused the functional and structural aspects of the psychological explanation *without* explicitly introducing the time parameter into the analysis (which he, however, later indeed tried to do—see Lewin, 1939, 1942, 1943a—but in these examples the emphasis on the nature of the boundaries in the field was negligible).

Lewin's major interest in the functional organization of the life space explains the prevalence of the concepts of 'locomotion', 'force', and 'valence' ('Aufforderungscharakter') over those of 'boundary' and 'zone' in his theoretical analyses of phenomena. In *his* theoretical 'life space' the concept of 'boundary' was narrowed down to the concept of 'barrier' which was defined strictly in connection with the 'force' concept:

> We shall call boundaries (boundary zones) which offer resistance to psychological locomotion 'barriers'. We shall speak of barriers of different strength according to their degree of resistance.
> We shall continue to use the concept of boundary in a purely topological sense. The term 'psychologically real' boundary therefore does not imply defined dynamic properties. (Lewin, 1936a, p. 124)

This definitional separation of 'barrier' and 'boundary' by Lewin illustrates the conceptual dilemma that the originator of the field theory in psychology was in. On the one hand, the topological use of the boundary concept could fit the description of the static structure of the psychological field sufficiently well, but it offered no direct connections with the dynamic concepts that Lewin put an emphasis on. On the other hand, some notion of structural organization of the field was necessary as the context within which the 'locomotion', the work of 'forces' and 'valences', can be clearly demonstrated. The concept of 'barrier' as a functional (=locomotion-related) boundary served well for Lewin's theoretical purposes. In his empirical studies (e.g. Barker, Dembo, and Lewin, 1941) it is exactly the 'barrier behavior' that was studied, rather than the structure of boundaries in the field, or the transformation of that structure. In summary, *Lewin's theoretical analysis of the microgenesis of psychological phenomena made use structural concepts as context for the dynamic ones* in his efforts to analyze the processes that determine person's actions within the environment. In contrast, the present theoretical framework sets up a balance between the context (structured environment) and the acting individual—the latter participates in the construction (or reconstruction) of the former, and the structured environment in its terms canalizes the development of the individual towards culturally acceptable and required achievements.

4.2.3 Definition of 'zone', and its different representations

The environment of the developing child is structured by sets of boundaries that define different zones of the child's environment. The environment is zoned, or—to use a rare but fitting term from Webster's *Dictionary* (1981, p. 2660)—it is *zoniferous*.

Webster's *Dictionary* (1981) also provides a range of meanings for the term 'zone'. The Latin root-meaning of the word *zona*—girdle or belt—has been subsequently extended to different domains of knowledge, particularly those where spatial areas of metaphors are used (as in geography, military organization, economics, anatomy, and physiology). One of the explanations that Webster provides—'a region or area set off or charcterized as distinct from surrounding or adjoining parts'—fits the general notion of the term as it is used in the present theoretical context.

Lewin's theoretical thinking included the use of the zone-concept. The concept of 'Zone of Free Movement' that constitutes a part of the present theory follows from Lewin's introduction of the concepts of region of freedom of movement (Lewin, 1933) and space of free movement (Lewin, 1939). Lewin's own use of the zone-concept itself was related to the question of boudaries in life space occupying an area of differenting width. He also discussed the issue of 'zones of undetermined quality'—the frequent cases in which the boundary zones contain 'undetermined sectors' or 'psychologically empty' areas (Lewin, 1936a, pp. 130–131). Compared to Lewin's use of the zone-concept, the present application of the term is wider in its meaning, including his notions of 'region' and 'space'.

The zone-concept as it is used here can be clarified by the use of a diagram. The zone can be an area that is characterized as distinct from its surroundings in different ways. Figure 4.3 provides some illustrations that serve the purpose of clarification of the concept.

First, the simplest way of depiction of such a zone is a region that is surrounded by a continuous and evenly sharp boundary (zone X in Figure 4.3(a). However, the surroundings of such a zone constitute a zone in itself (zone Y) which is observably bounded on the one side (by the boundary of zones X and Y), but the boundary of the other sides of Y is undetermined. This diagram helps to express the point that a zone need not be bounded (closed) on all of its sides. In fact, regularly bounded zones like X in Figure 4.3(a) are rare in reality. Instead, the majority of zones that enclose areas of space are *partially discontinuous* and *unevenly bounded*, like zone X in Figure 4.3(b). This example illustrates the case of semi-peremable boundary of zone X with zone Y in a particular locus. Furthermore, a zone may be specified by a *discontinuous boundary* (e.g. Figure 4.3(c)) that separates zone X from zone Y in some loci strictly, whereas allowing the two zones to be fused and inseparable in other areas. The example in Figure 4.3(d) moves one step further, specifying as zone Y all the field except for points a, b, and c which have strict boundaries with Y and are the only areas in the field

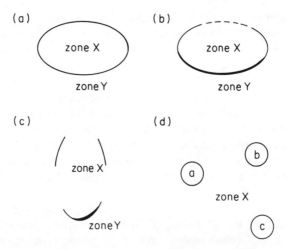

Figure 4.3. Schematic illustrations of different explications of the 'zone' concept: A. Separation of zones by homogeneous boundary with closed contour; B. Separation of zones by heterogeneous and semi-permeable boundary with closed contour; C. Separation of zones by heterogeneous and discontinuous boundary; D. Determination of a zone in exclusive terms ('zone X includes everything except a, b, and c')

that are excluded from zone Y. It is easy to see that the excluded points are similar to zone X in Figure 4.3(d), since a point constitutes a zone with strict boundaries but of infinitely small area.

The four examples of different zones given in graphic form in Figure 4.3 do not constitute the full list of possible versions of all conceivable forms of zones that one may think of. The function of these examples is to emphasize that the zone-concept need not be limited to the intuitively most obvious case—that of a continuously bounded area. Instead, it can include fuzzy or semi-permeable boundaries, or an undefined boundary in many areas of the zone. The epistemological usefulness of the zone and boundary concepts lies in their flexibility in capturing the often partially fuzzy or indeterminate nature of the phenomena, rather than in adding stricter preciseness to our description of inherently imprecise reality.

4.3 The constituents of the present theory

The present theoretical framework is individual–socioecological in its nature. The developing child is conceptualized in the context of his relationships with the culturally and physically structured environment, where the child's actions upon that environment are guided by assistance from other human beings—parents, siblings, peers, teachers, etc. The particular physical structure of the environment of a human child is set up by the activities of other human beings, and modified by them over time. In this respect, all physical environment of human children is cultural. Children are acting within the culturally structured environments, and under the direction of 'social others'.

The present theoretical framework uses three basic zone-concepts that are used to depict canalization of children's action within culture. These concepts constitute abstractions which under particular circumstances are 'filled in' with specific objects, places, actions, and their meanings. The mechanisms described by these concepts are construed as working as a system, so no direct causal properties can be attached to any of the concepts on their own.

4.3.1 The 'Zone of Free Movement' and its properties

In the context of child–environment relationships, the child's freedom of choice of action (and thinking) is limited by a set of constraints, that define the *Zone of Free Movement* or *Zone of Freedom of Movement* (abbreviated as ZFM) of the child at the given time and in the particular environment. The concept of Zone of Free Movement originates in the field theory of Kurt Lewin (Lewin, 1933, 1939). The ZFM structures the child's (1) access to different areas in the environment, (2) availability of different objects within an accessible area, and (3) ways of acting with available objects in the accessible area. As a result of development the child learns to set up ZFMs in his personal thinking and feeling—the ZFMs become internalized.

In the internalized case, the Zone of Free Movement provides a structural framework for the child's cognitive activity and emotions, as the latter are to be controlled in culturally expected ways in different social situations (see Cole, 1985; Lutz, 1983). Even in the internalized case, ZFMs regulate the relationships of the person with the environment. The Zone of Free Movement is therefore a *socially constructed cognitive structure of child–environment relationships* (Valsiner, 1984d, p. 68). It is 'socially constructed' as it is based on adults' (and older siblings') cultural meaning systems, and constructed in interaction with them. It is a 'cognitive structure' because it organizes child–environment relationships on the basis of cultural meanings of the society, that become internalized by the developing children in the process of their acting within these environments. The ZFM is simultaneously a structure of the child's actions within the environment at the given time, and the future structure of the thinking of the child. The development of internal cognitive processes starts from external acting of the child within its environment (Piaget, 1977; Vygotsky, 1956, 1960, 1978), and proceeds towards internalization of the external experience.

The Zone of Free Movement has a number of properties:

(a) It is always based on the child's relationships with the structure of the given environmental setting. At any time in life the child's (adult's) access to some areas in the environment is seemingly unlimited, whereas access to some other areas is blocked for the person. In addition, there can exist areas in a person's environment in respect to which their being 'in' or 'off' limits is not exactly specified at the given time. An effort to clarify that status may lead either to access to these areas, or their blocked-off status. The notion of 'area' can also be applied beyond the geographically organized space, and can include different objects in places, different actions with the same object. Last, but not least, it can also be extended to thoughts and feelings.

(b) It is based on the meanings of different aspects of the environment for the 'social other' (parent, sibling, schoolteacher, etc.), who is the leading organizer (but not the sole determiner) of Zones of Free Movement for the child. Either the 'social other' or the child may make the first move in structuring the ZFM. However it is the child's caregiver who is the gatekeeper of the ZFM as it is constructed, and reconstructed from time to time. For example, when a 2-year-old child and his mother enter a new environment (e.g. during a visit to a friend's home), it can be the child (who goes to a precious vase in the living room and tries to push it onto the floor), or the mother (who tells the child immediately when they enter the room not to touch the vase), who may start the construction of a particular ZFM. The construction of the ZFM may involve both proactive and reactive (see Holden, 1985) child-control techniques. Whichever of the two, adult or child, starts the construction, the resulting ZFM can be constructed by different routes. On the one extreme, the caregiver may play an overwhelmingly dominant role in its construction and the child is left with the option of conforming to the ZFM as it is unilaterally set up for him. On the other extreme, we have occasions where the 'social others' of the child participate minimally in the construction of ZFMs, and the major role in that ends up played by the child. In the majority of cases in the contemporary European and North American cultures, ZFMs are constructed in child–adult joint action. Through a series of alternate 'moves' by both sides (by the mother's efforts to set up limits on the child's action, and by the child's actions that either cross the limits, or stay within them) the ZFM is set up, maintained, and changed.

(c)   The ZFM is often set up on the basis of the parent's understanding of what the child *can* do in the given setting, in conjunction with what he is doing, or has done in the past. Orientation towards the future possible actions is thus a part the construction of ZFM.

(d)   The ZFM is reconstructed when the adult and the child enter a novel environment. The adult analyzes the new setting, on the basis of his/her knowledge of the former action of the child, and the potential future action afforded to the child by the new environment. That analysis—based on cognitive simulation of scenarios of possible events—leads to the basic understanding of how the ZFM could be constructed. Beyond that, the actual behavior of the child may lead to further refinement, or change, of the simulated ZFM.

Obviously, the ZFM is a means to an end, rather than the end itself. It is set up to organize child–environment relationships, and through that, to canalize the development of the child in directions that are accepted in the given culture at large. As a means, a particular ZFM can become obsolete, once the child is past a certain age, and his relationships with the environment are changed. It is particularly easy to bear this in mind, when one thinks of man-made physical constraining devices (playpens, baby-gates, cribs) that occupy the role of important organizers of infants' and toddlers' relationships with their Western middle-class environments. Once the functions carried out by them are no longer important in the child's development, these devices (and the ZFMs they helped to set up) are discarded and replaced by others. Within the ZFM, however, different actions are made differentially available to the child through selective support of these actions being provided by people in the child's environment. This unevenness of the organization of the ZFM requires the introduction of another zone-concept that characterizes further social structuring of the Zone of Free Movement.

4.3.2 The Zone of Promoted Action

If the ZFM is here conceptualized as an inhibitory psychological mechanism, then its counterpart is oriented towards the promotion of new skills. That zone is called the Zone of Promoted Action (abbreviated: ZPA) (Valsiner, 1984d, p. 68; 1985, p. 136). The ZPA is a set of activities, objects, or areas in the environment, in respect of which the child's actions are promoted. Parents may get involved in special efforts to promote the child's actions with an object that they consider important for the child's development. The child may, but need not, be interested in acting with that object. The parents, however, may try to do whatever they consider feasible to promote the child's action with that particular object. The ways in which ZPA functions in everyday lives of families are easily observable at any age of children. For example, during a session of 'free play' of the parents and their toddler in the living room at home, the parents may try to get (and keep) the child interested in reading a children's book, so that understanding of words and pictures, and knowledge of the alphabet, could be promoted. The child, however, may be captivated by the book reading only for a short while, and will move on to other activities soon. The parents may try to get the child to continue with book reading, but if many other activities are available within the ZFM for the child, parents' efforts may be to no avail.

The important characteristic of ZPA is its *non-binding nature*. Once a ZPA is set up but the child does not follow the lead of the parents' promotion effort but acts with other objects (in other ways) within the ZFM, there is no way in which the child can be made to act within the ZPA (unless the ZPA is turned into ZFM).

Perhaps a little analogy from the adults' world clarifies the difference between the ZFM and ZPA. Different producers of various products are interested in selling these products to the customers. However, in the case of free-market economy, a producer cannot force any buyer to buy its particular brand. Instead, the producer can only persuade the potential buyer to act in ways favorable for him. In this way, commercial advertisement acquires prominence under conditions of free-market economy. All sellers advertise their products in a hyperactive way, but it is up to the buyer to decide which of the competing products (if any) to buy. There is a direct analogy between that state of affairs in producer–consumer relations and the establishment of Zones of Promoted Action in adult–child relationships. In both cases, the side who establishes the ZPA cannot bind the other to accept it, but has to try to persuade him to that end. In contrast, the non-binding nature of ZPAs set in adults' consumer world disappears as soon as a monopoly on the production of some product, or its distribution, is established. In this case, the producer (or distributor) has full control over the market, and need not try to persuade the potential buyer in order to get him to buy his product—since everything that can be bought is produced by him anyway, and the buyer has no alternatives. State-controlled production and distribution systems in different non-Western countries provide many examples of how the economic life is organized under these conditions. The ZFMs in child socialization, that are set up by parents, resemble such monopolies—the only options available to the child are the ones he can choose among, and as long as it does not matter to the parent which is chosen, no ZPA need to be present.

More usually, both ZFMs and ZPAs are used by child caregivers in their socialization of children, at least in contemporary Western industrialized countries. It is more accurate not to separate the two zone-concepts from each other, but to consider them as parts of the same whole: the ZFM/ZPA complex.

4.3.3 Relationships between ZFM and ZPA

The two types of zone-concepts—Zones of Free Movement and Zones of Promoted Action—work jointly as the mechanisms by which canalization of children's development are organized. This applies equally to the development of children's actions and thinking. In the first years of life, the joint work of the ZFM/ZPA system is easily observable in naturalistic settings. Later during the childhood, however, some of the functioning of that complex becomes rarely observable as a result of children's internalization of the control over their own actions and thinking.

In some environmental settings, the ZFM/ZPA complex remains observable for a longer time over childhood. One of such settings in which the relationships between ZFMs and ZPAs can be traced both historically and cross-culturally is education. This is not surprising, since education involves a purposeful effort by the adults to educate children in domains of knowledge that require more skillful and mature persons to acquire it. Every form of education, informal or formal (see Greenfield and Lave, 1982), contains some limits set up to constrain the developing children's exposure to, and participation in, some aspects of adults' lives. Certain efforts by children to observe and/or participate in some activities of the adults are strictly prohibited. For example, contemporary American children do not learn about sexual activity by observing their parents engaging in it. In many traditional societies youngsters may get their sexual education vicariously by observing others. However, these same youngsters may be kept away from some other kind of knowledge (e.g. their cultures' secret rituals), until they get their knowledge in those domains during their initiation rites.

The situation is not much different in the case of Western formal schooling. Parallels between different aspects of Western educational settings and traditional initiation ceremonies are noteworthy (see Lancy, 1975). In different settings where children get their formal education, the ZPA and ZFM relationships can be very variable.

The history of Western education provides an interesting account of how the schooling of children gradually progressed from the prevalence of strictly limited ZFMs to include more emphasis on the student's individual goal-directed actions in the process of learning. That change was part of the large-scale social changes that surrounded the process of the Reformation

(Ozment, 1983). In Puritan England the increasing emphasis on the active role of the student within a ZFM (set by the teacher) can be observed in the child-oriented catechisms that appeared in the seventeenth century. Previous methods of educating children has emphasized rote memorization of texts (i.e. ZFM was set to equal ZPA—the rote-learning child was requested to repeat exactly the material that the teacher provided and not allowed to do anything else). The Puritan catechisms widened the ZFM in this learning situation. For example, Herbert Palmer's catechism *An Endeavour of Making the Principles of Christian Religion . . . plaine and easie* that appeared in 1640 approached the teaching task through a reflective method which would get the 'truth' out of the child through the child's *own* (independently dependent) answers, instead of letting the child merely repeat the teacher's words. The method included presentation of the main question and then suggested to the child possibilities that could be answered in yes/no format. The main question was then followed by the right answer, provided by the teacher. Hearing the questions and answers from the teacher would suggest the right answer to the child, rather than give it to him directly (Sommerville, 1983). An example of teacher–child interaction taken from that early catechism illustrates this issue:

QUESTION: What is a man's greatest business in this world? Is it to follow the world, and live as hee list?
ANSWER: No.
QUESTION: Or is it to glorifie God, and save his own soule?
ANSWER: Yes.
QUESTION: So, what is a man's greatest business in this world?
ANSWER: A man's greatest business in this world is to glorifie God, and save his own soule.
QUESTION: How shall a man come to glorifie God and save his own soule? Can they do so that are ignorant?
ANSWER: No.
QUESTION: Or, they that do not believe in God?
ANSWER: No.
QUESTION: Or, do not serve him?
ANSWER: No.
QUESTION: Or, must they not needs learn to know God and believe in him and serve him?
ANSWER: Yes.
QUESTION: So how shall a man come to glorifie God and save his own soule?
ANSWER: They that will glorifie God, and save their own soules, must needs learn to know God, and believe in him and serve him. (Quoted with minor textual modifications via Sommerville, 1983, pp. 391–392)

This example illustrates how the ZFM/ZPA complex became gradually restructured in the history of Western education and in conjunction with the reformation of the Christian religion. In this example, the teacher narrowly defines the student's ZFM to the role of the listener to the message, the organization of which involves examples of answers to the questions that are considered 'correct'. The reflective organization of the teacher's text, organized into the question/answer format, prepares the students to become independent in answering the given set of questions on their own but in the 'correct' ways.

This educational approach can be considered to be the historical forerunner to the widespread use of multiple-choice tests in psychology and education in contemporary times. The structural similarity of the two is astounding. In both the early catechisms and contemporary multiple-choice tests the responder is given the question and possible answers, together with the task of reaching the single 'right' one. This task requires the selection, rather than construction or reinvention, of the 'right' answer. The respondent is guided by the narrow ZFM that includes the choice of 'wrong' answers as possible answers but excludes the option of coming up with one's own answer to the question (the ZFM structure excludes respondent-initiated change). The availability of choice between different answers creates the illusion of independent decision making by the student (thus promoting the idea that the individual's choice is independent). In reality the individual's independent choice is dependent on the ZFM as it is set (see 4.3.1, above).

An illustration of how contemporary school systems in different countries organize the ZFM/ZPA system comes from a comparison of two examples from schools in the contemporary world. The first of the examples is taken from a description of a Qur'anic school in rural Morocco. In the Qur'anic school the ZFM and ZPA are set up in such a way that the students' freedom of choice is limited to the actions that the teacher is currently promoting. The limitation of the students' ZFM to the prescribed ZPA is evident from the following description of a lesson in a Moroccan grade school:

> The French writing lesson. The teacher calls for the chalkboards. . . . Teacher says, 'Ready.' Everyone is sitting up at his desk with chalkboard in left hand and a piece of chalk in the right. Right hands are poised. The teacher reads aloud a sentence from her notebook. Unexpectedly no one moves, right hands still remain poised. The teacher slaps the desk with a ruler. The children at once bend over their slates, working slowly and painstakingly with their chalk. Several minutes later the teacher slams the ruler again. All slates go straight up in the air at arm's length, facing forward in the fashion of a placard parade. The teacher marches up and down the aisles, saying 'Wrong, correct, correct. . . .' She slams her ruler for the third time and the boards are lowered, erased, and chalk poised for the next sentence. (Miller, 1977, p. 146).

This description illustrates the classroom situation where, during the dictation, literally every movement of the children was exactly constrained. In everyday language, we may be tempted to talk about such instances as extreme examples of 'discipline'. In such a case, the children's ZFMs in the situation equal ZPAs—they can act only in ways that are allowed by the teacher, and have no choice of acting in any other way (what children are required to do—ZPA—is their only option that they can possibly select—ZFM). This situation represents the widespread form of the structural organization of human actions that bears the label 'military discipline' in Western discourse. It is the military institutions that have developed to the maximum the cases of canalization of human actions where the boundaries of ZFM are narrowed down to match the boundaries of ZPA (the latter, though, occurring in its extreme form of not promoted, but *required* action—upon orders, of course).

A different way of organization of the ZFM/ZPA complex is evident in the context of a school in a middle-class neighborhood (in Canada), described by Smollett (1975). Here the students are provided with strict frameworks of ZFM by the teacher, who at the same time promotes the idea of personal choice (between strictly given alternatives) within the ZFM:

> A bright, well-equipped third-grade classroom. Miss Simms explains that today they will begin work on their Christmas pictures. They will draw with crayons again today, as they did such a good job on their last set of crayon drawings.
>
> She explains the task. They will do, altogether, two Christmas pictures each, one today in crayon, one next week in paint. One picture will be on the religious side of Christmas, such as a manger scene, the wise men, or the like (henceforward referred to in class as 'the manger picture'), the other on Santa Claus (St. Nicholas) or something on the non-religious side (henceforward referred to as 'the Santa Claus picture').
>
> 'Now, you have two choices,' she declares. 'You can do either the manger picture or the Santa Claus picture this week—as you like. Then you will do the other one next week.'. . .
>
> The children begin to draw. Miss Simms walks about, making suggestions, answering questions. 'Do the figures first, Janet, then the background.'
>
> Several children begin to put questions to Miss Simms, exploring the boundaries of their choices. 'Can we do it in pencil?' asks Tom. 'No, do it in crayon,' says Miss Simms, 'it must be in crayon.' Little Brenda whispers to another child: ' . . . hard to do manger in paint; . . . try it in crayon first.' 'Miss Simms,' asks Brenda, 'can I make both pictures of the manger?' 'No,' says Miss Simms, 'you have a choice—one subject for one picture, one for the other.' 'Can both pictures be in crayon?' asks a boy. 'No.' Brenda tries again: 'Miss Simms, can I make both pictures about the manger if I put Santa Claus in both of them?' Miss Simms walks to another part of the room without responding. After several minutes, Brenda begins to draw. (Reproduced with permission from Smollett, 1975, pp. 221–222).

This example of the student–teacher interaction about the ZFM boundaries in the classroom task may look at first glance very different from the Moroccan description. The students in this example are encouraged to make their own decisions about what to draw in what order, *but they are not allowed to alter the boundary set through the ZFM* for their drawing activity by the teacher. On the one hand, the teacher is available to the students to answer their questions (promoting active queries about different aspects of the drawing task), but she refuses to reciprocate any efforts by the children to redefine the ZFM of the task. The children are *free to choose only within the limits set*, and their use of this limited freedom of choice is promoted (by setting up the possibility to ask questions) by the teacher. Some of the questions asked are reciprocated by the teacher in a manner that leads to promotion of one or another of the children's drawing skills, but the basic issue of the ZFM boundaries remains inflexible in this case.

Finally, it is possible to add to these examples the case of the 'open classroom' type of organization of school lessons that became widespread in the USA in the 1960s. Here the ZFM boundaries are set quite wide indeed and the students are provided with excessive opportunities to make (and therefore—learn to make) their personal choices within the ZFM. Through setting up a set of different ZPAs for the students' actions (e.g. 'You can work on task A, or B, or C, or D, etc.'), the teacher leaves the choice to the students, which constitutes a step in the lengthy process of socialization of the American schoolchildren into the ethos of personal choice and 'self-made person' who is active in life and tends to attribute causality for events that happen in his relationships with environment to his own credit.

Thus, from the structural point of view of ZFM/ZPA relationships, the classroom settings in the Moroccan and Canadian schools as well as in the 'open classroom' contain the universal presence of the limits set on children's actions by setting up ZFMs. The examples differ greatly in the ways in which ZPAs are set up for the children—in the Moroccan case ZPA covers the (narrow) area of ZFM for the children; in the Canadian case the bifurcation between possible choices for children is strictly determined by the structure of the ZFM, but the ZPAs are set up so that the children can decide on their own what to draw in what order. The 'open classroom' is an example with perhaps less promotion of any particular task by the teacher, but with ZPAs set for the particular content domains to be covered in the lesson. In all three cases the teacher uses ZFM *to keep the children within the given field of actions*, not letting them leave that domain for another one (not allowing the children to redefine the function of the whole setting). The function of ZFMs is to block the possibility of the child to leave the present field of actions, while possibly (but not necessarily) promoting some actions within the ZFM by setting up ZPAs for the child. A child can learn a new skill, provided that it is within the range of accessibility (in ZFM) even without adults' efforts to promote its acquisition (by ZPAs). Or, if such promotion is present, the child also learns the same skill, possibly a little sooner or at the same time as without promotion.

4.3.4 Context-dependence of the ZFM/ZPA complex

The ZFM/ZPA complex depends on the cultural context of the meanings in the situation. These meanings serve as guidelines to the caregivers to organize the child's ZFM/ZPA in the given situation. The particular meanings of a situation can result in diametrically opposite ways of setting up the ZFM/ZPA complex—what ordinarily is strictly kept outside ZFM (and ZPA) may suddenly become included in ZFM and a specific ZPA may emerge within it. This is the case in situations where parents (or teachers) teach children skills which require learning before the child is allowed to act in the given setting without adults' supervision. An example of such a case is parental supervision of their infants' and toddlers' behavior in bathtubs, filled with water. Having a bath is a necessary hygienic activity for children which is recurrent. However, in the first years of life bathtub drowning can constitute a serious danger (Nixon and Pearn, 1977; Pearn and Nixon, 1977). Infants and toddlers in many families are not allowed to get into the bathtub in their ordinary playtime. In many homes this exclusion of the bathtub (and the whole bathroom) from the children's ZFM for playing is introduced strictly by external (keeping the bathroom door shut, punishing the child for going into bathroom alone, etc.) boundaries. This situation, however, changes when the bathtime setting arises. Specific restrictions are usually enforced for the child's ZFM in that setting. Toddlers are usually put into the bathtub, washed there, and promoted to play in the bathtub with water and toys, only when the setting is organized by the adult for the purpose of taking the bath (ZPA) and when a caregiver is around constantly to control the child's actions in the bathtub. Once the bathtime is over, the usual restrictions on the child's actions in the bathroom are reinstated. Parents who are aware of the danger of bathtub drowning would be motivated to keep bathroom/ having a bath outside the toddler's ZFM until they can be sure of the child's safe conduct. However, since *supervised* taking of a bath is a must, the parents organize the ZPA concerning the bathtub and activities in it, for the special time when the child is given the bath, and for no other time. Many other examples of adults teaching children the use of different objects (ZPA) before the children are allowed to operate these objects independently (i.e. before those become parts of their ZFM) illustrate the case where the ZFM/ ZPA system is set up temporarily under parental supervision so that actions, that ordinarily are outside ZFM, suddenly not only become parts of ZFM but also of ZPA. Not surprisingly, such situations usually involve relatively limited extent of ZFMs where the parental supervision is used to constantly monitor the child's actions and keep them within limits. At the same time parents promote new skills that are important to learn first so that later (when they are within individual ZFM) the child is sufficiently prepared to continue using them on his own.

The ZFM and ZPA are psychological means through which the child's development is gradually socially canalized by shaping his relationships with the environment. The ZFM reflects the current structure of child–environment relationships, and the ZPA reflects the desired direction of the child's further development. Whether or not that expected direction is indeed going to become actualized in further development, depends upon how the particular aspect of child–environment relationships that is actively promoted by the adults (i.e. lies within ZPA) relates to the child's current motor and cognitive capabilities. The latter can be conceptualized through the use of the concept of the 'Zone of Proximal Development'.

4.3.5 The Zone of Proximal Development

If the parents promote certain tasks to their child that are too far away from the child's present capabilities, then these new tasks are unlikely to be assimilated into the action schemes (and cognitive schemata) of the child. On the other hand, the lack of parents' purposeful efforts to guide their child's development would eliminate the role of parents from child socializ-ation. Although both these extremes can be observed in reality, it is more usual to observe situations where the parents' efforts to promote the develop-ment of their child's new skills is based upon both their understanding of what the child can already accomplish, and what they think he can learn to accomplish with parental help. This perspective—the interdependence of the child's actual capability and his near-future possible capability—has been an important feature of Vygotsky's concept of the Zone of Proximal Develop-ment (abbreviated: ZPD). In contemporary international psychological discourse, the ZPD is usually taken to be defined in terms of a figurative explanation that Vygotsky provided: 'It is the distance between the actual develomental level as determined by independent problem solving and the level of potential development as determined through problem solving under adult guidance or in collaboration with more capable peers' (Vygotsky, 1978, p. 86).

This definition of the concept of ZPD is not fully accurate from Vygotsky's original standpoint, since it constitutes the *pars pro toto* replacement fallacy. That fallacy is not often recognized, all the more that Vygotsky's own expla-nation of his notion of the ZPD is scattered into different places in his original writings. Only the narrower description of the concept (quoted above) is directly and easily accessible for readers of Vygotsky's work. It was largely meant as a figurative device to let his audience (which was well acquainted with psychological testing traditions) get the basic idea of what Vygotsky had in mind (see also Valsiner, 1987, Chapter IV; and 3.5.2 in this book). In the context of the present analysis, the term will be used in connection with the ZFM/ZPA complex.

The ZPD is a term that helps us to capture those aspects of child develop-ment that have not yet moved from the sphere of the possible into that of the actual, but are currently in the process of becoming actualized, interde-pendently with the activities of the 'social others'. Vygotsky outlined the idea of ZPD only in a very general form, without concrete elaboration of how the concept refers to the complexity of actual adult–child interaction. Recent work by a number of investigators has been aimed at further elaboration of the concept within the empirical realm (Cazden, 1983; Greenfield, 1984; Rogoff, Malkin, and Gilbride, 1984; Rogoff and Gardner, 1984; Saxe, Gearhart, and Guberman, 1984; Wertsch, Minick, and Arns, 1984). In addition to that extension to the empirical reality, further theoretical elaboration of the concept is called for. Wertsch's (1984) treatment of the ZPD through the notion of qualitative transformation in the situation definition extends the original theoretical context in which Vygotsky's ideas of ZPD were cast. In the context of the theoretical framework presented in this chapter, the ZPD has a decisive role to play in child development, as it provides a link between the ZFM and ZPA. That link can be characterized by the following:

(a) If the ZPA is set up in ways that have no overlap with the ZPD, then any effort to promote the child's development within the ZPA thus set, will necessarily fail. In real life, if parents try to teach the child a new skill which, given the child's present state of development, is beyond his immediate learning possibilities, then the effort will fail. However, the promotion of the same skill in the same way, sometime later in development of that child, may succeed—if the child by that time has reached a state from which he can learn that new skill with the adults' assistance and instruction. The practical question that is asked by parents and educationalists over and over again, is familiar—when is the 'right time' to begin teaching the child how to use the spoon, or toilet-train the child, etc.? It illustrates the layperson's concern with the issue of setting up ZPAs that would not be outside ZPD.

(b) In cases where the range of ZPA exactly matches the range of ZPD the instruction provided for the children by others can have the maximum possible effect—in terms of everyday life, if parents were knowledgeable about the full extent of what their child *could* learn with their help at the given developmental state. If the parents wanted to provide the full range of such instruction, then the child may show the expected development of new skills, provided that the child actively participated in the tasks that parents instruct him/her in.

(c) The relationship between ZFM, ZPA, and ZPD is constantly 'filled in' with new content that depends on what is important in the life of the particular child at a given time. For example, a toddler starts to climb different objects in the home. This constitutes a new motor skill, which is canalized through ZFM and ZPA. The parents deny the toddler the possibility of climbing certain objects in the home (e.g. window sills, kitchen table, etc., which belong outside ZFM at the time), and at the same time may promote the development of safe climbing habits up, and down, the stairs (ZPA—cf. Valsiner and Mackie, 1985). If the given toddler's previous motor development has created a basis onto which the new skill of climbing stairs can easily be integrated, with instruction from the adults, then ZPA fits into ZPD, and the new skill is learned relatively quickly and without difficulty. If the motor basis for learning to climb stairs in that particular toddler is not yet sufficient to fit the parents' preferred ways of teaching the child to climb, then the ZPA does not fit the ZPD at that time, and the efforts to teach the child to climb may fail, or remain unsuccessful for a longer period of time. Some parents, of course, do not bother to teach their child how to climb (no ZPA set), but let their toddler try to ascend and descend the staircase (ZFM). In accordance with both the equifinality principle and Vygotsky's original notion of the ZPD, the child whose climbing is not 'pushed', but who is allowed to try it on his own, will also develop the capability for climbing stairs. However, after the child has learned to climb stairs, the whole issue of climbing may be redefined to include only ZFM (e.g. certain objects remain unavailable for the child to climb), and no ZPA is set up for the child's further development of that particular skill, despite the possibility that the child might be capable of further advancement of that skill under instruction by an adult, or in his own play (ZPD). Instead, another content domain may become important for the adults to promote after climbing skills have developed sufficiently, so the whole system of ZFM/ ZPA that should fit ZPD is filled with that new content domain.

4.3.6 Paradoxes of ZPD: empirical unverifiability of its boundaries

It is easy to see the paradoxical status of the ZPD that poses serious difficulties for any directly empirical use of that concept. The idea of the ZPD relates to what kinds of further developmental accomplishments are possible for the given child at the given time in ontogeny. Therefore it is impossible to determine the empirical boundaries of ZPD. If the boundaries of ZPD are determined inductively, on the basis of empirical observations, the result of such study is the actualization of some subset of the ZPD, from which it is not possible to determine the full set of ZPD that was existing before the given subset was studied (and actualized by the study). Once a child has learned to read with grandmother's help (proving that reading under the conditions of instruction that the grandmother used while teaching the child were indeed in ZPD when the teaching started), it would be impossible to find out whether the same function (reading) could have been within the ZPD set up with the help of somebody else, using different methods of teaching (e.g. mother, father, teacher). For the purposes of the study of the boundaries of ZPD, the child will not relearn the important skill (reading) with the help of another instructor. What has been learned with the help of an instructor in a certain way cannot be learned again, as a totally novel function, with the help of another instructor, or by himself. This basic nature of development renders the full extent of ZPD in principle empirically unverifiable. Whereas ZFM and ZPA can be empirically verified, only the part of ZPD that reflects the actualized part of the whole range of what is possible may be available for empirical study. This empirical unverifiability is not a theoretical obstacle for research, since the explanatory value of the ZPD concept can be demonstrated on limited empirical model data sufficiently well.

4.3.7 Alternative existing conceptualizations: scaffolding, formats, frames, and scripts

The conceptual framework outlined in this book is not without its more recent relatives or predecessors. Two lines of thought in the cognitive psychology of the 1970s have wandered along similar structural-dynamic paths in their search for explanation of acting and thinking of human beings. First, various research efforts emerged in conjunction with the intellectual stimulation by Jerome Bruner (1975, 1976, 1978, 1981). The emphasis on understanding the psychological role of instruction (tutoring) in child development that has been consistently present in Bruner's interest (Bruner, 1960, 1972) has been ultimately connected with Vygotsky's explanations of development through the ZPD concept (Bruner, 1983, 1984).

The empirical research efforts around Brunerian perspectives on development have led to the use of the metaphor of 'scaffolding' to describe the process of adults' instruction of children in the solving of specific tasks (Wood, 1980; Wood and Middleton, 1975; Wood, Bruner, and Ross, 1976; Wood, Wood and Middleton, 1978). The explanation of the meaning of 'scaffolding' reveals its explicit similarity in its empirical coverage to the ZFM/ZPA/ZPD complex that constitutes the core of the present theory:

> Adult and child together were achieving success on a task, but the nature of their individual contributions varied with the child's level of ability. Once the child could be lured into some form of task-relevant activity, however low level, the *tutor could build around him a supporting structure which held in place whatever he could manage.* That supporting activity served to connect the child's activity into the overall construction and to provide a framework *within which the child's actions could lead to and mean something more general than he may have foreseen.* As the child mastered components of the task, he was freed to consider the wider context of what he could do, to take over more of the complementary activity. The adult could 'de-scaffold' those parts which now stood firmly on their own. Thus tutor and child shared in doing the task, the tutor helping the child succeed with those aspects he could not manage, thus supporting his gradual mastery of the task. (Wood, 1980, pp. 281–282; italics mine— J.V .)

This quote illustrates how 'scaffolding' relates to the same aspects of empirical reality as those covered by the concepts of ZFM and ZPA in the present framework. The child is 'lured' into task-relevant activity which can be promoted through ZPA while excluding alternative action options by ZFM. Once the child is 'on task', the adult keeps him acting by setting up constraints that help the child (ZFM) and suggests ways of acting (ZPA) that would contribute towards the solution of the problem. Once a particular action is perceived by the adult to be mastered by the child to a sufficient extent, the 'de-scaffolding' process rearranges the set of constraints on the action mastered by the child, progressing to erect a similar 'scaffold' around some other actions. The decision by the adult of how to proceed from supporting the development of child's previous action to promoting and constraining some new action depends upon the perception of child's developmental possibilities on the adult's side. It is in this respect that the ideas covered by Vygotsky's ZPD concept relate to 'scaffolding':

> . . . successful instruction involves more than the child's recognition of goals and the adult's encouragement to achieve them. It also involves what we have called the scaffolding of means. The successful teacher regulates his or her instructions, demonstrations, descriptions, and evaluations to the child's current attentions and abilities. The adult provides *just that level of intervention which is necessary to get the child over his current difficulties*; when the child can successfully take responsibility for a particular constituent of a task, the adult abandons that particular form of intervention and reacts at a more general level. Thus, adult intervention is contingent upon the child's activity, and the contingency is based upon the adult's interpretation of the child's errors and the fate of earlier interventions. (Wood, 1980, p. 294; italics mine—J.V.)

The process of matching the instructor's actions to the child's particular ZPDs in Wood's conceptualization was originally related to the empirical domain of children solving construction problems in laboratory settings. In such settings, the whole environment (the fixed-feature space of the laboratory, the objects present in it, and the social expectation that the child will stay in the room and act on experimental tasks) reveals the connection between the instructor's actions within ZFM/ZPA and the particular organisation of the ZPD. The more exclusive role of ZFM—keeping the child 'on task'—may have been easier thanks to the laboratory setting. It is in the sense of the role of the structures of general settings in organization of action that the concepts of 'script', 'frame', and 'format' are close to the present perspective.

All these three concepts capture the *structural* aspect of the phenomena that they describe. Bruner's concept of 'format' parallels 'scaffolding' in substantial ways. It is 'a little microcosm, a task, in which the mother and child share an intention to get something done with words. At the start, what the child cannot manage in the format, his mother does for him. Once he can, she requires him to do it thereafter. The format 'stores' presuppositions that become shared by the two partners' (Bruner, 1983, p. 171).

Bruner's empirical analysis of different formats (e.g. 'peek-a-boo': Bruner and Sherwood, 1976; 'book reading': Ninio and Bruner, 1978) revealed how the development of children's speech is canalized in the context of these formats. The idea of formats is related to two other concepts that are in use in cognitive psychology and anthropology—'scripts' and 'frames'. Both of these concepts are rooted in the concept of 'schema' that has been used in psychological thinking in the past (Bartlett, 1932; Piaget, 1970a) and that has become used in contemporary psychology in conjunction with talk about 'knowledge base' or 'knowledge structures' (see, Abelson, 1981; Schank and Abelson, 1977). Scripts are defined as 'conceptual representations of stereotyped event sequences' (Abelson, 1981, p. 715) that become activated when necessary to help the person to organize actions. A similar concept, although approaching the issue of knowledge from a slightly different angle, is Minsky's 'frame'— 'a collection of questions to be asked about a hypothetical situation: its specific issues to be raised and methods to be used in dealing with them' (Minsky, 1982, p. 379).

All these concepts—format, script, and frame—are slightly different reincarnations of the recognition of the structured nature of organism's psychological phenomena and their environments (see 4.1.1 and 4.1.2). These structurally oriented concepts, however, are largely assumed to pre-exist in some static (normative) structural form. Such assumption of the *existence* of these structures may be sufficient for the majority of non-developmental tasks in psychology, anthropology, and artificial intelligence research. However, in the case of developmental psychology it becomes important to explain the emergence of the knowledge structures and action schemes. The theoretical framework outlined in this book can explain the development of scripts in children's ontogenies (see Nelson, 1981) through the general canalization explanation which is made empirical by the notions of the ZFM/ZPA/ZPD complex as it works in particular conditions of child–environment relationships under the supervision of other people.

4.4 Conceptualization of development: the transformation of structures

Our discussion of the three zone-concepts that make up the theoretical system outlined here points to two aspects of organization of child development. The first of them—the description of the child's actions within a structured environmental setting—involves the ZFM/ZPA complex as it was described previously. It is obvious that the ZFM/ZPA complex serves both immediate and longer-term goals. It both organizes the child–environment relationship at any given time, and at the same time prepares the child for future development. It is in conjunction with that latter task that the Zone of Proximal Development becomes an important addition to the theoretical system. It is the ZPD that organizes the child's psychological development on the ontogenetic plane. It moves the ZFM/ZPA complex along a trajectory on ontogenetic transformation. At every developmental period, the ZFM/ZPA complex is being transformed into a new state under the demands of the given context on the one hand, and in accordance with the ZPD on the other.

The idea that development is to be considered in terms of structural transformations is not new to developmental psychologists (see Basov, 1929, 1931; Brent, 1984; Piaget, 1970b, 1977; Van der Daele, 1969). However, it has very often remained obscure what kinds of structures are being transformed in the course of development, and in what ways. Piaget's conceptualization of equilibration (see 3.2.2) provided only the most general and abstract answers to that important question. Furthermore, Piaget's main focus of interest has been in the realm of cognitive structures and their transformation, which provides different investigators with great freedom to posit the existence of very different structural units in the children's minds. A similar difficulty interferes with the efforts of those investigators who try to describe the change in the structure of children's observable actions (e.g. Basov, 1929, 1931)—the context-dependency of the action within a particular setting, and the emerging internalization of the control of the child's own actions render descriptions of a behavioristic kind very difficult to provide.

It is in this respect that the effort to provide a constraint-based theory of child development may prove to open some new opportunities for empirical analysis of the developmental process. First, it puts an emphasis on context-dependency of children's action as the general rule, rather than an exception. That implies that an investigator needs to analyze the constraints on the child's action that are present in the particular context in which the child develops. Such analysis provides an empirical basis for understanding the set of possible actions as the background for further analysis of actually occurring actions. Further, the course of development of the actual actions of the child can then be charted in the process of empirical observations. These newly emerging novel actions lead to the transformation of the immediate (actual) constraint structure of the setting first, and may lead to changes in the structure of what is generally possible as well. For example, the onset of the child's independent walking (together with exploratory interest in the garbage can in the kitchen) leads the mother to introduce new physical constraints into the child's environment (e.g. blocking access to the garbage can in the kitchen by a chair). At the same time, she may start actively preparing the child for understanding the complicated cognitive difference between 'garbage' and 'non-garbage'. As the child's motor skills develop further and reach the stage where the physical blocking of the garbage-can access is no longer effective (e.g. the child can pull the chair away from its place, or climb over it to the can), the physical constraint can be taken away by the mother since the internalized meaning of garbage as something not to be played with may already be in place. That meaning constitutes an internalized cognitive constraint that guides the child's actions in *all* situations (with occasional relapses in its effect still expectable), rather than only in those where the mother watches and controls the child's actions. Thus, the temporary nature of the external structure of action constraints is transformed into a cognitive internal structure of constraints. More specific examples of the development of actions as transformation of external constraint structures over time, and their eventual transition to the children's internal cognitive sphere, are provided in chapters 6 and 7. In chapter 6, the analysis of the cultural structuring of the set of possible actions in toddlers' mealtime settings is performed. In chapter 7, empirical observational data on individual children's actions in mealtime settings over the longitudinal period of 1.5 years are used to illustrate the empirical use of the theory outlined in this chapter.

The description of the process of ontogenetic transformation of constraint structures is further complicated to the rare interest in structurally oriented empirical analyses methods that has been noteworthy in psychology. At best, microgenetic descriptions of the structure of action in different situations have been provided: Lewin's descriptions of adolescents' psychological functioning (Lewin, 1939), dynamics of social groups (Lewin, 1948), and solving marriage conflicts (Lewin, 1951) involved the use of illustrations in the form of topological schemes. However, Lewin's fascination with topology did not go much beyond superficial use of its concepts (see London, 1944; Sorokin, 1956). It did not lead to development of more adequate structuralistic formal tools for psychological applications. Most possibly, psychologists' own dogmatic emphasis on quantification of their research materials is to be blamed in that respect.

The scarcity of formal structuralistic methods that might be suited for developmental psychology makes it necessary to analyze some formal approaches used in other sciences, which may be useful for formalizing the theoretical system presented in this book. This task is undertaken in chapter 5, and is necessarily of limited scope. However, it is expected that it provides the reader with insight into those areas of mathematical sciences which a developmental psychologist with structuralistic interests might find some leads as to how development of structural transformation could be studied. Needless to say, the contemporary state of affairs (as will be demonstrated in chapter 5) is quite meagre in this respect.

4.5 Summary

In chapter 4, theoretical concepts that constitute the core of the theoretical system were outlined. The theoretical system is built using the individual-socioecological reference frame, which implies the presence of child–others–environment interdependence in the process of child socialization. This perspective requires the analysis of particular instances of children's actions within structurally organized settings under the guiding influence of other people. Such an analysis has to use terminological and empirical tools that are quite novel in contemporary developmental psychology.

This chapter included the description of the terminological means to which child socialization can be conceptualized. The theoretical system is set up on the core idea of *canalization* of children's development by its purposeful and selective limiting by *constraint structures*. Such constraints specify the expected *direction* of children's future development in relatively deterministic ways, while leaving the particular actual course of the future development of a particular child largely *indeterministic within the limits of the direction specified*. The theoretical perspective overcomes the traditional determinism-versus-indeterminism issue in psychology by a structured concept of determination of the *range* of possible future trajectories of development, while allowing large freedom (and the influence of unaccountable, 'chance' factors) in the determination of the actual developmental course of any particular child.

At the empirical level, the theoretical system makes use of three zone-concepts. First, the Zone of Free Movement (ZFM) is a term used to characterize the binding constraints set first by people around the child to regulate the child's relationships with the environment in ways that fit the cultural meaning system. These constraints are later internalized by the child, and become cognitive control mechanisms that keep the child within a culturally acceptable realm of thought and action. The concept of the Zone of Free Movement and the notion of constraints originate in Kurt Lewin's field theory, and are accepted in the present theoretical system with some significant modifications.

Secondly, the present theory relies on the concept of the Zone of Promoted Action (ZPA). People who take care of children very often try to promote the children's action to proceed in some, rather than other, directions. Their efforts to guide the childrens actions (and in later childhood—thoughts) are subsumed under the concept of the Zone of Promoted Action. The ZFM and ZPA are constructed theoretically to be parts of the same wholistic scheme of the organization of child–environment relations. The particular content of such a ZFA/ZPA complex depends upon the particular setting within which it is used.

Thirdly, the theoretical system makes use of Lev Vygotsky's concept of the Zone of Proximal Development (ZPD). That zone provides the conditions under which any particular ZFM/ZPA complex can be instrumental in guiding the child's further development. The unit of ZFM/ZPA on the one hand and the ZPD on the other provides for organization of child development through its *canalization*—a term suggested by Conrad Waddington but used here in a slightly modified meaning.

Finally, the theoretical system outlined in this chapter is structuralistic in its nature. It is based on the early structural-dynamic ideas of Mikhail Basov on the one hand, and Jean Piaget's concepts describing structural transformation as the essence of development, on the other. The presently incomplete aspect of the theory is its lack of formal-mathematical organization. However, as will be seen in chapter 5, that limitation is characteristic of most of psychology and other social sciences.

Mathematics and the study of development

> Very often efforts in mathematical biology depend upon existing mathematics
> and try to make the biology fit these existing theories. But the biology is the
> real world, and the models must fit it rather than the reverse.
>
> Guckenheimer, 1978, p. 38

The structured nature of both the developing person and his/her environment
(as discussed in chapter 4) makes it necessary to analyze the epistemological
background of any system of formal mathematical descriptions that is used
to describe (or even explain) psychological phenomena and their development. In psychology and other social sciences, the idea that mathematical
methods increase the precision of scientific analyses is widespread. This belief
has led psychology of the past five decades to become increasingly filled with
formalisms the use of which supposedly guarantees the scientific rigor of the
discipline. Quantification of psychological phenomena, and the overwhelming
use of the inter-individual reference frame, have become the accepted
tradition in empirical psychological research. The basic subjective belief that
quantitative analysis grants objectivity of the research seems to be shared by
the majority of psychologists, and emphatically propagated by a few (e.g.
Eysenck, 1985).

However, there are good reasons to be skeptical about the strong belief
that quantitative analysis of psychological phenomena opens a direct route
to objectivity in our science. Even if quantitative methodology may fit *some*
kinds of psychological phenomena well (e.g. test results, data from simple
experimental settings in which elementary phenomena are studied, its application to *all* possible phenomena in the science of psychology is no panacea
for the serious theoretical shortcomings. If in some instances quantification
may result in increased precision, then in others it can lead to misplaced
precision. Misplaced precision ('Type III error'—see Mitroff and Feather-

ingham, 1974) involves the production of precise but illusionary answers to questions that preserve little or no connection with the reality—the phenomena from which the data are derived. The worry about dissemination of such misplaced precision in sociology and psychology led Pitirim Sorokin to a rather outspoken evaluation of such 'quantophrenia':

> At the present time quantitative study of psychosocial phenomena is one of their main methods of investigation. So long as the method is genuinely mathematical and is applied to those psychosocial facts which lend themselves to quantitative analysis, it provides fruitful and deserves ever-increasing cultivation. But when the true quantitative method is replaced by pseudomathematical imitations; when the method is misused and abused in various ways; when it is applied to phenomena which, so far, do not lend themselves to quantification; and when it consists in the manipulation of mathematical symbols in a vacuum or in the mere transcription of mathematical formulae on paper without tying them to the relevant psychosocial units—then the approach misfires. Under these conditions, use of mathematical method becomes a mere quantophrenic preoccupation having nothing in common with mathematics and giving no cognition of the psychosocial world. (Sorokin, 1956, p. 103)

Explanation of complex, structured psychological phenomena is the main realm in which contemporary psychology has become infested by the fallacy of misplaced precision. In the first half of our century, Gestalt psychologists were active to remind others that 'the whole is not equal to the sum of its parts'. With the disappearance of such reminders from contemporary psychology's discourse, many psychologists have overlooked the structured nature of their objects of research. This has coincided with technological modernization of the research process, which has led many psychologists to follow the fashion of computer-based consumerism in empirical research. Such consumerism has often created paradoxical situations where the researchers themselves do not exactly know what is being done to their data when the computer analyzes them, while great pride may be displayed by such researchers on the occasion of their use of a currently fashionable data analysis technique.

The overwhelming majority of data analysis techniques that are in use in psychology at the present time are quantitative in their nature. If a psychologist is eager to use such techniques, the original (usually qualitatively structured) phenomena have to be transformed into some conventionally assembled 'quantitative measures'. Such derivation of quantitative 'measures' from the structurally organized original phenomenon inevitably alters the nature of information that the research process can provide (see 2.4). It is evident that phenomena of child development that are the target of the study in this book cannot be reduced to quantitative depictions without the complete loss of those phenomena (or of research questions that are addressed in this book).

The purpose of this chapter is to provide a brief overview of alternative formal mathematical systems that are used mostly in sciences other than psychology to capture different structural aspects of the objects of investigation. It is evident that in different sciences where the structure of the phenomena cannot be eliminated from consideration, because it constitutes the object of study, application of different mathematical systems—both quantitative and qualitative—have been attempted. The structure of phenomena cannot be replaced by quantitative measurements in such disciplines as linguistics, biology, many areas of chemistry, and physics. It will also become evident that it is the static structure of phenomena that is more frequently being studied in these disciplines—instead of the questions about the process by which a structure is transformed. This is evidently due to two reasons. First the disciplines themselves have only rarely posed developmental questions which would require the construction of new branches of mathematics. Secondly, even if the phenomena under study are explicitly developmental (e.g. in embryology), the kind of mathematical systems that are being applied may be built on axioms that do not fit the developmental nature of the phenomena. Thus, neither do the phenomena lead to the immediate understanding of the need for the development of mathematics, nor do the existing mathematical systems fit the phenomena. In the long run, of course, the phenomena and their mathematical models can arrive at a state of mutual fit, but it is certainly not an automatic development in science. Instead, it is wrought by the purposeful efforts of scientists and mathematicians to find a common ground for collaboration. As with any social interaction, such collaboration is sometimes full of mutual misunderstanding, of frequent quarrels about primacy, and—occasionally—of mutual exclusion. In this chapter I shall consider some approaches which involve the formalization of structures and their transformation. One aspect of these approaches is their relative specificity. The majority of them may fit fairly well the particular object of investigation for which they were constructed. Their application to other phenomena is often questionable on the grounds of how their axioms fit those phenomena.

5.1 The closed nature of mathematics and the open nature of development

Development entails constant innovation in form and function. In this sense, developmental processes are open-ended, so that it is impossible to predict the exact form and final state of the developing system. In contrast, formal mathematical systems are closed and incapable of developing themselves without the intervention of their creators. Pankow has contrasted the closedness of mathematics to the openness of philosophy:

> By definition, formal languages are incapable of recognizing themselves and . . . are therefore also incapable of recognizing any other position. Thus, a formal language does not link positions, but constitutes itself a fixed position. It is not, like philosophy, an open eye to the outer world, but a closed eye which may also be called a logically isolated eye. (Pankow, 1976, p. 22).

The status of 'logically isolated eye' attributed to formal mathematical systems is crucial for any psychological application of the rigour of mathematics. *Every mathematical system carries with it its axiomatic basis. Its nature is firmly fixed on that basis. When applied to the phenomena of a particular field of science, the system's axiomatic basis sets the conditions that guide what kinds of data can be derived from the phenomena by the given mathematical system.* These conditions determine the outcomes of the application effort *prior* to the effort itself, rather than provide for any post-application empirical decision about the adequacy of the given system for the target phenomena. Thus, an empirical discovery of 'goodness of fit' between a formal model of a phenomenon and its empirical characteristics does not prove the conceptual adequacy of the model in general.

All mathematical systems are embedded in their philosophical frameworks, and it is the latter that make the application of a particular system potentially adequate for a certain class of phenomena. This stipulation is particularly important to bear in mind in the case of developmental biology and developmental psychology. The majority of available formal systems are based on assumptions that exclude development from their focus. Therefore it would be impossible to apply such systems to the study of development, since such application necessarily leads to a non-developmental description of the object of investigation.

The picture is even more complicated because different formal-mathematical models (e.g. geometric, logical, game-theoretic) which belong to different subdisciplines of mathematics and may have few if any connections between them. All this has contributed towards making the effort to apply mathematics to the description of structured phenomena and their change highly compartmentalized and domain-specific. The application of mathematics for its own sake cannot help developmental sciences, but the application of *adequate* mathematics for the sake of understanding how developmental processes work may lead us to better understanding of the structured complexity of development.

What is meant by 'adequate mathematics' in this context depends on the abstract-philosophical analysis of the research questions requiring empirical investigation in psychology. Contrary to the widespread emphasis on quantitative methodology as almost synonymous with 'mathematical' in contemporary psychology, the present-day mathematics is a highly heterogeneous discipline that includes a variety of non-quantitative domains. Nigel Howard has emphatically illustrated the misunderstanding between mathematicians and others:

> Non-mathematicians often think that mathematics is primarily concerned with numbers. That is not so today. In fact, while twentieth-century social scientists have tried desperately to become more quantitative in the belief that this would make them more mathematical, twentieth-century mathematicians have become increasingly nonquantitative. . . . The idea that mathematics is the science of

quantity is a nineteenth-century notion, and social scientists who pursue it are immersing themselves in dead ideas. (Howard, 1971, p. 2).

However, even among qualitative mathematical systems of this century, examples of immediate applicability to developmental phenomena are very rare. The following short overviews of some of these domains will bring the theoretical separation of developmental from non-developmental ideas again into the centre of attention.

5.2 Space structures and the geometries of contour change

Some structures of phenomena can be described as spaces that are limited by their outer closed contours, and the change of these space structures may be reflected in the change of the contours. The geometric description of such cases interested D'Arcy Thompson (1942) who offered mathematical solutions to both the description of such spaces and their transformation. Largely the methods he suggested involved finding formal systems to describe biological forms that undergo transformation during development. For example, methods introduced by Thompson have been useful in the prediction of human craniofacial growth in two-dimensional (Mark, Todd and Shaw, 1981; Todd, Mark, Shaw and Pittenger, 1980; Todd and Mark, 1981) as well as three-dimensional versions (Mark and Todd, 1983). The relevance of different geometries to characterize the perceptual and action space of organisms is likewise important for theoretical issues in ecological psychology (Shaw and Pittenger, 1977).

Despite the success in the application of different geometries to describe the growth of biological forms, the geometric formal descriptions provide little for the task of exaplining the developmental processes involved in children's acting and thinking. These formal geometries may fit particularly well for description of those biological forms the growth of which is relatively strictly genetically determined, rather than a result of organism–environment epigenetic process. Without doubt the structural development of the human cranium is a good example of such forms. In contrast, the main aspect of children's psychological development involves constructive acting by the child that transforms his environment, which is set up for the child by his 'social others'. The mathematical description of the space within which the social agents act may be useful, but cannot serve as the definitive formal model for all aspects of development.

5.3 Syntactic models: Chomsky's application of context-free grammars in linguistics

Describing the form and function of human language and explaining its development, in both ontogeny and cultural history, provides a difficult and as yet unsolved set of problems. These problems are partly due to the fact that language is structured interdependently within its syntactic, semantic, and pragmatic aspects. Historically it has been the syntactic aspect that has been of primary concern to linguists and philosophers as the questions of language grammar have been held to be of relevance by language users.

The contribution of Noam Chomsky towards the formal analysis of language has been a much disputed system over the past two decades. It has been the subject of fierce attacks by its opponents, and equally fierce defence by its proponents. Such active discussion of Chomsky's program of formal analysis has largely been based on extra-scientific and epistemological issues that become the foreground of societal discourse in conjunction with the active exposure of Chomsky's methods and ideas to the public. Since Chomsky's contributions to societal discourse cover a wide area, ranging from computer science through linguistics and philosophy to social politics, the discussions of his ideas have often borrowed from one aspect of that range to concentrate on another.

From the perspective of developmental psychology, Chomsky's philosophy and formal models constitute a 'fascinating mix of geneticism and Cartesianism' (Piaget, 1970b, p. 87). Chomsky's geneticism is reflected in his effort to provide the formal description of the generation of language performance as it functions in the case of the 'idealized speaker-bearer'. This abstract person is constantly involved in the *creative production of new sentences*, or in other terms, the construction of performance (actual speech) on the basis of competence (implicit language knowledge). Chomsky states:

> The most striking aspect of linguistic competence is what we may call the 'creativity of language', that is, the speaker's ability to produce new sentences, sentences that are immediately understood by other speakers although they bear no physical resemblance to sentences which are 'familiar'. . . . Normal use of language involves the production and interpretation of sentences that are similar to sentences that have been heard before only in that they are generated by the rules of the same grammar, and thus the only sentences that can in any serious sense be called 'familiar' are clichés or fixed formulas of one sort or another. (Chomsky, 1966, p. 11)

As is evident from this quote, Chomsky's emphasis on the microgenesis of speech (the production of sentences) involves the notion of construction (novel sentences are constructed by the speaker) which is based on the fixed generation mechanism. The fixity of the latter constitutes the non-developmental basis of Chomsky's linguistic thinking which is most explicitly evident in his arguments about the ontogeny of language. His conceptualization of the ontogenetic side of language is built on the belief in the innate and genetically determined 'language faculty' which specifies the class of 'humanly accessible grammars' (Chomsky, 1980a). Chomsky's use of exclusive separation (see 2.1) of the organism and its environment leads to the denial of interactionist viewpoints in the explanation of development (Chomsky, 1976, 1980b) and to genetic preformationism as the only alternative explanation that would fit his assumption of the static nature of the kernel of linguistic competence.

Chomsky's non-developmental theoretical perspective is also evident in his efforts to formalize the rules by which language competence can be turned into language performance. The fundamental idea of Chomsky's 'transformational generative grammar' is that surface structures are formed through the application of at least two types of rules. The base rules generate an abstract phrase structure representation, and transformational rules move elements and otherwise rearrange structures so that those become acceptable language sentences, and only such sentences. Since the adequacy of a formal grammar is determined on the basis of the fit of its output to the reality, the sequence in which different rewriting rules of the formal system are applied in order to generate sentences is irrelevant. Different sequences of rule application can produce the same (fully adequate) outcome, but these sequences themselves need not be adequate descriptions of the actual sentence-generation processes that the speaker uses to produce the sentence. In contrast, developmental research has its goal to *adequately represent the reality of the generation process* for the microgenetic and ontogenetic phenomena in psychology or biology. Instead of reaching satisfaction in finding a formal system that accurately describes all the possible outcomes of a productive (i.e. outcome-generating) psychological process, the goal of developmental research is to describe all the possible versions of the time-dependent (sequential) structure of the process itself—even in cases when the process produces in some sense 'deficient' outcomes. Furthermore, developmental research includes the option that the set of different versions of the process is not finite, and that new versions of the process can emerge in the course of development. Contrasting these characteristics of developmental research with Chomsky's thinking, it becomes evident that Chomsky's 'generative grammar' is a formal description of little or no value for the study of development. It is true that Chomsky's emphasis on linguistic creativity looks at first glance developmental (in its microgenetic aspect). However, in reality it represents a non-developmental view on the production of performance given the static limits of the competence. In that 'generative process', the *outcomes* of the production process are the actual object of the study, while the actual production process is of no relevance in the course of formal model building.

5.4 Context-sensitive grammars and the description of structure

The formalisms involved in Chomsky's application of the transformational generative grammar to linguistic analyses represent the *context-free type* (Type 2) of formal grammars. The productions (application of rewriting rules to symbols) are not dependent on their context and take the general form of $[a \rightarrow b]$. In contrast, the Type 1 formal grammars include the dependence upon the context of the symbols. These are called *context-sensitive grammars* and they differ from their context-free counterparts in how the context is taken into account in the description of transformations. That involves the form of the rewriting rules of symbols used to depict transformations. The rewriting rules of context-sensitive grammars take the form [x/a/y→x/b/y] where a and b are symbols, x and y represent the context (Fu, 1974, p. 28). In the case of context-sensitive grammars the rewriting of a symbol by another (a→b) can take place only in the appropriate context (x/y), and in no other context.

Incidentally the distinction between context-free and context-sensitive grammars was introduced into the theory of formal languages by Chomsky (1959), who then proceeded to concentrate on the application of the context-free type to linguistic material. Context-sensitive formal grammars have remained largely underdeveloped mathematically but potentially useful formal descriptive systems. As long as the ethos in most of the scientific enterprise has been to generate context-free abstract knowledge about the objects of investigation, the ideas of context-sensitive formal systems may have been found superfluous to the goals of science. The few efforts to discuss context-sensitive formal languages have been largely confined to the realm of computer languages and pattern recognition (Fu, 1974; Kasai, 1970; Rosenkrantz, 1969).

From the developmental perspective, context-sensitive grammars fit the inevitably context-dependent nature of developing systems, as they take into account the contextual conditions under which a structural change (rewriting in a symbol structure) can take place. This constitutes a clear advance over the context-free grammars. The environmental embeddedness of context-sensitive grammars does not yet make them adequate developmental models as such, since the open-endedness (innovation) of developmental processes is not included in the version of existing grammars of that kind. If a context-sensitive grammar is developed so that it specifies the *contextual conditions under which the grammar would generate new rules within itself* that would restructure the grammar and its relationships with the environment, it is only then that the possibility that context-sensitive grammars can become adequate formal models of developmental processes arises.

5.5 Automations in describing structure and its change

Contemporary automata theory has developed its own tentative answers to the question of how to model change in a system. Not surprisingly, the efforts to develop mathematical models of such change grew out of learning theory in psychology (Bush and Mosteller, 1955). The theory of learning automata (Fu, 1970; Narendra and Thathachar, 1974) is aimed at specifying the formal system which involves a stochastic automation nested in an exchange relationship with the environment, and which changes as a result of that exchange relationship. The basic operation that is carried out by a learning automation is the updating of its action probabilities depending on the feedback from the environment. The environment (as it is defined by the feedback regime that it provides for the learning automation) can be conceptualized as either stationary of non-stationary. The environmental feedback regime has usually been conceptualized using the ideas of reward and punishment which are highly familiar for psychologists. Usually the probability distributions of reward versus penalty that the environment feeds back into the automation following its particular actions are the core data on which the automation's learning is based. Traditionally, binary probability distributions (probability of the reward = p; of the penalty = 1−p) have been used by the learning automata theorists to characterize the environment, but some applications have also experimented with continuous probability distributions (e.g. Fu and McLaren, 1965, cited via Narendra and Thathachar, 1974, p. 332). The resemblance of this way of describing the learner's environment to the traditions of learning theory's use of probabilistic reinforcement schedules is quite obvious. That resemblance brings into the learning automata theory both the theoretical strengths and weaknesses of psychological learning theories. Among the former the emphasis on learning as reorganization of the learner should be mentioned. This emphasis on the reorganization of the learner makes the learning automata theory closer to the needs of developmental psychology. On the other side, however, the assumption of *inevitable* and *direct* feedback to the learner from the environment—which the learning automata theory seems to have implicitly taken over from behavioristic learning theories—may limit the applicability of the learning automata as potential formal models of actual developmental processes. This point requires explanation. The assumption of 'inevitable feedback' includes the belief that whenever the organism/automation acts in manner x, it will elicit from the environment either a reward (with probability $p(x)$) or a penalty (probability $1−p(x)$), e.g. Lakshmivarahan and Thathachar, 1973), while any other outcome is excluded. In real-life learning outside Skinner boxes, however, the third option of receiving *no* feedback is always possible, and very often the case. The environmental feedback to the learner (organism or formal automation) is better characterized by conditional dependence on the situation at a given time. That aspect of environmental feedback makes the use of the stationary environment as an assumption highly unrealistic for any reality-linked advancement of learning automata theory.

The assumption of 'direct feedback' from the environmental relates to the learning theory's acceptance of the assumption of causality being *elementaristic* in its nature (see 2.7). Both the 'reward' and 'penalty' are considered to 'cause' change in the organism (learner) in a direct manner. In contrast, many aspects of the learning process are in reality *catalyzed* by the simultaneous presence of other conditions, either in the learner or in its environment.

It is easy to see that learning automata with stationary environments—where the probability distribution of the environmental feedback options remains constant over the time during which the automation is studied—constitute the simplest possible case which does not fit developmental phenomena. The assumption of stationariness of the environment as its basic nature is unwarranted for all open systems, and thus for all systems that undergo development. This does not rule out the possibility that a developing system's environment is stationary for a limited period of time, but this is a special case of no-change of a dynamic environment, rather than the normal state of the environment.

Learning automata theory has provided advancements that go beyond the environmental stationariness assumption and allow learning phenomena to be dealt with in ways closer to reality. First, the environments have been conceptualized as switching between different stationary states. Secondly, environments have been considered to vary in a periodic fashion. Thirdly, the environments can be thought of as 'slowly-varying' (Narendra and Thathachar, 1974, p. 331). It is the direction of considering non-periodically (but not necessarily slowly) varying environments that would bring the learning automata theory the closest to becoming useful for the developmental sciences.

Another aspect of developmental relevance that contemporary lerning automata theorists have attempted to formalize is the hierarchical nature of organized and developing systems. This is accomplished by constructing a multilevel system of automata, where each action of an automation at a certain level triggers automata at the next lower level. The basic problem to be solved in the formal analysis of such a hierarchical system is to find an algorithm suitable for each level that ensures the coordination of the whole structure in the optimal action (Thathachar and Ramakrishnan, 1981a, 1981b). The issue of the coordination of the whole structure in the process of development is indeed important for developmental psychology to which learning automata theory may have relevance. However, until the theory of learning automata with changing environments is applied directly to developmental phenomena it remains unclear exactly what it can offer to the developmental sciences in terms of any new understanding of the process of development.

5.6 Modelling the growth of multicellular structures: L-systems

Lindenmayer-systems (abbreviated: L-systems) are a special family of formal descriptions of the development of multicellular patterns of biological phenomena. In mathematics the theory of L-systems belongs in the realms of automata theory and the theory of formal languages (cf. Lindenmayer and Rozenberg, 1976).

The introduction of L-system into developmental biology was related to the empirical question of how to model the growth of branching plants in botany (Lindenmayer, 1968, 1975). The phenomenology of filamentous growth processes in botany constitutes an empirical domain where the abstract modelling efforts can be verified against the observation of the actual growth process of plants. Furthermore, the L-systems theory was constructed to fit the structured (multicellular) nature of developing botanical structures. The growing filament is not homogeneous but is made up of a multitude of cells, some of which are immediate 'neighbours' of others. Furthermore, the whole structure—a tree-leaf for example—grows to take a final general form which is invariant for the leaves of the given tree species, although there exists variability in the exact outer contour forms that individual leaves may have. The structured nature of the growth of multicellular plants requires the use of mathematical formalisms in its description which consider the structural aspects of that growth. Lindenmayer (1978, p. 38) contrasts his formalisms with preceding efforts to model growth:

> As frameworks for the description of growth and morphogenesis in time and space mathematical formalisms have been borrowed from mechanics and dynamics, primarily based on differential equations, which are suitable for changes of form of homogeneous objects like crystals or clouds, but are entirely unsuitable for complex heterogeneous systems like developing organisms. Precisely the cellular aspect is missing from most of these models. In terms of the above formalisms the description of a multicellular growing body would require at least as many separate differential equations as there are cells in it. Since the number of cells, or whatever other units one might choose, increases in the course of development, sometimes without limit, this would imply a mathematical description with increasing numbers of differential equations. Systems described in this way cannot be handled with any presently available analytical method.

L-systems, like generative grammars, can be *context-free* or *context-sensitive*. In the case of context-free L-systems (OL-systems, also called 'zero-sided' or 'informationless' Lindenmayer systems) the growth of the multicellular organism depends only on the lineages of its constituent cells which are independent of their neighboring cells. The growing biological structure goes through a series of changes (modelled by the rules of the OL-systems) where the growth at the next time interval depends solely on the cells in the previous interval. At each step (time interval) each of the cells in the structure can either changes its state (including remaining in the same state), or it can disappear from the structure ('die').

Lindenmayer (1975) has demonstrated that context-free (OL) systems are in principle incapable of generating complex forms that could fit the form of the majority of biological species. For example, sets of adult forms of tree-leaves with three or more equal-size lobes cannot be produced by OL-systems, and require taking the intercellular interaction into account. This limitation of the context-free L-systems leads to the necessity of modelling processes of growth in ways that are context-sensitive. The 'context' in the particular case of L-systems constitutes taking the status of a cell's neighboring cells into account when modelling its developmental course. A context-sensitive L-system consists of a set of states of the cells, a set of transition rules, and the starting structure. The transition rules specify for each state of a cell and each combination of its neighboring cells what the state of the given cell during the next time interval would be. Both the context-free and context-sensitive L-systems can be either deterministic or probabilistic. The deterministic L-systems assume that any transition rule used in modelling the growth process is either applicable with full certainty, or not applicable at all. Deterministic OL-systems (called 'DOL-systems' in the literature on L-systems) use fully determinate application of transition rules independent of the simultaneous context of the given cell. Probabilistic OL-systems ('POL-systems') incoude the application of transition rules independently of the simultaneous structural context on the basis of the probabilities of the application of these rules (e.g. Jurgensen, 1976). The deterministic context-sensitive L-systems include absolute (probability=1) conditions for application of transition rules, given the required state of the complex of the neighboring cells. Probabilistic context-sensitive L-systems add to that aspect the probabilities of the application of different rules given the particular context.

Since the purpose of this chapter is to analyze the most general aspects of different mathematical systems with claims to usefulness in modelling development, the specific formalisms and examples of the L-systems are not given here. The interested reader may want to study Lindenmayer's original work (Lindenmayer, 1968, 1975, 1978) or its introductory and simplified presentation (MacDonald, 1983, chapters 18 and 19). What is of relevance in the present context is the question of what novel opportunities for formal modelling of developmental processes the L-systems afford. Since the L-systems were constructed starting from the empirical problem of understanding the principles of multicellular organisms, their applicability in other developmental sciences aside from the study of botanical growth can be expected to be relatively straightforward. The L-sytems framework also provides the rare case of proof that the growth of complex structured organisms cannot be modelled by context-free formal systems (Lindenmayer, 1975). On the other hand, the use of context-sensitive L-systems can be complicated when applied to developmental phenomena that are not characterized by a relatively stable pattern of units (like a multicellular anatomical structure) where the neighborhood of the units in the pattern cannot be simply determined. For example, psychological structures involved in child development (either motor action patterns or cognitive schemata) may be difficult to model with L-systems because the 'neighborhood' of different action patterns and the contexts in which they are applied cannot be described by straightforward mapping as is possible in the case of a growing tree-leaf. However, despite these limitations it is potentially the context-sensitive probabilistic Lindenmayer-systems that are the closest to the task of modelling epigenetic developmental processes. The difficulty that may still appear insurmountable is how to determine the origin of the probability values that get entered into such formal models. If the aim is to use the formal model for better understanding of the reality, then the probabilities cannot be assigned to transition rules *ad hoc*, but have to be based on some aspects of the reality. There exist many different empirical possibilities of finding the probabilities on empirical grounds and (or all) of which is dependent upon the particular investigator's often implicit assumption of what probability is.

5.7 Catastrophe theory and the explanation of development

René Thom's topological 'catastrophe theory' was developed explicitly for the purposes of formalizing of morphogenesis, a process of qualitative change from previous form to a new morphological state. It is aimed at the construction of 'an abstract, purely geometrical theory of morphogenesis, *independent of the substrate of forms and the nature of the forces that create them*' (Thom, 1975, p. 8). As has often happened with abstract theoretical systems in the history of science, the dissemination of knowledge about Thom's catastrophe theory led to selective retention of the non-developmental aspects of his originally developmentally oriented system. For example, Gilmore's (1981) overview of catastrophe theory and its applications in science makes no mention of the theory's explicit historical conceptual roots in problems of embryology. 'Morphogenesis' is not even included in the subject index of the book! A similar fate has followed the application of catastrophe theory in psychology. Both the majority of efforts to apply it and its active critics (e.g. Zahler and Sussmann, 1977) have similarly been non-developmental in their emphasis. The case of the application of catastrophe theory in psychology is an example of the recurrent situations where an originally developmentally oriented abstract system of thought is turned into a non-developmental basis for local 'theories', which are subsequently discounted because they may be found not to provide 'better predictions' (cliché used in psychology widely and often in an indeterminate way) of 'behavior'.

Thom's definition of 'catastrophe' in the context of the 'morphology of a process' involves the observation of forms created by the location of points in the four-dimensional time-space structure:

> Suppose that a natural process, of any kind whatsoever, takes place in a box B; we then consider B × T (where T is the time axis) as the domain on which the process is defined. Also suppose that the observer has at his disposal probes or other means to allow him to investigate the neighborhood of each point x of B × T. As a first classification of points of B × T we have the following: if the observer can see nothing remarkable in the neighborhood of a point x of B × T, that is, if x does not differ in kind from its neighboring points, then x is a *regular point* of the process. By definition the regular points form an open set in B × T, and the complementary closed set K of points in B × T is the set of *catastrophe points*, the points with some discontinuity in every neighborhood;

'something happens' in every ball with center c where c belongs to K. The set K and the description of the singularities at each of its points constitute the *morphology* of the process. (Thom, 1975, p. 38).

The emphasis in Thom's formal system is clearly on how to describe structural-dynamic processes which take place in the space-time. This constitutes the aspect of catastrophe theory which is of primary relevance for developmental biology and psychology. On the other hand, the catastrophe theory was also based on the typological (static) world view. It is fundamentally a classificatory theory the predictive power of which (like in the case of other similar theories) is weak. It includes a typology of different elementary catastrophes that can be described topologically and are found to fit different morphological phenomena in nature and society (Thom, 1973). The actual complexity of the biological phenomena has made it necessary for catastrophe theorists to go beyond the types of elementary catastrophes (Thom, 1973; Zeeman, 1977) and to provide mathematical descriptions of their form. That typology-based descriptive application of the theory is non-developmental in its nature and therefore largely irrelevant for developmental sciences. In other terms—a sophisticated mathematical description of a biological form that fits any of the list of elementary catastrophes need not yet constitute an explanation of its development. For example, knowing that a certain form can be characterized as a version of the 'cusp catastrophe' does not allow us to consider the formal-mathematical description of the cusp the explanation of that form. Even less adequate would it be to consider that formal description an explanation of its development.

The developmental relevance of catastrophe theory is similar to that of geometric efforts at describing changing forms (see 5.2)—both kinds of formalisms can provide adequate descriptions of complex static and even dynamic (changing) forms, but as abstract descriptive systems they need not be sufficient for explanation of the development of particular structured biological or psychological phenomena. Guckenheimer's cautious criticism of the catastrophe theory is worthwhile mentioning here:

> Without a better understanding of *both* the geometry of morphogenesis and the answers to a variety of mathematical questions, the relevance of catastrophe theory to problems of development will remain an open issue. Moreover, it is not clear that catastrophe theory can ever provide strong evidence for the correctness of any explanation of development. It may be limited to suggestive analogies between the mathematical theory and reality. (Guckenheimer, 1978, p. 15)

Thom himself has admitted that catastrophe theory has turned out to be of little use for modelling living systems. He argues that catastrophe theory' at least . . . does not dissociate the genesis of a system (and its death) from its adult behavior, as do all existing schemes' (Thom, 1976, p. 252). This emphasis on non-dissociation of development from static (albeit structural) being may actually be the reason why the theory does not easily afford explanation of development, as Thom consistently intermingles developmental and non-developmental approaches in his epistemology (e.g. see Piaget, 1980; Thom, 1980).

Perhaps the key to a productive integration of catastrophe theory with developmental sciences lies in the presence of empirical developmental research issues. In its beginning Thom's theory was explicitly developed (see Thom, 1975, p. xxiii) to provide formalization of Waddington's ideas of epigenesis and the chreod which were introduced into biology within the framework of a developmental approach. Thom's mathematical formalization of the concepts of chreod (Thom, 1975, p. 114) and his discussion of the process of canalization (pp. 142–143) provide formalized leads towards further advancement of the developmental side of catastrophe theory. Likewise, Zeeman's (1974) analysis of the primary and secondary waves in cases of biological growth may provide interesting leads for formalizing the development of boundaries and structure of real developing organisms. Last (but not least), the introduction of catastrophe-theoretic ideas to linguistics in the framework of Gestalt linguistics (Wildgen, 1984) may provide a more sophisticated and a more suitable formal method than has been available in linguistics thus far. The direction taken in Gestalt linguistics has relevance from the standpoint of the theory esponsed in this book. The catastrophe-theoretic semantics is based on the axiomatic assumption that the meanings of propositions are vague, and that semantic theories which do not take the user and his social context into account are nonsensical (Wildgen, 1981). The basic vagueness of the phenomena and their context-dependence are also the cornerstones of the present theory. In both Gestalt semantics and in the theory presented in this book, catastrophe/theoretic thinking may prove to be useful for the analysis of boundaries between different zones involved in the microgenesis of children's actions or word meanings (Wildgen, 1983).

5.8 Game theory and problems of development

In various social sciences, the use of game-theoretic ideas has become widespread. Perhaps that has been due to the fact that the game-theoretic branch of mathematics has been constructed in analogy with phenomena in society and individual psychology that are of primary interest to social scientists. Among the topics in the study of which game-theoretic thinking has been used are the understanding of conflicts and ways of their resolution, individual and collective interests and moral decisions, the formation of coalitions, and ideas of economic processes and rationality involved in economic decision making. Many of these central problems of social life include developmental aspects. For instance, conflict *resolution* is a process that covers (ideally) the movement of a system from a conflict state to a non-conflict state. Likewise, any moral decision outcome involves the process of economic decision making leads to one or another economic outcome. On the other hand, all real-life phenomena to which the game theory has any links can (and most often are) also be thought of in static, non-developmental terms.

5.8.1 Traditional emphases in game theory

Beginning with the real-life analogue of a 'game' where different 'players' make certain choice between the options that are available to them, and where certain specific goals are sought, the traditional game theory has proceeded to formalize game-like phenomena in their abstract form. The historical starting point of these ideas was the nature of strategies used in economic decision making and their 'rationality' (Von Neumann and Morgenstern, 1944). This guaranteed the inclusion of complexity of the motivation of participants in the analyzed phenomena from the very beginning of the game theory. Economics may be the most complex of human inventions, but its importance is too central for it to be disregarded or brushed aside as 'too messy' to study. On the other hand, the specific nature of economic processes (often based on the idea of obligatory maximization of benefits in relation to costs—see also 2.5) may set the stage for game-theoretic applications in social sciences outside economics in ways that may be inadequate for the phenomena.

Psychological application of game-theoretic ideas has varied from one of its branches to another. Game theory has been quite widespread in some areas, like in social psychology (particularly in the fields of small group studies and interpersonal processes). At the same time it has been virtually unused in others, e.g. in child psychology, with the exception of some use of game-theoretic experimental situations with school-age children (Graves and Graves, 1978). There are two major ways in which game theory is applicable in psychology. First, it can be used as *a means* for the study of different psychological phenomena. In this case the game theory is applied as a part of the independent-variables complex. Social psychology experiments that are conducted in laboratory settings usually reflect the use of game theory as a means to some end. Experimental subjects are given 'payoff' matrices and asked to 'play the game' under different experimentally manipulated conditions. The latter are often made up so as to fit the requirements of the game-theoretic thinking, rather than reflect the ultimately more complex conditions of persons' interaction in real life. In such experimental settings, different extra-game 'variables' (e.g the subjects' 'competition' or 'cooperation') are studied with the help of the game theory based experimental manipulations. The game itself does not function as a model of the inherent psychological processes involved in interpersonal transaction in these experimental situations. Instead, it creates the conditions for specific ways of interaction between the subjects to which the participants are expected to conform, at least during the experiment.

The second way of using game-theoretic thinking in psychology involves the modelling of psychological phenomena. Here, the game theory is used as part of the dependent-variables complex: the particular phenomenon is studied using other methods, and the results of that study are used in the attempt to reveal which of the different formal models best fits the reality. In such applications, game theory is part of the end goal of establishing the formal model of the phenomenon.

It could be argued that it is the second type of application that is closer to the philosophical goals of mathematics. Paradoxically, it is the first kind of use which has been widespread in psychology, despite the difficulties of inference from the laboratory game tasks to the reality of daily life and experience. In the game theory, a number of abstract assumptions (constraints) were developed under which its formalizations are applicable. These constraints upon conditions under which an abstract game is assumed to be played determine the domains of reality to which the particular game-theoretic formalizations are applicable. For example, consider the widespread use of ideas from traditional game theory in the practice of social-psychological experiments where two previously unacquainted subjects are instructed to make choices between given (and immutable) action options based on a given payoff matrix. The subjects' choices are supposed to made independently of each other and at the same time, after which the outcome (determined on the basis of the payoff matrix) of the conjunction of their choices is established by the experimenter and made known to the subjects. As the experimental game progresses, the partners may shift their choices of strategies (e.g. from 'cooperative' to 'competitive' domain, or vice versa, as determined by the payoff matrix). However, the partners are constrained by the way the game conditions are set up—they cannot construct a new action option, or change the payoff matrix during the game, and neither of them can wait until the other's choice has become known and make his only then. Such constraining conditions effectively limit the applicability of game-theoretic formalisms to real-life domains where such constraints do not apply.

A good example of the constraints set up for a widely popular type of game used in many investigations, particularly in the late 1960s, is a possible dilemma that a pair of prisoners may face, and which has given rise to the 'Prisoner's Dilemma Game' (e.g. Rapoport, 1974). Two prisoners who are kept in separate cells are accused of the same crime. They both—independently of each other and on the basis of their own rational decision—have to choose whether to confess or not. If both confess, both receive a medium-severity sentence. If one confesses and the other does not, the first one is freed and the second one gets a high-severity sentence. If neither of the prisoners confesses, they both get a minimal sentence.

The prisoner's dilemma is a situation where two kinds of advantages for the decision makers are set against each other because of the limitation of communication opportunities between players. The *individual* advantage ('I would better confess, since there is a chance that he will not') and the *cooperative* advantage ('If we *both* do not confess, then we *both* get the minimal sentence') are in contradiction under these circumstances, which do not allow any modification of the situation on behalf of the prisoners. The latter can choose between two courses of action, and cannot make up a new action option. In fact, the prisoners are not playing *their* 'game', but they are just trapped by the law enforcement system which tries to make them confess by eliminating the most adequate (from the prisoners' standpoint) option of communicating between themselves, and thus preventing cooperation while making their choices.

In other terms, the Prisoner's Dilemma Game may indeed reveal psychological issues that are applicable to the real-life domain of prisoners' dilemmas of the sort, but *not* to psychological phenomena outside prisons and prisoner–law–accomplice relationships where the two (or more) side caught in such dilemmas can establish information-gathering systems and communicate in negotiations about possible actions. The proliferation of different kinds of espionage to counteract the limits of access to relevant information, and the extension of negotiations about real-life decisions over lengthy time periods, illustrate the freedom of preparatory actions that people outside prison-like situations use to avoid getting trapped in the Prisoner's Dilemma Game.

Many of the traditional assumptions of the classical game theory have served as effective limits to the adequacy of its application in different real-life contexts. First, the players in real-life 'games' are usually not limited in their communication during the decision process that lsads to their choices. The traditional game theory is not adequate as a model of phenomena where limitations on communication are not enforced. Secondly, the set of options for people 'playing games' in real life includes the possibility of *constructing new action strategies* which can usually including the choice of no-action under the given circumstances, or moving away from the given situation that requires action. The 'games' in real life are constructed (and reconstructed) in all of their aspects—the set of strategies, their 'payoffs', conditions of decision making, rules of acting, recruitment of arbiters, etc.—all of which can be reorganized. In other terms, 'games' in real life are embedded in processes of change and development (psychological, social, cultural), and are thus open-ended, whereas the formal models of any kind of game theory are necessarily closed and therefore always of limited rather than universal applicability (see 5.1, above).

Some contemporary developments in game theory have moved the formalization efforts closer to fitting the completely of real-life problems. Not surprisingly, efforts of this kind have mostly taken place in conjunction with applied problems of conflict resolution in politics and industrial relations (e.g. Bennett and Dando, 1979; Fraser and Hipel, 1979; Howard, 1971;

Kuhn, Hipel, and Fraser, 1983). Two extensions of the traditional game theory are noteworthy—the metagame and hypergame theories.

5.8.2 The metagame theory

The metagame theory, advanced particularly by Nigel Howard (1971, 1974), takes its beginning in Von Neumann and Morgenstern's (1944, p. 100) conceptualization of the 'minorant' and 'majorant' games. The conditions of these games eliminate the constraint of simultaneous independence of the players' actions. In the *minorant* game, Player 2 acts after gaining knowledge of Player 1's action. In the *majorant* game, Player 2 has to make his choice before Player 1 acts. The minorant/majorant games introduce temporal reciprocity to the players' actions in the game. The metagame concept involves the notion of meta-level reflections used to guide one's reactions to the other player's actions:

> If G is a game in normal form, and if k is a player in G, the (first-level) metagame KG . . . is the normal-form game that would exist if player k chose his strategy in G in knowledge of the other players' strategies (in G).
>
> Hence, by recursion, the second-level metagame jkG, where j and k are players, is the game in which j chooses his strategy (in kG) in knowledge of the other's strategies (in KG); in terms of strategies in G, it is a game in which j reacts (a) to k's reactions to the actions of the players other than k; (b) to the actions of the players other than j and k. (Howard, 1974, p. 261).

The metagame approach makes its application more suitable to those real-life phenomena which have action/reaction reciprocity at their core. However, it assumes that the outcomes of the players' actions (which, of course, are decided upon by their partners' previous choices) are stable, even if the information about these outcomes is imperfect (i.e. includes probabilistic information).

As a rule, the game theory has avoided modelling reality where information is incomplete. Of course, gaps in information are an inevitable part of the reality. These gaps usually get interpreted in game theory as an indication of *imperfect rather than incomplete* information. Incompleteness is theoretically de-emphasized by the assumption that the information is in principle complete although it may be imperfect (Harsanyi, 1982, p. 215). Avoiding the fact that information is incomplete may be a crucial feature of both the traditional and metagame theories that reduces their usefulness as formal systems in modelling processes of development. Development necessarily involves incomplete information about the outcomes of different events that occur as it proceeds. A game-theoretical formal system that can be assumed to fit developmental phenomena has to take the open-endedness into account. Hypergames have features that seem to satisfy this requirement better than other game types that have been discussed thus far.

*5.8.3 Hypergames and the requirements for game theories that would be
adequate for developmental phenomena*

Hypergames are games where one or more players are not fully aware of
the nature of the game situation. This unawareness may include lack of
knowledge of the consequences of their own and other players' different
choices. The players may have an inaccurate understanding of the preferences
of others, or they do not possess full and correct information on the range
of options available to them and to other players. Furthermore, they may
be unaware of the identities of all the players involved in the game (Fraser
and Hipel, 1979, p. 811).

The existing few efforts to analyze complex phenomena have concentrated
on the understanding of the process of decision making in political or military
situations (Bennett and Dando, 1979; Berresford and Dando, 1978; Fraser
and Hipel, 1979; Kuhn, Hipel, and Fraser, 1983). Usually these applications
cover the series of events within a specified time frame, rather than conceptualize event sequences over a longer time period. An example of the limited
time frame of hypergame modelling is the study of the fall of France to
Germany in 1940 (Bennett and Dando, 1979). It covered events that led to
the decision of the German troops to attack via a route (in 'the Ardennes)
that the Allied leadership discounted as an option. What the hypergame
modelling of that short period in the history of World War II provided was
the *emphasis on the difference* in the perception of the situation by the two
sides. However, the hypergame model covered only the static rationale that
led to the outcome (choice of an attack route), rather than provide a dynamic
analysis of the process via which that outcome was reached. In this sense,
the hypergame theory in its present form is not applicable directly as a
model of developmental phenomena. Although it includes the highly relevant
feature of incomplete information about the game in its premises, it excludes
some aspects relevant for capturing development. Hypergame theory still
assumes that the players' options are stable, rather than emerging or disap-
pearing. It likewise excludes the fact that the whole payoff matrix can be in
a flux so that its stable state cannot be determined.

What, then, are the conditions under which a game-theoretic formal model
can be considered to fit the developmental nature of phenomena? First, it
should share the assumption of incomplete knowledge by the participants
with the hypergame theory. Beyond that, it should emphasize the context-
bound nature of the strategies used. It also should allow the conceptual
restructuring of the whole game *at each action* of a player. Every move by
a player, be this choosing an already existing action option, refusing to act
(which is included with the set of existing options), or making up a new
option, restructures the whole game. *The game is thus constructed by the
participants rather than played as provided for the players.* Game-theoretic
endeavors that incorporate these issues seem to be absent in that branch of

mathematics at the present time, although the issues of dynamic game theory have captured the attention of mathematicians (e.g. Baser and Oldser, 1982). A developmentally relevant game theory may integrate the irreversibility of developmental processes (see 5.9) with the notion of the constructive role of the agents who create themselves in their transaction with the environment.

5.9 Modelling non-equilibrium-based changes of form

Among the physical sciences it has been the field of non-equilibrium thermo-dynamics that has been closest to the study of developmental phenomena in nature (see 3.2.4, above). That domain of physics and chemistry deals at the present time with problems of how quantitative fluctuations in the system give rise to qualitatively new structures of the phenomena. The theoretical interest concentrates on how to model such qualitative change stemming from fluctuations. This task is diametrically opposite to the modelling efforts in the social sciences which have traditionally depended upon believing in the 'law of large numbers'. In fact, the emergence of new structures as a result of disequilibration is an issue that the traditional statistical world view cannot explain because of its emphasis on averaging as a means to the end of obtaining 'true' information (cf. Valsiner, 1984b). The 'order through fluctuation' approach *depends upon the breakdown of the 'law of large numbers'—during the emergence of new form it is the fluctuations that take place far from the 'average' of the system that are instrumental in the qualitative transition* (Nicolis and Prigogine, 1977, p. 9). When for Quetelet's 'social physics' the average served as an ideal towards which all phenomena strive, then from the standpoint of the 'order-through-fluctuation' school of thought it is the development of a system due to far-from average fluctuations that constitutes the nature of the system.

The other crucial feature by which contemporary thermodynamics has enriched science is the emphasis on the time dimension. The *irreversible* nature of thermodynamic changes under conditions that are far from equilib-rium should make clear the obvious aspect of all developing phenomena—*all developmental processes take place in irreversible time.* Shotter has pointed to the lesson which scientists who study development should learn from contemporary thermodynamics:

> . . . organic structures (processes) only exist (live) in a state of exchange with their surroundings—they are 'rooted' in them. And in the course of such exchanges, they transform themselves from simple individuals into richly struc-tured ones—without having to wait, so to speak, to be 'switched on' to act once the 'last part' is in its place. They live and grow as individuals from the moment of their 'birth'. They grow in such a way that their 'parts' at any one moment owe, not just their character, but their very existence both to one another, *and* to what the 'parts' of the system were at some earlier moment in time—that is, if it is legitimate at all to call the different regions in each phase of a temporarily evolving process its 'parts', for there is never a moment at

which they cease their growth. Thus they are always in the process of becoming *other than* what at any moment they already are. Their growth is an essential and irreducible aspect of nature; it cannot be partialled out and 'added in' later, when convenient. Temporal processes cannot be made up from parts themselves devoid of temporality. Truly temporal processes are *continuous* or *indivisible* in the sense that, the very process of differentiating them into phases of *before* and *after* serves, not to separate them into a 'patchwork of disjoined parts' . . . but . . . to relate their phases of aspects of the same dynamic unity. It is a unity which is perceived as a unity, and in spite of its novelty in every moment, but because of it; for while clearly changing in one sense, like a swirl or eddy in a stream it remains recognizable in another sense as continually the same. (Reproduced with permission from Shotter, 1983, p. 21).

The time dimension that has been of little relevance in classical physics, becomes an integral part of dynamic processes studied in contemporary physics and chemistry. This change requires theoretical rethinking of the concept of 'sameness' (as is attempted by Shotter in the quote above), and the development of new formalisms to capture the dynamic aspects of thermodynamic change.

The kinds of formal models that are used by investigators who apply the 'order-through-fluctuation' theoretical framework to social science stem from the traditions of thermodynamics that use different kinds of equation to describe the laws inherent in the phenomena. The kinds of equations used are non-linear in nature. In a non-linear system the whole system is not given by the simple sum of its parts. The non-linear character of equations used in research that is based on the philosophy of non-equilibrium thermodynamics is thus in principle suitable for solving the historically long-ranging conflict in psychology between the investigators who reduce the phenomena to their elementary constitutents, and others who follow the Gestalt psychology based ideas of the nature of psychological phenomena (see 2.4 above).

Different formalisms used in the paradigm of dissipative structures are not always connected with one another (see Jantsch, 1980, for an effort of unification). Thus, applications of the disequilibration paradigm to different empirical domains in biological and social sciences may include formal descriptions that need not resemble one another, although they all may be built on the idea of disequilibration as the process that creates novel structures.

In the social sciences the efforts to model economic and social systems like those of urban areas (Allen, 1981, 1982; Allen and Sanglier, 1980) or economic analysis (Berry and Andresen, 1982) have emerged in the framework of contemporary disequilibrium thermodynamics. Urban units (towns, cities) illustrate the kind of problems that the modelling by 'dissipative structure' models can afford. The emergence, maintenance, and development of a town is a process within which the input and output flows (e.g. food, building materials, capital flowing into the town; waste, products, etc., flowing out of the town) between the town and its surroundings are of decisive character. The interdependence of these input/output flows illustrates how the developing town is treated as being an open system. Among different formal systems with claims to capturing laws of development that have been overviewed in this chapter, it is only the disequilibration approach that treats its objects of investigation consistently as open systems.

The input/output flow in the town example is certainly a quantifiable process, which leads to qualitative outcomes in the form of the structural development of the town. A step-by-step illustration of the development of a town can be easily constructed. Some enterpreneur with capital (input flow) constructs a road through a forest. Once that road is completed, the forest will never by the same—its structure is irreversibly altered by the road. The use of the road now makes it possible for another businessman to build a fuel station somewhere along the road, which again leads to irreversible alteration of the existing structure. However, the decision to build the station may depend on the flow of drivers along the new road which, if sufficiently high, makes the construction of the station economically profitable. The personnel of the station may decide to build houses nearby, and in conjunction with that the need for shops emerges. Once a shopping center is constructed, the people living in the locality may provide profitable labor for an industry to set up a plant nearby. After many qualitative changes in the locality a small town emerges, which may become a bigger town, etc. However, if the services/products that people in the town provide/produce (i.e. output flow) become non-competitive in the outside markets, the companies that have set up their plants in town may decide to close them, introducing another new (regressive) development into the structure of the system. Allen's simulation of the development of the urban system formalizes exactly such kinds of growth and regression processes—starting from the formal equations it is possible after every iterative step to determine the particular structure of the urban system, and observe dramatic (catastrophic) changes in it wrought by the quantitative changes in the exchange of the urban system with its wider environment.

The efforts to model dynamic processes, treating them as leading to new order through fluctuations, has also slowly entered psychology (Kugler, Turvey, and Shaw, 1982). The empirical domain in which formal modelling of this kind has occurred has been the area of motor functioning and motor development (e.g. Kelso, Holt, Rubin, and Kugler, 1981; Kugler, Kelso and Turvey, 1982). The disequilibration approach to modelling developmental phenomena is also unique among the formalisms described in this chapter in its acceptance of the systemic version of causality (see 2.7, above). The factors that instigate the system's development involve a multiplicity of cycles or loops between its parts. These cyclic relations lead to development of the system dependent upon its exchange with the environment. The use of the 'morphogenetic causal loop models' (see Maruyama, 1982) makes this framework more suitable for the study of developmental phenomena than is afforded by other formal systems that either reject systemic causality or avoid the issue of causality.

Disequilibration-based formal models, if applied in developmental psychology, will have a difficulty similar to that which emerges in the application of L-systems. If in the case of L-systems the difficulty was related to the specificity of the nature of the suitable objects of modelling (multi-part structures which can be directly represented by a topographic map) then in the present case problems emerge on the opposite side of high generality of the basic ideas behind the equations that fit the phenomena. For example, the development of a toddler's acting within his environment includes both qualitative change and some quantitative aspect (e.g. frequency or time spent in a certain activity) that could be modelled through such equations. However, the basic parameters by which the general input/output exchange relationships of the toddler (as the system) can be conceptualized leave a wide range of open possibilities for the modelling-oriented child psychologist, only some of which may be adequate as far as the reality of children's action development is concerned.

5.10 Summary: possibilities and limitations of formal models of development

This chapter has sought to show that borrowing formal descriptive systems from mathematics for developmental psychology is a complicated enterprise of fitting the nature of formal systems with the nature of developmental phenomena. Given the structured nature of developing children and their environments (as outlined in 4.1.1 and 4.1.2), currently widespread quantitative strategies for deriving data from the original phenomena are quite inappropriate. Furthermore, different currently existing branches of qualitative mathematics tend to be specific to the domains in conjunction with which they have emerged (e.g. L-systems, non-equilibrium thermodynamic formalisms, etc.). Developmental sciences need their own kind of mathematics that starts from the essentials of development (e.g. its open-systems nature, and time-dependency) at its axioms, and constructs particular formal models for developmental processes *per se*. The mathematics used in developmental psychology must fit the developmental phenomena and not the other way round.

Mathematics is essentially a conglomerate of different kinds of philosophies that are turned into formal systems within which statements can be deductively proven. However, the axioms these systems use are often selected on some *ad hoc* basis stemming from the psychology of the particular mathematician as a philosopher. It is exactly in the realm of these axioms where the usefulness (or principal uselessness) of a mathematical system for the purposes of a scientific discipline is determined. Once the axioms of a mathematical domain fit the basic characteristics of the phenomena under study, then that particular mathematical system may be valuable for furthering our understanding of the phenomena. Likewise, if there is no fit between the two, or if there is a basic discrepancy between the characteristics of the phenomena and the axioms of the mathematical system, then the application of that mathematical formalism is likely to lead only to an illusion of greater precision, or the 'Type III error' as described by Mitroff and Featheringham (1974).

Developmental psychology has been particularly ill-served by the mismatch between the phenomena of development and efforts to make the study of child psychology more mathematical in the mistaken belief that this has led to a more scientific psychology. Usually the mathematical tools that have filtered into developmental psychology have been outgrowths from linear statistical models which originated in the mathematics of the last century. The linear model itself is ill-suited for psychological phenomenas (see Thorngate, 1986).

Unfortunately, the alternative mathematical approaches which could be of value in developmental psychology are either absent or insufficiently developed. They are often deployed in the service of very specific tasks, mostly within developmental biology, and the design and construction of computer systems that can learn new information. The systems which have been briefly examined illustrate the gap between developmental thinking and existing mathematics. This gap is not surprising, since developmental questions have rarely been posed in different sciences. In this sense, biology is not much better off than psychology. Curiously, it is in the framework of contemporary physics and chemistry where the need for adequate formal descriptions of qualitative (structural) change has emerged.

Of the different formal systems considered, none was found to fit the needs of developmental psychology directy. Non-equilibrium thermodynamics is closest to capturing the general nature of development, but its actual use in developmental psychology is complicated because of the high fluidity of the structures observable in the empirical research on children. The mixing of developmental and non-developmental approaches in catastrophe theory renders it of doubtful value—despite the fact that it originated in an attempt to solve the basic developmental problem of epigenetic canalization. The static assumptions involved in most versions of game theory were also found to be unpromising, with the possible exception of the hypergame theory. The latter, however, is a relatively new line of theorizing within game theory and has so far not been applied to the study of developmental phenomena. The Lindenmayer-systems were developed for the modelling of a specific developmental issue (growth of filament structures in botany) and they are difficult to apply to more heterogeneously structured phenomena. The learning automata theory deals with modelling of complex organismic learning, but its assumptions of the environmental structure of the learning automata are too much simplified to fit the reality of ontogeny in their present form. Finally, Chomsky's widely known philosophy of 'generative grammar' captures the important issue of what the formal models of development should allow (i.e. the generation of all possible cases of the class of phenomena), but fails to capture the context-sensitive open-systems nature of not only psychological but also of linguistic phenomena.

The inadequacy in matching the goals of developmental psychologists with those of mathematicians need not be blamed on either side. Rather, it is more fruitful for developmental psychology to carry out mathematics-free empirical research—to observe selected processes of development in ways that retain their systemic and context-bound nature. Close empirical description of child–environment relationships from an explicit theoretical point of view, especially if the change in these relationships is follows longitudinally, may provide a picture of developmental processes that is of interest to mathematicians. The following two chapters constitute an attempt in that direction. The setting of infants' and toddlers' mealtimes, their structural and cultural organization, will be analyzed in chapter 6. Chapter 7 includes empirical data derived from the observation of children as they actually had their meals in such settings in a very limited cultural niche—that of middle-class American families. It will become obvious from these empirical data that the processes by which children develop involve their own actions within the structured settings, which sometimes lead to new states of the settings, and—thereby—of the children's actions.

CHAPTER 6

Theory and phenomena: the organization of children's mealtimes

In any science, the links that connect a particular theory with a phenomenon to which that theory is applied are of crucial significance. As was demonstrated above (chapter 2), psychologists' implicit assumptions about the psychological phenomena often guide them to build theories and derive data in ways that eliminate some essential aspects of the phenomena. This is particularly true in developmental psychology, where the non-developmental assumptions accepted by many investigators prohibit them from direct empirical study of the developmental processes. Only few theoretical perspectives (overviewed in chapter 3) have dealt with developmental issues in epistemologically adequate ways. Furthermore, little or no help from existing mathematical systems used in other sciences can be immediately available for developmental research, as the analysis in chapter 5 revealed.

Given that state of affairs in the science of developmental psychology, the task of relating an abstract theoretical system (outlined in chapter 4) to real-life developmental phenomena is a formidable task. The main strategy for accomplishing it is to start from the general type of reference frame, which in the present case is the individual–socioecological one (see 3.1.4). That framework involves the emphasis on the dynamics of child–environment relationships that are organized by another person, usually the child's parents or other caregivers. As was emphasized before (in 4.1.1. and 4.1.2.), both the child's actions and the environment in which he acts, are structurally organized entities. The structural organization of the environment, as well as of the child's actions, must therefore be observed and described in empirical research performed within the individual–socioecological reference frame. Furthermore, the 'another person' who organizes child-environment relationships is not an occasional, or random, participant in the whole scheme of things. Just the contrary—she organizes these relationships in an active way, working towards *her* particular goals as the parent, teacher, youth group leader, etc. The setting of goals by people who organize child-environment relationships is canalized by their cultural background.

This brief reminder of how developmental phenomena are conceptualized within the individual–socioecological reference frame brings us to the goals pursued in this chapter. The real-life setting that is selected as the empirical illustration of the theory presented in this book is that of mealtimes of infants and toddlers, over the age range 6 to 24 months. This setting involves the eating of different kinds of solid or liquid foods, using various utensils and containers. The aim of this chapter is to analyze the structure of children's mealtime settings from different angles—its physical and cultural-historical sides. The role of empirical data in theoretical discourse, and the meaning of 'action' as it constitutes an important empirical unit of analysis, will also be discussed in this chapter. Chapter 6 serves as preparation for the next chapter (7), in which longitudinal observations of children's actions within mealtime settings will be presented.

6.1 Theory, reality, and data in psychology

What is the role of empirical phenomena in theory construction? This basic question can be answered in different ways, depending upon investigators' philosophical foundations. In the present context the empirical *reality*—i.e. psychological events in people's acting and thinking—plays the role of the determiner of the adequacy or inadequacy of different local aspects of the theory, as well as of the adequacy of acceptance or rejection of the basic assumptions onto which the theory is built. It is evident that in the present context I am carefully avoiding the use of the term 'data' which dominates empirically minded psychologists' discourse and thinking. The reason for this avoidance is the ambiguous and indeterminate meaning of that term. It is often the tradition among psychologists to think that the data are 'objective' in and by themselves, and that any theory must be verified (or falsified) on the basis of the data. For instance, 'let the data speak for themselves', is a frequently honored call among psychologists. The cult of such empiricism (see Toulmin and Leary, 1985) has largely concealed the actual relationships between empirical reality and psychological theories. The latter are not haphazardly assembled sets of independent propositions of different (usually low) levels of abstractness—like the majority of what are called 'theories' in contemporary psychology are (Smedslund, 1978). Instead, theories are hierchically organized systems of propositions about reality where every single proposition is related to others and follows from some more general assumption that the theory-constructor has accepted. Such systems are more likely to be adequate if they are constructed by a scientist who knows the empirical phenomenology well—in this sense many aspects of theories grow out of the author's intuitive integration of the empirical knowledge with the abstract bases of the theory. Explicit testing of the theory in research process involves only some aspects of the theory that the constructor considers important. Depending on the theory constructor's psychological tolerance for failure, different scientists react to the disconfirmation of the selected aspects of their theory in variable ways (see Mitroff, 1974; Wertheimer, 1981). Some may accept the disconfirmation and reject the theory. The believers in the absolute truthfulness of the data in their role as 'final judges' might react in this way. Others may refuse to accept the disconfirming empirical evidence.

Neither of these two extreme reactions is likely to improve the theoretical status in the given discipline. The empiricist extreme is unlikely to construct a viable theory, since the empirical reality is sufficiently rich for anybody to generate some kinds of data that would disconfirm at least part of any theory in psychology. An extreme empiricist's activity in theory construction (especially if s/he accepts the demand for falsification) resembles children's build-and-bash games—a tentative theory is erected, and then disconformed by data. As a result, it is disassembled, so that the construction process starts anew. On the opposite side, the extremes of the refusal to accept disconfirming evidence lead to the making of the theory into an ideology (religion) that is accepted as an *a priori* true and unmodifiable corpus of beliefs.

What, then, is the role of empirical material in theory construction? In the present context it is accepted that *access to empirical reality that occurs in the process of empirical research clarifies the adequacy of the connection between parts of the theory at different levels of abstractness.* The data do not exist separately from the investigator but are the result of the investigator's relationship with the empirical reality *from the perspective of the given theory.* For that latter reason the data cannot be considered to be 'objective' independently from the theory which is used as their basis. The data that are derived from reality to prove a certain theory cannot prove it (or disprove it) in full—they can only be informative about the particular part of a theory to which they are related. Thus, they can prove or disprove that *part* of the theory, but not necessarily the whole theory. On the other hand, a theory that is based on abstract premises that (on the basis of conceptual anslysis) can be argued not to fit the reality can be rejected in full. The present conceptualization of theory–data relationships involves a certain asymmetry between inductive (empirical) and deductive methods of the analysis of the theory: *the empirical research is relevant for verification (or falsification) of the adequacy of parts of the theory, whereas conceptual analysis of the bases of the theory affords testing of the adequacy of the theory as a whole.* In other terms, a theory can be fully rejected if one can prove that its basic assumptions are unwarranted (given the state of empirical reality), but empirical research *per se* can lead only to rejection or reformulation of particular aspects of the theory. Theories are abstractions of reality—and as such cognitive constructs their fate is determined in the investigators' thinking and not in the real world which continues to be organized in its own ways independently of how well a theorist has captured that organization in his theory.

6.2 The meaning of 'action'

On the side of empirical reality this book deals with the development of children's action. The concept of action has been defined differently in different schools of thought in psychology. In its different versions, though, it has centered around the invariant emphasis on the *goal-directedness* and *conscious planning* of acting (Chapman, 1982; Harré, 1980; Herzog, 1984; Leont'ev, 1975; Von Cranach, 1982; and others). The conceptual roots of action theories lie within the German cultural-philosophical traditions where the concepts of 'Handlung' and 'Tätigkeit' have served as the language basis for action theories.

The English-language terms 'act' and 'action' both relate to the Latin verb 'agere' (=to do, see Webster's *Third New International Dictionary*, 1981, pp. 20–21). The closeness in the meanings of these terms in the English language has facilitated the use of them in scientific discourse in more electic ways than the German equivalents afford, which has certainly contributed to the translation difficulties of German or Soviet contributions to action research in psychology or sociology into English.

6.2.1 Summary of concepts of action in psychology

In different theoretical systems in contemporary psychologies the meaning of ACTION and ACT and their relationships is conceptualized in various ways. Within one tradition, Harré (1980, Harré and Secord, 1972) and Von Cranach (1982) view ACTION as goal-directed behavior while the term ACT is reserved to denote the meaning of some set of actions within a culture. For example, the act of greeting can be accomplished by different actions: kissing, hand shaking, nodding, smiling, saying 'Hi!', bowing, etc. All these actions (which can occur in combination, and/or in a sequence, e.g. saying 'hi!', followed by shaking hands) accomplish the same social act of greeting. Thus, the term act may be in different relations with the action: the relation can be one-to-one (e.g. in cases where a specific action has a specific meaning), or one-to-many (a certain act is carried out by a sequence of partially parallel actions, like the example of greeting).

In research on children's motor development, the term 'action' is used in connection with the more general term 'skill'. A skill (e.g. walking, singing, using a spoon while eating, etc.) can be defined as a sequentially organized programme of actions towards the attainment of a goal (Connolly, 1973, 1975), which is composed of different subroutines (Connolly, 1970). In the domain of motor skill research the issues of the cultural meaning of the skills are usually not considered important, thus the discrepancy between the term 'act' and 'skill'. This discrepancy may be remedied by assuming partial overlap between 'skill' and 'act': all motor skills of human beings are, or become, acts (or parts of acts) as their goals are culturally meaningful. However, not all acts involve readily available skills, as the meaningful frame of an act may direct the development of a motor skill (action programme) for its fulfillment.

The traditions of thinking about actions that have emerged within the Soviet psychology have branched off from the German traditions of viewing action in an object-related manner (exemplified by 'Tätigkeit'). Vygotsky's writing about the role of cultural tools in human development (e.g. Vygotsky and Luria, 1930) served as a beginning stage for increased interest in the concept of activity in contemporary Soviet psychology. The most well-known effort in the Soviet psychology to construct a theory of activity is found in A.M. Leont'ev's thinking. His (Leont'ev, 1975) 'theory of activity' (*deyatel'-nost* in Russian) involves a different use of the terms. Different ACTIVITIES (that are forms of human relationships with the object-world, distinguished and guided by their motives) include ACTIONS (*deistvie* in Russian—processes that are guided by conscious goals). Leont'ev explicitly defines action as 'the process that is subservient to the representation of the result that must be reached, i.e., the process that is subservient to a conscious goal' (Leont'ev, 1975, p. 103). Actions, in their turn, consist of OPER-ATIONS (behaviors that are immediately dependent upon the context of attainment of concrete goals). Leont'ev explains his use of the term 'operations' in the following way:

> Every goal—even such like 'reach point N'—exists objectively in some object-related [environmental] situation. Of course, for the subject's consciousness the goal may be in the form of an abstraction from that situation, but his *action* cannot be abstracted from it. That is the reason why, aside from the intentional aspect (*what* must be accomplished) action includes also its operational aspect (*how*, in what way it can be accomplished), which is determined not by the goal in itself, but by the objective object-related [environmental] conditions of its accomplishment. In other words, the *action that is being carried out* matches the task; the task—that is the goal which is given under certain circumstances. That is why action has a special character that in special ways 'creates' it—the ways for whch it is carried out. I call these ways of accomplishment of action *operations* (Leont'ev, 1975, p. 107).

Whereas the Harré–VonCranach tradition of thinking emphasizes the relevance of behavior and its existing social function, Leont'ev's emphasis is rooted in his understanding of motives as results of person–environment transaction. Motives, for Leont'ev, constitute the object (which either exists in reality, or is constructed in the ideal sphere of a person) that directs the activity of the person towards himself. Leont'ev posits the absolute existence of motives—according to him, 'non-motivated' activity cannot exist (if it seems to exist, ir represents a case with hidden motives—cf. Leont'ev, 1975, p. 102).

6.2.2 The concept of action in the present theory

Any developmental perspective on children's actions has to deal with the issue of validity of teleological understanding of the young infant or child. Under what conditions is it reasonable to assume that the child's activities are goal directed? This question, however, is flavored by its non-developmental ethos—it is asked to verify the *existence versus non-existence* of the child's purposefulness and even intentionality. It overlooks the developmental aspect—how do purposefulness and intentionality develop from a state of the young organism in which it is not *yet* present? The latter question helps us to overcome the theoretical duality of action-theoretic handling of infancy, which either has to posit the existence of intentionality in the infant and then analyze its actions, or to deny the existence of intentionality and consequently refuse to analyze infants' behavior as related to actions. A developmental solution to the problem of actions among infants is suggested by Thelen and Fogel (1986) in their effort to explain infants' motor coordination and interaction with adults in terms of *coordinative structures*—synergistic forms of organization of the particular functional structure (e.g. muscle complexes of the infant's body, or mother–infant interactive behavior) that are capable of advancing into qualitatively new states of organization. In this sense, conscious goals are not necessarily part and parcel of action, but emerge in its process and continue to participate in actions once they have emerged. The present perspective on children's action development emphasizes the *teleogenetic* nature of actions—human capacity and practice of generating their goals and acting towards attainment of such self-constructed goals (Coulter, 1973). This perspective contrasts with both the teleonomic (goal-seeking) view of action, as well as with the rich behavioristic traditions in psychology that have attempted to eliminate the notion of future-oriented purposeful behavior from the realm of scientifically studied phenomena. The theory presented in this book is aimed at explaining how children's actions (observable behavioral episodes) and acts (culturally meaningful events) are *constructed in the process of transaction of the developing child and his social others, as that transaction regulates the relationship of the child to the particular environmental context.* In the process of such transaction, the directedness of the 'social others' of the young child can be assumed from the beginning, but the child's intentionality and goal-direction constitute emergent developmental phenomena. In other terms the development of child's actions starts from a state of no intentionality and goal-directedness and is gradually canalized towards culturally acceptable and prescribed forms of goal-setting and goal-attainment, as well as towards the cognitive construction of intentionality as a psychological device that underlies human actions in their adult form.

The empirical study of psychological phenomena from a teleogenetic perspective confronts with three conceptual difficulties. First, the possible construction (and/or presence) of multiple goals makes it complicated to explicate the whole goal-network that is functioning at a given time. Furthermore, some goals in that network may be eliminated from the network, and new ones constructed, at the next time moment—the goal-network is a dynamic entity that changes in connection with the actions related to it. Secondly, many of the goals in the goal-network may be *fuzzily defined* at a given time. This is a very likely state of affairs because of the constructed nature of the goals—their construction starts from a state in which the given goal does not exist, moves through a state where its existence is unclear and its nature fuzzy, and only finally may reach a state of high clarity and clear differentiation. Since at any given time, some of the goals in the goal-network are in the intermediate state of emergence in which they cannot be exactly delineated in an analysis, the empirical study of goal-directed action has to assume their existence without their clear delineation. Finally, the third difficulty of empirical research relates to the temporal organization of the goal-network: some goals are set up to be attained sooner than later, some more immediate goals serve as means of the reaching of more far-off and more general goals, etc. Since analysis of any future goals involves explication of an organism's projection of expected outcomes in the future, such analysis depends heavily on the conscious self-reports of the organism. The latter is accessible to the investigator if the organism involved is a human being capable of introspection. Infants and toddlers are not particularly suitable subjects for introspective accounts of their goals, although from their behavior goal-directedness is easily implied by the socialized *adult* observer who treats his projections of goal-directedness into the child's actions as if these were necessarily true.

6.3 Strategies of search for relevant empirical reality

The theoretical system outlined in this book is based on assumptions that determine where to look for empirical phenomenology that would be relevant for the theory. First, the structured nature of the organism and its environment leads to looking for empirical phenomena in those domains where one can expect constraining of the actions of developing children to take place. This direction of search is quite opposite to the strategy of many child psychologists who want to observe children's 'free' behavior in their habitats. A good example of the latter is the overwhelming interest in contemporary studies of adult–infant interaction in the setting called 'free play'—where the adult and the baby 'act naturally' in a situation where they 'play freely'.

From the perspective of the present theory, such a 'free play' situation is the *least* interesting domain of empirical phenomena—exactly because the potentially present constraints on action (and thinking) are least likely to become evident in observations of such situations. The 'free' (=constraint-free) nature of 'free play' makes it highly unsuitable for the purposes of the present theory, whereas exactly the 'free' (='natural') aspect may make it valuable to investigators whose theoretical background is not based on the central relevance of limits or constraints. Furthermore, from the perspective described in this book, *no play, or any behavior of any organism, can be 'free' in principle, since all behavior is embedded in its context which sets some limits on its 'freedom'*. Even if it is difficult to point to the constraints operating in the mother–child 'free play' situation, the constraints are actually there; only since they are unlikely to be reached (because of the wide range of possibilities they afford) it is possible to imagine that they do not exist.

The everyday life of developing children is full of both highly constrained (e.g. diapering, eating, riding in a car-seat, or on mother's back, etc.) as well as low-constrained (e.g. unsupervised play, sleep) events or happenings. The domain of toddlers' lives that is represented in this chapter (mealtimes) was selected because in that domain adults purposefully limit some of children's actions and promote others, thus canalizing the toddlers' further development. It is also important to view the functioning of the present theory inside the adults' minds when they think about children in the role of parents, or about child-related activities. In both cases, the thinking of adults is canalized by some cognitive constraints that allow the adults to solve old problems under new circumstances. Such sets of cognitive constraints o thinking can be viewed as results of the internalization process of external constraints on action—internal reconstruction of external reality (Vygotsky, 1956, 1960). The question of the correspondence between thinking and acting as both of these are organized by sets of constraints remains beyond the scope of this book.

6.4 The cultural organization of children's mealtimes

It would be trivial to state the importance of feeding from the perspective of any living organism. The fundamental importance of the alimentary functions make human actions in feeding settings prime targets for cultural regulation. As Lévi-Strauss (1966, p. 587) has emphasized, cooking shares with human language the status of being truly universal forms of human activity—there is no society without a language, and also no society which does not cook in some manner at least some of its food. The discovery of controllable fire and its purposeful use have been important milestones in the history of the human cultures that set human beings apart from other species. Some non-human primates may, under special circumstances, acquire artificial semiotic systems that may be called language—but no non-human primate has been observed or taught to cook himself a meal, either in the wild or in a laboratory!

The cultural organization of cooking and eating includes many facets all of which are relevant for the developing child. In fact, the ontogeny of feeding constitutes the microcosm for the infant within which cultural patterning of behavior begins and where the child is confronted with cultural knowledge about the world of foods, tools, and feeders. Gesell and Ilg (1937, p. 33) remark:

> One of the basic developmental problems of the human infant is to use his hand adaptively, to grasp food, and to manage implements for conveying food through the short but troublesome route from hand to mouth. The beginnings of self-feeding by hand in the very primitive child would make a fascinating evolutionary tale if it could be reconstructed. The introduction of cooking and the development of feeding utensils are important chapters in the history of civilization. Cup and spoon are sufficiently sophisticated implements of culture to come into conflict with the infant's capacities. There is a discrepancy between his immature equipment and the demands of adult culture.

The child's knowledge about the cultural meanings embedded in food-related activities is gradually acquired both by observing others cook and eat what was cooked, onself eating under the supervision of others, and observing (and participating in) the practices of the disposal of the left-overs. The following specific aspects of cultural organization of eating are important in the process of child socialization in any culture:

(1) The distribution of meals and occasional snacks in the culture within the day/night cycle.
(2) The nature of raw foods, the length of time spent in food preparation, and the public verses private nature of cooking different kinds of foods.
(3) The distinction between feasts and everyday meals and the meaning of the former within the religious belief system of the culture.
(4) The rules of social organization of a mealtime (the social closeness and positioning of the people present; inclusion/exclusion of women and children in the mealtime; rules of serving food—who serves what in which order, rules of eating—'table manners'—and social interaction during the meal; beginning- or end-rituals marking the mealtime and connecting it with the religious belief system of the culture).
(5) Rules of dealing with the left-overs: disposal or preservation.
(6) The meaning of 'clean' versus 'dirty' distinction as applied to food objects before, during, and after the meal.
(7) Rules for children's behavior in the context of the mealtime of the household: changes in expectations for children's behavior dependent on age and capabilities.

All these cultural issues are intricately intertwined with the nutritional and psychological events that take place during mealtimes. On the other hand, these events also depend on the physical structure of the particular settings, which itself is culturally organized.

6.4.1 Accounts of children's mealtimes in psychology

The process of acquisition of cultural knowledge by children in conjunction with eating has been very rarely of interest to psychologists, at least as far as times after weaning are concrned. Earlier studies devoted directly to children's eating included topics such as eating habits (Baldwin, 1944) or food preferences and appetite (Duncker, 1938; Katz, 1928). It has happened mostly that psychoanalytically oriented researchers have been more akin to paying attention to psychological events that take place in connection with eating. Anna Freud (1963) interpreted the development of children's relations with food in the context of transitions in their relations with the mother. She outlines six approximate steps in the progression to fully self-controlled eating:

(1) Being nursed at the breast or bottle, by the clock or on demand, with the common difficulties about intake caused partly by the infant's normal fluctuations of appetite and intestinal upsets, partly by the mother's attitudes and anxieties regarding feeding; interference with need-satisfaction caused by hunger periods, undue waiting for meals, rationing or forced feeding set up the first—and often lasting—disturbances in the positive relationships to food. Pleasure sucking appears as a forerunner, by-product of, substitute for, or interference with feeding;

(2) weaning from breast or bottle, initiated either by the infant himself or according to the mother's wishes. In the latter instance, and especially if carried out abruptly, the infant's protest against oral deprivation has adverse results for the normal pleasure in food. Difficulties over the introduction of solids, new tastes, and consistencies, being either welcomed or rejected;

(3) the transition from being fed to self-feeding, with or without implements, 'food' and 'mother' still being identified with each other;

(4) self-feeding with the use of spoon, fork, etc., the disagreements with the mother about the quantity of intake being shifted often t the form of intake, i.e., table manners; meals as a general battleground on which the difficulties of the mother—child relationship can be fought out; craving for sweets as a phase-adequate substitute for oral sucking pleasures; food fads as a result of anal training, i.e., of the newly acquired reaction formation of disgust;

(5) gradual fading out of the equation food–mother in the oedipal period. Irrational attitudes toward eating out now determined by infantile sexual theories, i.e., fantasies of impregnation through the mouth (fear of poison), pregnancy (fear of getting fat), anal birth (fear of intake and output), as well as by reaction formations against cannibalism and sadism;

(6) gradual fading out of the sexualization of eating in the latency period, with pleasure in eating retained or even increased. Increase in the rational attitudes to food and self-determination in eating, the earlier experiences on this line being decisive in shaping the individual's food habits in the adult life, his tastes, preferences, as well as eventual addictions or aversions with regard to food and drink. (Reproduced with permission from Freud, 1963, pp. 251–252).

Anna Freud's interpretation of the sequence of development of children's relations with food is strongly (and unsurprisingly) influenced by the explanatory system of Freudian thinking, which is cast within the intra-individual frame of reference (see 3.1.1). Similar intra-individual emphasis is often present in clinical-psychological literature on children's eating *disorders*, mostly concentrating on later childhood years and adolescence (Diepold, 1983; Garfinkel, Moldofsky, and Garner, 1980; Minuchin, Rosman and Baker, 1978; Schwartz, Thompson, and Johnson, 1982; Slade and Russell, 1973; etc.). Some research involving children's mealtimes in its social-interactional aspect has been conducted within studies of mother–infant interaction (Benigni, 1974; Golinkoff, 1983; Kindermann, 1985, 1986; Leenders, 1983). These studies, however, have only made use of the mealtime setting without explicitly analyzing its constraint structure, since they have theoretically been based on context-free conceptual systems.

The most explicit and structured description of children's mealtime social interaction with adults that is currently available in psychological research literature is part of the extensive longitudinal study of child development that has been conducted in Nottingham (Newson and Newson, 1963, 1968, 1976; Shotter and Newson, 1982). The theoretical perspective of the 'Nottingham school' of psychology (see also Gauld and Shotter, 1977; Shotter, 1975, 1983, 1984; Wood, 1980) emphasizes the relatedness of the emerging 'selfhood' in children with the organization of their social environments. Mealtimes, among other settings, turned out to be situations around which much of the social interaction was found to center in the Nottingham longitudinal study, especially around the children's age of 4 years (Newson and Newson, 1968, chapter 8). The mothers' accounts of their 'problems' with their children's eating revealed three basic themes: concern with children's nutrition, their table manners, and the parental strategies for coping with children's eating at mealtimes. Newsons' interviews (Newson and Newson, 1968) with mothers of 4-year-olds revealed very interesting qualitative aspects of mothers' worries and action strategies at mealtimes. Literally any aspect of 4-year-olds' behavior at mealtimes *may* become a 'problem' for the mother, depending upon *her* (and the whole family's) ways of structuring the mealtime settings. The 'problem' status of the child's actions is determined by the adults' thinking regarding these actions within the context of social norms that the adults accept and impose upon children.

Some aspects of Newsons' empirical findings about mealtimes of 4-year-olds in Nottingham are of direct relevance for the empirical data on American toddlers' mealtimes (reported in chapter 7). By the age of 4, the sample of mothers in the Nottingham study showed overwhelming (although not absolute) institution of special rules for mealtime actions. Thus, 73 per cent of mothers did not allow the child to bring toys or books to the table, 25 per cent did not allow the child to get up from the table during the meal, and 65 per cent minded about the order in which the child eats things during the meal. The rules of using utensils for getting food in the mouth reveal some surviving flexibility on mothers' side at that age of children. Only 10 per cent of mothers admitted that they would not let the child use a spoon instead of a knife of fork. The times at which the use of fingers by the child, in situations where utensils are culturally prescribed to be used, was allowed were almost an event of the past for most of the sample: 79 per cent of mothers admitted that they would not let the child use his fingers while eating (Newson and Newson, 1968, p. 233).

Although utensils were used overwhelmingly within the sample, in individual instances the issue of the child's reverting to the use of fingers while feeding was reported to acquire greater specificity as a 'problem'. Thus, the wife of a metal polisher described her son's actions:

> He does tend to use his fingers, but we try to break him of that habit, you know. It is a delicate situation at the moment as regards that, because he would *like* to use his fingers; but we keep pushing the fork in his hand. He knows about it—once I've spoken about it, he won't actually use his fingers for the rest of the meal. But every meal he *starts* to use them. (Newson and Newson, 1968, p. 236).

This example illustrates the possible reality of many 4-year-olds' mealtimes—where the child's actions are aimed at keeping the Zone of Free Movement at its wider state (i.e. to include hand use to transport food for which adults' culture prescribes a utensil). On the other hand, parents' canalization of the child's actions involves gradual (and future-oriented) promotion of utensil use. What emerges as a basic finding from Newsons' data on 4-year-olds' mealtime behavior is the long ontogenetic period (essentially covering all the preschool years). The lengthy time tht it takes children to begin to accept the cultural regulation of mealtimes may be due to the intricately structured nature of these settings. A view into our own cultural history may help us better to understand the complexity of the setting.

6.4.2 Cultural organization of children's mealtimes in European history

In written records about European cultures and their history, information on children's behavior at mealtimes is scarce (Braudel, 1973; Elias, 1978). This is not surprising, given children's status in our cultural history: (a) long-term breast-feeding of children on demand, and no great motivation to force them to succumb to adults' mealtimes rules at an early age; (b) once the children are expected to learn new social rules they do so without raising many problems; and (c) child-related aspects of everyday life have been largely left outside the sphere of interests of chronicle writers or social scientists, since these aspects have been considered too natural to be of relevance for the understanding of history or society. However, from the perspective of understanding how child socialization works the history of everyday life of children within their families is highly informative.

The cultural history of mealtime settings is determined by two interdependent lines of historical inventions. First, the history of cooking and eating technology (tools for food preparation, utensils for eating) provides a sequence of external objects that make it possible to restructure the mealtime setting in different novel ways. Each of these inventions: from the discovery of the usefulness of fire for roasting meat, to the invention of the microwave oven—cater for some cultural and alimentary needs of the users of these inventions at a particular historical period. Secondly, the history of cooking/eating technology is closely intertwined with the history of social rules that have been constructed to regulate the processes of food preparation and eating, and which make prepared food into an object of social exchanges with particular meanings in the culture (e.g. gifts of food as regulators of kinship ties—see Fortes and Fortes, 1936). The feeding utensils lead to new rules of using them at mealtimes, which in their turn may lead to the invention of new utensils.

The developing child has inevitably been the participant in, as well as an observer of, the mealtimes as those were organized in his/her culture at the particular time. The following is an excerpt from a text by C. Calviac, influenced by Erasmus Rotterdamus, from the year 1560:

> When the child is seated, if there is a serviette on the plate in front of him, he shall take it and place it on his left arm or shoulder; then he shall place his bread on the left and the knife on the right, like the glass, if he wishes to leave it on the table, and if it can be conveniently left there without annoying anyone. For it might happen that the glass could not be left on the table or on his right without being in someone's way.
>
> The child must have the discretion to understand the needs of the situation he is in.
>
> When eating . . . he should take the first piece that comes to his hand on his cutting board.
>
> If there are sauces, the child may dip into them decently, without turning his food over after having dipped one side. . . .
>
> It is very necessary for a child to learn at an early age how to carve a leg of mutton, a partridge, a rabbit, and such things.
>
> *It is a far dirty thing for a child to offer others something he has gnawed, or something he disdains to eat himself, unless it be to his servant.*
>
> Nor is it decent to take from the mouth something he has already chewed, and put it on the cutting board, unless it be a small bone from which he has sucked the marrow to pass time while awaiting the dessert; for after sucking it he should put it on his plate, where he should also place the stones of cherries, plums, and suchlike, as it is not good either to swallow them or to drop them on the floor.
>
> The child should not gnaw bones indecently, as dogs to.
>
> When the child would like salt, he shall *take it with the point of his knife and not with three fingers*.
>
> The child must cut his meat into very small pieces on his cutting board . . . and he must not lift the meat to his mouth now with one hand and now with another, *like little children who are learning to eat*: he should always do so with his right hand, taking the bread or meat decently with three fingers only. (Elias, 1978, pp. 90–92; italics mine—J. V.)

This description of 'good' eating habits of children (of indeterminate age range—most likely in mid-childhood) in the sixteenth century illustrates a number of concerns for child socialization in conjunction with the increasing complexity of the social rules that regulate mealtime behavior. It is interesting to note the socially transformed meaning of a food object once it has been in the person's mouth (offering others—except servants—things that had been in the child's mouth, putting food remains from mouth back to cutting board).

Another text that dates back to the sixteenth century originates in the German town of Gotha, where it was written by a local shoemaker, Hans Sachs, in 1534:

Listen you children who are going to table,
Wash your hands and cut your nails.
Do not sit at the head of the table; this is reserved for the father of the house.
Do not commence eating until a blessing is said.
Dine in God's name, and permit the eldest to begin first.
Proceed in a disciplined manner.
Do not snort or smack like a pig.
Do not reach violently for bread, lest you may knock over a glass.
Do not cut bread on your chest, or conceal pieces of bread or pastry under your hands.
Do not tear pieces for your plate with your teeth.
Do not stir food around in your plate orlinger over it.
Do not fill your spoon too full.
Rushing through your meals is bad manners.
Do not reach for more food while your mouth is still full, nor talk with your mouth full.
Be moderate; do not fall upon your plate like an animal.
Be the last to cut your meat and break your fish.
Chew your food with your mouth closed.
Do not lick the corners of your mouth like a dog.
Do not hover greedily over your food.
Wipe your mouth before you drink, so that you do not grease up your wine.
Drink politely and avoid coughing into your cup.
Do not belch or cry out.
With drink be most prudent.
Sit smartly, undisturbed, humble.
Do not toast a person a second time.
Fill no glass with another.
Do not stare at a person as if you were watching him eat.
Do not elbow the person sitting next to you.
Sit up straight; be a model of gracefulness.
Do not rock back and forth on the bench, lest you let loose a stink.
Do not kick your feet under the table.
Guard yourself against all shameful words, gossip, ridicule, and laughter, and be honorable in all matters.
If sexual play occurs at table, pretend you do not see it.
Never start a quarrel, quarreling at table is most despicable.
Say nothing that might offend another.
Do not blow your nose or do other shocking things.

Do not pick your nose.
If you must pick your teeth, be discreet about it.
Never scratch your head (this goes for girls and women too), or fish out lice.
Let no one wipe his mouth on the table cloth, or lay his head in his hands.
Do not lean back against the wall until the meal is finished.
Silently praise and thank God for the food he has graciously provided, and you have received from his fatherly hand. Now you rise from the table, wash your hands, and return diligently to your business or work. (Reproduced with permission from Ozment, 1983, p. 143).

The general inhibitive nature of the particular 'do not . . .' rules in this text may perhaps illustrate the relevance that had been given to proper structure of actions at mealtimes in our cultural history. It may be also reflect the difficulty of forcing children to succumb to the rigorous cultural rules of adults, which were related to the general life conditions of all people at different times in history (e.g. the rule concerning 'not fishing out lice' in the 1534 Gotha text).

In general, the cultural history of mealtimes in the European cultures is characterized by increasing differentiation of the individual participant's food and food-use utensils from communal usage, and by increased external mediation of food handling during mealtimes by specific tools. The European cultural traditions of eating have developed from the sharing of a communal dish in which food is presented and from where it is extracted by hand, towards highly differentiated social organization of the meal setting where each participant has a varied set of food-handling tools (plates, bowls, glasses, forks, spoons, knives, etc.) for his or her use only, and where these private tools are kept strictly separate from similar but jointly used utensils (e.g. forks or spoons for the delivery of food from a common plate t the person's plate) in the process of eating. This cultural-historical development leads to a situation where

On many occasions, not only the plates are changed after each course but the eating utensils, too. It does not suffice to eat simply with knife, fork, and spoon instead of with one's hands. More and more in the upper class a special implement is used for each kind of food. Soup-spoons, fish-knives, and meat-knives are on the one side of the plate. Forks for hors d'oeuvre, fish, and meat on the other. Above the plate are fork, spoon, or knife—according to the custom of the country—for sweet foods. And for the dessert and fruit yet another implement is brought in. All these utensils are differently shaped and equipped. They are now larger, now smaller, now more round, now more pointed. But on closer consideration they do not represent anything actually new. They, too, are variations on the same theme, differentiations within the same standard. And only on a few points—above all, in the use of the knife—do slow movements begin to show themselves that lead beyond the standard already attained. (Elias, 1978, p. 105)

Undoubtedly, such cultural-historical development of the mealtime setting makes the task of learning to act in such a setting increasingly more complicated for the developing child. In this respect, *mealtimes are one of the very few recurrent settings in the lives of developing children where they experience the cultural organization of the social life of their culture in its full complexity.* The contemporary state of cultural organization of children's mealtimes in Europe-rooted societies on both sides of the Atlantic is an outcome of the cultural histories of these societies. However, when we view children's mealtimes in a synchronic comparative-cultural perspective, the variability in the ways in which mealtimes are organized becomes very evident. As will be seen in 6.4.3, the ways in which contemporary Euro-American parents structure their children's mealtimes constitute very particular setting structures of little cross-cultural generality.

6.4.3 Cross-cultural diversity in organization of mealtimes

Among the variety of descriptions of mealtime customs in different cultures, only a few have included information about children's actions in these settings (Fortes and Fortes, 1936; Goody, 1982; Lévi-Strauss, 1963, 1966; Richards, 1939; Richards and Widdowson, 1936). This oversight stems from the logic of interest in the stable cultural organization of the adults' society which has traditionally been characteristic of anthropologists. Children, from that perspective, are not yet fully competent informants about their culture, since they are still in the process of being socialized. This view is on the one hand a reflection of the dominance of non-developmental thinking in cultural anthropology, and on the other it may characterize the difficulty of observing and recording children's actions during fieldwork.

It is not surprising to find very high diversity across cultures in the ways children's food intake is organized. First (and foremost), that organization depends on the *availability* of food. It would be ridiculous to present the situation of a child from some middle-class European or North American family as in any way a 'typical' example of children's eating and mealtime organization. Such a child may have a surplus of food in front of him at every mealtime. Contrary to the expectations of his parents, he may choose not to eat what is offered to him and end up being considered a 'problem' eater by parents. Newson and Newson (1968) reported a number of cases where British parents expressed serious concerns about their 4-year-olds' eating habits, and described in very vivid terms how they try to deal with the problem. Furthermore, the two clinical disorders of adolescence and young adulthood that have eating problems in their core, anorexia nervosa and bulimina, are mostly problems of the affluent part of the world's population. In contrast, a child in a Third World country who is malnourished because of the simple lack of food, would provide a very different perspective on the role of food-related actions in child socialization.

However, the cultural diversity of organizing children's food-related actions is not of unidimensional dependence on the availability of food. The whole organization of life in a culture sets the stage for structural organization of children's food-related actions. For example, accounts of child care in different African cultures have regularly stressed the difference that mothers' constant tactile contact with the infant (attached to her back) creates (e.g. see in Curran, 1984; or Konner, 1976). Such 'infant niche' prepares the child for a different way of relating to the mother, as the following description of a recently weaned young Wolof boy (age 2 years 2 months) having a snack illustrates:

> Lying against his mother's back Abdou is whimpering slightly and then clearly asks for something to eat. An elder brother brings him some rice. The mother tries to lift the child on to her lap. But he grumbles, pushes her away and spontaneously presses himself against her back, becoming immediately quiet. She hands him the bowl of rice over her shoulder; the child takes it and begins to eat all by himself, still leaning against her back. The mother lifts her arm and passes the child a small tin of water; he leans over, grabs the tin which the mother still holds and drinks in the same position. (Zempleni-Rabain, 1973, p. 224)

This description illustrates quite clearly how culture-specific the contemporary Western toddler in his high-chair is. The same nutritional actions can be performed in front of the mother (as in the case of a child in a high-chair) or behind the mother's back (as in the case of the Wolof boy), but they are performed anyway. It is also obvious from the Wolof example that it is not necessarily the mother in other cultures who is the primary helper of the younger child's eating, but an older sibling (in this case, an elder brother). The primary role of older siblings in taking care of young children (following the latter's weaning) is a dominant feature in the organization of home life in the majority of world's cultures (see Weisner and Gallimore, 1977). The traces of effectiveness of such a caregiving arrangement even in European-type cultures becomes evident if we return to Karl Duncker's research on the role of social suggestion in children's food preferences (Duncker, 1938). He discovered the fact (which may be intuitively obvious for parents with two or more children) that an older child's example in the area of food preferences coincided with the younger child's similar preference (in 26 out of 28 cases, children not siblings). The mothers in the cultures where sibling caregiving is used retain the leading (albeit indirect) role in the child care. Only the mother's role is changed from being that of the immediate caregiver (breast feeder) to that of the supervisor of the older siblings' work at caring for younger siblings (e.g. Ochs, 1982).

It is the child's elders—parents, relatives, older siblings—who play the key roles in the organization of the childs mealtimes. It is they who set up the mealtime setting in everyday life, provide the utensils and foods that are considered acceptable or necessary for the child, conduct or supervise the feeding process, and try to direct the child towards the acquisition of appropriate action patterns and culture knowledge in respect to foods and mealtime settings. The social role of meal organizers includes multiple facets—from planning the menu to actual food preparation, and to the plan for feeding the child. First, the decision about what sources of nutrients are in principle edible is culturally determined knowledge (see Fortes and Fortes, 1936; Tambiah, 1969) which guides the decisions about what the menu of a meal would incoude. The knowledge about the distinction between edible and inedible objects need not be simple or strict, and in many cases it can be age-bound. For example, Tambiah's ethnographic materials from Thailand reveal that certain animals (house rat and to some extent field rat) are eaten only by children, but not by adults (Tambiah, 1969, p. 448). Likewise, Tallensi children in the 1930s were found to eat field or domestic mice, a species of toad, and harmless snakes—all of which were despised by adolescents and adults (Fortes and Fortes, 1936, p. 251). These examples pertain to kinds of animals that children kill and use sporadically in their eating, rather than to the menus of the regular meals in the context of their families. In the context of regular meals, the issue of how and when a child begins to participate in the regular adults' diet is important. In traditional cultures where food preparation for adults as a rule is a time-consuming process, and where the basic set of used nutrients is limited, the foods for participating children are unlikely to be foods that are different from those prepared for adults. In this sense, children's participation in adult meals involves their sharing of the adults' food. Only in Western industrialized cultures could the practice of cooking separate foods for children that would be eaten by children at the general mealtimes become possible—under the conditions of relative affluence and food preservation.

The social organization of mealtime settings is the next aspect that is under control of the adult participants of the meal. It is obviously dependent on the occasion (e.g. the difference between a freast and a regular meal), which itself includes a different set of participants (i.e. the presence of many visitors of kinspeople is likely during feasts, but not necessarily at everyday meals). The participants of the meal are located spatially in the meal setting, which may take place in one of several places, public or private. The particular marriage form and the rules of relationship between sexes have an input to the spatial location of meal participants. Among the Tallensi the practice of the separation of the sexes during mealtimes provides an example: within the family compound, the husband usually ate with his senior wife (in the case of polygyny), and received food from the kitchens of his other wives as a prescribed donation. The man used to eat with his youngest weaned child (the even younger offspring who was still suckling stayed with their mothers)—a practice that was explained by the need of the recently weaned child to 'eat properly in order to grow, and must be taught to do so' (Fortes and Fortes, 1936, p. 271). The role of the teacher of the child at mealtime was thus played by the father—who in other settings in traditional Tale life had little contact with the child. Older boys eat nearby, but by forming a separate group. Women and older girls formed still another separate eating group. This organization reflects the two basic principles of separation of social roles in the society: male/female and child/adult distinctions. In societies where such distinctions have been weak (or lessened), the spatial arrangements at mealtimes reflect it (see Dreyer and Dreyer, 1973, about the ethnography of contemporary middle-class American family dinners). Or, the subsistence needs of the given society may be cognitively related to the expected behavior at mealtimes, as the following description of Yurok Indians by Erik Erikson implies:

> The concentration on the sources of food is not accomplished without a second phase of oral training at the age when the child 'has sense'—i.e., when he can repeat what he has been told. It is claimed that once upon a time, a Yurok meal was a veritable ceremony of self-restraint. The child was admonished never to grab food in haste, never to take it without asking for it, always to eat slowly, and never ask for a second helping—an oral puritanism hardly equaled among other primitives. During meals, a strict order of placement was maintained and the child was taught to eat in prescribed ways; for example, to put only a little food on the spoon, to take the spoon up to his mouth slowly, to put the spoon down while chewing the food—and above all, to think of becoming rich during the whole process. There was supposed to be silence during meals so that everybody could keep his thoughts concentrated on money and salmon. (Erikson, 1963, p. 177).

The spatial arrangement of participants of a meal and the cognitive activity prescribed for the occasion set the stage on which the whole spectacle of the meal is played out. First, cultural rules govern the sequential organization of the meal (see Douglas, 1975; Douglas and Gross, 1981). The meal may consist of any number of courses, and each course may involve the use of a different set of utensils. A transition from one course to the next is connected with actions that emphasize the sequential nature of the meal. For example, after the main course, the foods and dishes/utensils with which that course was served are taken away from the table, and a new course (dessert) is introduced by the use of new food and tools for its manipulation (e.g. a cake is brought to the table, on a special plate, and every participant in the meal receives a new—often visibly different—plate and utensil for eating the dessert). A young child who observes or participants in such a meal is socialized towards accepting the sequential organization of the meal, as well as understanding it cognitively. Furthermore, *parents' direct efforts to provide an infant or toddler with some foods first, followed by others, constitute the beginning of multi-course meals in the life of the young child.* For example, a toddler's meal may start with some crackers, followed by the 'main dish' of lasagna, and end with fruit as dessert. The dessert (fruit) may be served by the mother only after the remains of lasagna are removed from the highchair tray and the child's hands wiped after the 'mess' that this second course involved. Such sequential organization of the toddler's meal is a step in the long process of socialization of the child towards accepting the society's eating traditions.

Secondly, there are psychologically relevant issues that occur during the meal that are of important socialization value. The major relevant issue is the adults' regulation of the child's relationship with food, and of the child's relationships with other people which are played out around the handling of food. As far as the child's eating is concerned, it is the adults who decide which social rules are applied to the child's actions. This involves social regulation of the child's initiative in getting food (e.g. whether the child is given things to eat, or expected to demand them, or to choose between different foods), accepting (or trying to modify) the child's noisiness or diversion from eating, rules about dealing with food that the child has left over (e.g. demanding that the child finish eating it, or accept the left-overs—including the way of disposal of them: throw away, give to other children or domestic animals, the parent eats them him/herself, etc.), and the regulation of child–child relationships in case of several children participating in the meal. An example from the organization of child socialization during mealtimes among the matrilocal Bemba in Zambia (in the 1930s) provides a suitable contrast with the European cultural traditions:

> . . . food is also something that has to be shared, and in this attitude the Bemba baby is definitely trained even in the first year. Children share from one dish and the mother or elder sister tears off for each a lump of porridge with a little drop of relish rolled inside. An unexpected present or find must be divided with any other babies sitting near. . . . I have seen a woman seize a lump of pumpkin out of a baby's hand and say in most vehement protest: 'You give some to your friend you child, you! You sit and eat alone! That is bad what you do.'. . .
>
> In a society in which individual initiative is on the whole encouraged, and age has no particular prerogatives, we tend to see that the youngest child gets his fair share at the dinner table or in the nursery school and often teach the elder children to 'Give it to Baby first'. The Bemba mother on the contrary always says: 'Let your elder brother have it! Give it to him first', and on this recognition of precedence the whole organization of daily life as well as the political system finally depends. (Richards, 1939, pp. 197–198).

It is evident that the social rules of relating to other people in the given society are particularly obvious in the context of meals, and thus mealtimes are the naturally occurring settings in which much of the cultural knowledge is acquired by the children. The examples provided here thus far have been of how children's actions at mealtime are *directly* constrained by the caregivers with some cultural goals in mind. However, the opportunities for cultural learning at mealtimes are not limited to such direct socializing actions and constraints—*within* the structured occasion of meals children are *indirectly exposed* to different ways of acting and thinking by others. Cultural transmission takes place at mealtimes, both in a goal-directed and an occasional manner. Consider the following example of American family talk at a meal

FATHER: Well, I'm sorry, but I forgot to bring home some whiskey for cocktails tomorrow night.

MOTHER: It's all right. I don't think we better serve cocktails.

FATHER: How come?

MOTHER: Well, the Pearsons are coming, and you know him.

SON: Is Dr. Pearson coming, mother, is he? Is he, mother?

MOTHER: Yes he is, and Mrs. Pearson is coming too.

DAUGHTER: Why don't we serve cocktails when Dr. Pearson comes?

MOTHER: Well, Dr. Pearson is a doctor, and he thinks cocktails aren't good for people. He says too many people have the cocktail habit.

SON: I like Dr. Pearson.

FATHER: Well, I like him, too. But this means a stupid party. (This to wife)

MOTHER: I think I'll serve tomato juice. Do you think that will be all right? The red glasses will look nice on that black tray.

FATHER: If Pearson doesn't want to drink that's O.K. with me, but I don't see why that should spoil the party for the rest of us.

MOTHER: Well, I do think that out of deference to his views we should have a dry dinner.

SON: I like Dr. Pearson. Is he a good doctor, mother?

This conversation carries these implications for the children: (a) A doctor whom I like does not approve of the social use of alcohol; (b) Father thinks a dry party is dull; (c) Mother sees her obligation as a hostess; (d) a difference of opinion is resolved with deference to a guest, regardless of the wishes of the host and hostess. There is no preaching, no moralizing. All the ideas are transmitted in a matter-of-fact way, incidental to a table conversation, chiefly between the parents, concerning a small dinner party. (Reproduced with permission from Bossard, 1948, pp. 174–175).

An important aspect of the indirect cultural transmission at mealtimes (or other settings) is its *co-constructive* nature on behalf of the recipients (children). The children who listen and observe what happens between adults at the dinner table have to integrate the information into the children's already existing knowledge structures *by the children's own active efforts*. The active role of the recipients of cultural messages leads to the possibility of novel ways of information integration. Rather than taking the parents' messages in their original form, the children adjust the information they receive to their own needs. In this sense, all cultural transmission involves parents' and children's joint construction of new culture, rather than children's passive acceptance of the teaching provided by the parents.

Apart from the social organization of participants' actions at mealtime in direct and indirect ways, cultural implements that are used during mealtimes tell the story of how child socialization in a particular culture takes place. Therefore, an analysis of these tools—furniture, covers, plates and bowls, eating utensils—constitutes a valuable source of information that has usually been little noticed by psychologists in their feverish quest for the limited access to reality called 'behavioral observations' or highly 'controlled' experiments.

6.5 Cultural tools for food-related actions

The whole meal setting and utensils used in it by human beings is a culturally structured environment where both the use of the cultural tools and the meaningful aspect of these tools coexist. The invention of implements to be used in feeding is not limited to *Homo sapiens*. In fact, the cases where higher primates have been observed to prepare and use an implement that supplements the capacities of the body largely occur in conjunction with feeding. Thus, wild chimpanzees' habit of making and using implements for catching termites (McGraw, 1977; McGrew, Tutin, and Baldwin, 1979) or making and using sponges to get water out of tree-holes (Kitahara-Frisch and Norikoshi, 1982), as well as the Japanese macaques' invention of washing technology to separate food from sand, occur in connection with fulfilling their alimentary needs. The same connection with food is widely exploited by animal psychologists who follow time-honored traditions of rewarding pre-hungered animals with food, after their sucessful solution of a problem.

The history of human cultures is closely tied in with the history of technology, among which food-processing and food-handling technologies constitute an important part. Within the history of food-related technologies, special inventions that enrich the scope of possibilities for the feeding of young children is the particular issue of interest in the present context.

It is the physical character of foods that determines the nature of utensils used to contain and transport foods. In the case of *liquid* foods, the problems of feeding children might not have required extensive development of tools, since the norm of feeding young children these foods has all through human history been breast feeding. The breast has largely made it unnecessary to develop many additional utensils for normal feeding of milk toobabies, at least up to the times in history when early weaning became emphasized in the culture. When the mother could not nurse, a lactating woman (wet nurse) was often hired to feed the child. Quite naturally, the need of utensils to be used to give milk to infants relates to the acceptance of milk produced by organisms other than humans (e.g. cow, goat) as an appropriate nutrient for babies. In the Middle Ages, special tools made of animal horns (with an aperture made in their end) were used to feed cow milk to infants. The invention of 'bubby pot' in the eighteenth-century England—the forerunner of the modern nursing bottle that was even named after the old word for female breast—made the practice of feeding cow milk to infants more convenient (Gesall and Ilg, 1937, pp. 37–39). The 'bubby pot' lacked the softness of the natural breast but guaranteed that no milk got spilled in the process of its intake—a quality that no cup-feeding or even horn-type tool applied to very young infants could grant. The invention of the rubber nipple followed suit (in 1861), from which time onwards different kinds of milk containers furnished with nipples have developed into the contemporary baby-bottles as a substitute tool for the female breast.

164

The problem of cultural child-feeding utensils emerges more basically in the case of the handling of *semiliquid* foods that, having been produced outside the maternal organism, could not be handled by the feeder's or child's hands only. Such semi-solid foods may have been necessary supplements to mostly breast-fed infants whose masticulatory capacities were yet underdeveloped. These foods require containers for keeping them—either for a longer time, or for the period from their preparation to consumption. Furthermore, these foods require implements for their transport from the container to mouth (unless the containing implement is also usable as a transport implement). Ontogenetically it means that the semi-solid foods were to be transported from the container into the child's mouth by the person feeding the child at first, followed by the child's gradual learning of the handling of the utensils and acquisition of the eating rules. It is under the demand characteristics of making and eating semi-liquid foods that we can view the cultural history of food containers (bowls, plates, saucers, bottles, pots) and transport utensils (spoons, forks, chopsticks in the Orient). Some kinds of feeding utensils emerged in history that are containers and transport utensils at the same time. For example, cups and glasses are used in both of these functions—on the one hand, these implements may contain liquid or semi-liquid foods for the necessary period of times on the other hand, these implements are used to transport the foods into the mouth repeatedly. The spoon is an interesting combination of the cup/bowl and a lever—its bowl-part is essentially a container capable of handling a *sufficient amount of food for one-time intake*. Its handle functions as a lever that can be used to extract food from another container without inserting the hand that holds the spoon, into the food.

Feeding utensils for semi-liquid supplementary feeding of infants are young children have been documented over a long period of cultural history. Special urns, cups, saucers, and flasks that were made to fit children's needs were used centuries BC by the Greeks, Romans, Egyptians, Assyrians, and others (Gesell and Ilg, 1937, p. 37). Spoon-like tools date back to paleolithic times.

Differently from spoons, personally used forks are a relatively recent cultural invention that emerged in the European eating settings only around the fifteenth and sixteenth centuries (Braudel, 1973). One can trace the history of the fork back to the dagger—a sharpened metal stick that can be used to transport pieces of objects of solid consistency. It is interesting that the history of personal forks had been influenced by the spoon—prior to the fifteenth century the forks lacked the bowl-like curve of the end which comes into contact with food, that is so characteristic of contemporary forks, and which developed under the conditions of similarity with spoons. That curvature, together with widening of the contact region of the fork (due to the addition of times—from two in the first forks in history, to four in the majority of contemporary ones), made the fork closer to the spoon, so that it could be used as an imperfect substitute for the spoon if necessary (e.g.

try eating semi-liquid purée-like food with a fork!), although that substitut-ability may work poorly in practice. Some contemporary forks made for children are exaggerated in their form to resemble spoons functionally, as the ends of the spikes are not sharp (the danger of hurting oneself leads to the elimination of the major role of the fork as the instrument entering hard objects of food).

However, forks are useful in the case of food objects that are of proper size for handling and eating. To get food into that size usually requires additional tools, which in cultural history has led to the invention of knives. Knives are the proper tools for cutting different objects, including food objects of hard consistency that cannot be reduced to smaller pieces other-wise. The use of knives to cut food may be the most ancient human-made tool-using activity that has been important for nutritional purposes. Isaac's (1978) findings of the use of stone tools for cutting meat by protohominids in Africa at least 1.6 million years ago illustrate the ancient nature of these implements that are useful for solid food objects that are either too hard or too big to be handled by teeth. In contrast to this long history of cutting instruments in general, the use of a knife as a personal eating utensil has had quite different fates in different cultures. Even in the present day one can observe differences even between some Western industrialized cultures in the use of knives during meals—the majority of present-day Americans find the European habit of continuous handling of knife by the right hand and the use of fork in the left, too complicated. Instead, they proceed to cut out a number of pieces of food of appropriate size, using the fork in the left and knife in the right hand, and then abandon the knife and continue eating the just cut pieces, handling the fork by the right hand. That difference between Europe and the United States illustrates the subtle differences, in the sequential organization of the meal (i.e. meal divided into 'cutting'-then-'eating' episodes versus continuous 'cutting and eating') in cultures that share much historically.

The contemporary utensils meant for feeding infants and toddlers reflect in their form the cultural expectations for the children to become socialized eaters within their society. An analysis of the affordances for different actions that are purposefully coded into the structure of these cultural tools is enlightening. First, the objects of furniture that are used as the basic frame for infants' or toddlers' mealtimes—the high-chair, infant seat, infant walker, special toddlers, seats that are either attached to the table, or put on a regular chair to bring the child to the level of the table—all share certain structural characteristics that represent cultural ideas (apart from serving as pragmatically useful in the meal process).

By far the most standard furniture for toddlers' mealtimes in our empirical observations is the *high-chair* (see Figure 6.1). The high-chair is a cultural tool into which the emphasis on toddlers' constrained freedom of action is coded in full accordance with the culture. On the one hand, it is a device

Figure 6.1. Child within a constraining device: the 'high chair' (photograph by the author)

that limits children's freedom of behavior for the mealtime. This is accomplished by the tray that does not allow the child to leave the meal situation, as it blocks exit from the chair. That limitation is further assisted by strapping the child to the high-chair so that the remaining alternative routes for leaving the situation of mealtime *by the child himself* (e.g. by sliding down under the tray, or standing up on the seat and climbing out of the chair over the tray) are excluded from the realm of possible actions. On the other hand, however, the high-chair *affords the child a limited field of freedom of behavior*—including the set of those actions which are possible to perform on the high-chair tray (e.g. banging on it by hand or object, manipulating objects on it, throwing objects across the board from it, etc.). Compared to the child's Zone of Free Movement before s/he is confined in the high-chair for a meal, the stay in the high-chair includes greater restrictions on the child's behavior. However, if the high-chair is compared to the arrangement where an adult keeps the child on her/his lap while feeding (e.g. using the left arm to limit the child's ZFM while feeding with the right hand), the high-chair provides the child with greater *local* freedom of action *outside immediate tactile contact with the feeder*. On the feeder's side, of course, the high-chair makes it possible to move around in the environment during the meal (e.g. for the purpose of fetching a new food, or to do other tasks). The high-chair also brings the child to the level at which adults eat their meals, thus promoting participation (through the possibilities for observation and imitation, as well as direct intervention) in the adults' activities during the meals.

A number of cultural tools are used in the infant/toddler meal setting in the contemporary American middle-class subculture. These can be divided into *direct-action utensils* (e.g. spoons, forks, cups, bottles, bowls, plates) and *indirect-action utensils*. The latter category includes tools that set the stage for direct feeding actions—bibs that prevent the child's clothing from becoming dirty, special toys set up on the high-chair tray that serve the function of keeping the child occupied, etc. Some objects of the direct-action utensils category can be used in the function of keeping the child occupied—for instance, the widespread practice of providing an extra spoon for the child for manipulation in order to keep the child from grabbing the spoon used by the feeder to spoon-feed the infant.

The specialized indirect-action utensils are themselves a product of a certain cultural patterning of infants' mealtimes. For example, if the infant were not provided with a certain local freedom of action during the meal, there would be no need for using objects to capture its attention and keep it away from intervening in the feeding process. That need for redirection of the infant's attention *emerges only in conjunction with the situation where the infant has the possibility to intervene in the feeder-controlled actions*. First, the adults provide the child with a ZFM, the child begins to use its resources in ways that counteract adults' goals, and consequently the adults have to deal with the situation. One way for them is to constrain the child's ZFM further so that the particular disturbing action possibility is eliminated. This, for example, happens when a parent holds down an infant's hands that try to grab the spoon, while continuing to spoon-feed the child. The other way out of the situation involves the creation of a ZPA with the help of an indirect-action utensil that is expected to occupy the child, retaining the present structure of ZFM.

The 'Wiggl-Egg' (see Figure 6.2) is one of the ingenious inventions of modern infant-feeding technology that constitutes an example of an indirect-action utensil *par excellence*. The function of the 'Wiggl-Egg' is explained to the potential buyers (parents) thus:

> *A plaything that always remains within reach is an excellent way to keep a baby entertained while in his high chair or any other seat*—especially when a parent's attention must be temporarily elsewhere, such as during meal preparation. Wiggl-Egg's sure-grip suction base holds it securely no matter how hard a baby bats it to and fro. The colorful duck design will attract an infant's attention while the pleasant rattle encourages further interaction.

Certain cultural practices, based on the cultural meaning system (as well as practical considerations of parents' activity), are evident in this description of the tool. First, the idea that *the baby should be entertained* is explicitly taken for granted—in direct conjunction with the accepted necessity that the

168

Figure 6.2. The 'wiggl-egg' (photograph by Albrecht and Elzbieta Lempp)

child's freedom of behavior has to be limited (but not fully eliminated) on some occasions (like a hungry child intervening in the parent's meal preparation activity in the kitchen). The tool invented for the purpose of providing the infant with an alternative action opportunity, thus redircting his/her attention from what the adults are doing, has additional characteristics that promote the culutrally valued positivity in expression of emotions. The duck figure on the Wiggl-Egg is depicted as smiling, and it is assumedthat the egg will be set on the high-chair tray *facing the child*. For the sake of an exercise in the strength of our culturally given expectations of what kind of environments we create for children, consider two versions of the Wiggl-Egg in Figure 6.3, and ask yourself which of the two eggs you would prefer to give to a fussy and hungry infant who is strapped into a high-chair, while you as the caregiver are nervously preparing the meal for the child.

The redirection of the child's interest thus involves canalization of the child

Figure 6.3. Cultural coding of promotion of happiness: which of the two wiggl-eggs would you choose for a child? (photograph by Albrecht and Elzbieta Lempp)

towards the expression of positive emotions. The socialization of children's cultural 'display rules' (Cole, 1985; Ekman, Friesen, and Ellsworth 1972) of emotional expression may start from everyday life situations where parents surround the child with objects (indirect-action tools) that mark the environment of the child, thus gradually leading the developing child towards internalizing these rules.

The use of indirect-action utensils among cultural tools used in different child-inclusive situations obviously goes beyond the limits of children's mealtimes. A highly interesting example—a set of toy cooking utensils—is presented in Figure 6.4 The toy set in Figure 6.4 constitutes an effort by adults to redirect the young child's play from adults' objects (real pots, pans, and food) to their toy replicas. Again, like in the case of the egg in Figure

170

Figure 6.4. The 'smiling pot' (photograph by Albrecht and Elzbieta Lempp)

6.2, the pot is furnished with a schematic smiling face on one side. The goal of directing children towards play with toy replicas of cooking utensils is related to a potential danger, though. The text on the label of the toy set reveals it most directly:

> Important:
> Never allow your child to place the pieces of this set on the kitchen stove, in the oven or over any open flame.

Turning to the category of direct-action utensils, it becomes evident from the ways these are constructed how in the given culture the use of such utensils is guided. A promotional statement on the back of a infant spoon and fork training set package illustrates that:

> *Allowing your baby to help spoon-feed himself as early as 9 to 12 months of age can help develop his independence and self-esteem.* Early attempts at using a spoon are bound to be messy, but with practice your baby will learn to manipulate it with minimal spills. Use of a fork should follow at about two years of age.

This promotional message from the reverse side of the spoon and fork package makes use of a number of cultural ideas that are prominent in the minds of contemporary American parents and that guide their actions in canalizing their children's development. First, the cultural core concepts of *independence* and *self-esteem* are explicitly emphasized in conjunction with the parents allowing a 9–12-month-old infant to manipulate the spoon on his own. Secondly, that spoon manipulation by the infant is referred to as 'help' to the parent in the process of feeding the infant. That 'help', of course, is necessarily connected with non-feeding actions with food by the child, which is culturally given the meaning of 'being messy'—a price that parents, realistically, will have to pay if they give a spoon to their infant early. Note that the promotional test explicitly acknowledges the 'messy' aspect of early spoon manipulation by the infant, *and compensates for that with the use of another core idea of the American culture—that of 'practice'*. That idea is based on the emphasis on independent (=individual himself against environment) work and learning to work that have guided the process of child socialization in the cultures where the Protestant work ethic has been dominant over some time in history. Finally, the *expectation of positive outcome* as a result of the child's individual learning of spoon use is emphasized—parents are told essentially that 'practice makes perfect' and that it is their responsibility to introduce the particular utensils *at the specified age period* (spoon at 9–12 months, fork 'should' follow at about 2 years).

Furthermore, important information about the psychology of child socialization is available from an analysis of the form of utensils that are meant for children at different ages. The case of infant spoons is highly instructive in this respect. Infants' and toddlers' spoons are sometimes constructed to promote the use of one hand over the other. Figure 6.5 shows a spoon and a fork with handles which make the left-hand use of these utensils in an appropriate manner increasingly difficult. At the same time, the twisted handle of these utensils make it easier to use the right hand while self-feeding.

Furthermore, the first forks given to toddlers are often designed so as to eliminate sharp ends of the tines, which make the use of such forks increasingly difficult, and reduces their function practically to that of spoons (see Figure 6.6).

Cups, glasses, bottles, and other devices used for drinking at children's mealtimes occupy a unique position in between the categories of *containers* and *transport utensils*—being simultaneously both. A bottle, or a cup, are containers in which the drinkable liquid is held, and in which it is transported to the child's mouth—either by the adult or the child himself. Bottles, of course, appear on the scene of infant feeding earlier than cups (although in some families bottle feeding may be fully bypassed). The form of contemporary baby cups (see Figure 6.7) reflects a complex relationship between the goal of promotion of infants' self-feeding skills early in life, and the goal of preservation of the liquid in the container. Thus, the cups are provided either with a spout in the lid or with a trainer lid with apertures. The spout

172

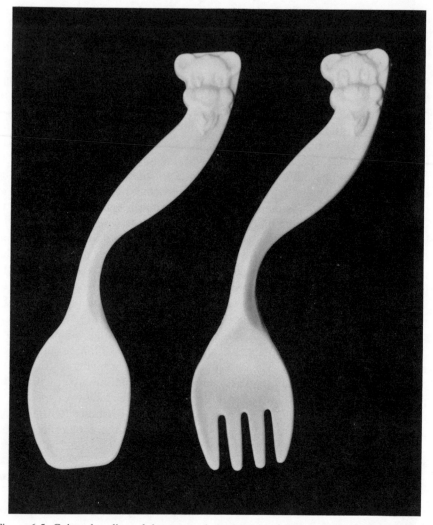

Figure 6.5. Cultural coding of the promotion of right-handedness: children's fork and spoon with twisted handles (photograph by Albrecht and Elzbieta Lempp)

serves as an intermediate device between the infant's handling of the nipple (of the breast, or bottle) and 'true' cup handling. The trainer lid with apertures (see Figure 6.7) is the device meant to make the child's cup handling even closer to the adult skills of drinking. The weighted base of the cups helps to bring it to the normal position if put down on its side—thus reducing spilling of milk by the child's handling of the trainer cup by himself.

The present little excursion into the analysis of cultural ideas and expectations that are coded into the cultural tools and structural units of the environment in which a child lives leads to the important conclusion that *cultural canalization of children's actions starts from the coding of some suggestive cultural messages into the form and function of objects which surround human beings.* This analysis illustrates the principle of the structured nature of the environment (cf. 4.1.2) in the particular setting of infants' or toddlers' mealtime environments—high-chairs, trays, eating and attention redirection utensils—all of which are man-made objects that carry cultural expectancies for some golas-directed function from the makers to the children via their caregivers. Usually behaviorally interested psychologists have bypassed the presence of these 'silent messages' that are available to the acting child as long as they constitute the environment. It should become evident that an approach in psychological research that claims to be cultural-historical in its scope cannot leave these objects outside the sphere of empirical analysis.

Obviously, the cultural structure of children's mealtimes is only one domain of factors that act as bases for constraints that emerge in parent–child transaction in the process of canalization of actions. The ontogeny of motor capabilities provides the complementary set of structurally organized possibilities for the development of children's self-feeding skills. An analysis of psychological knowledge about the precursors of toddlers' self-feeding development in the motor development in infancy is therefore in order.

Figure 6.6. Child's fork and adult's fork: compromises between functionality and potential stabbing danger (photograph by Albrecht and Elzbieta Lempp)

6.6 Development of motor skills necessary for self-feeding

The infants's self-feeding behavior is dependent upon both the nature of the food and the coordination of head-mouth-arm-hand-finger movements that can be used to transport the food from an external location to the mouth. Once an infant gains access to foods of different characteristics (beyond the first liquids—milk or otherwise—that are fed to the infant by the caregiver via breast or bottle), the food-transport problem emerges. The principal possibility of infants' self-feeding requires the development of certain motor coordinations. The requirement of such coordination differs for the case of infants' 'finger feeding' (the *natural line* in the development of feeding behavior) as compared to their use of a tool (utensil) for feeding purposes (the *cultural* developmental line). The latter case is, of course, the domain where the cultural organization of eating becomes most intimately inter-twined with the children's developing motor behavior, since all self-feeding tools carry cultural information that is coded into their form and the social rules of their use.

Figure 6.7. Toddlers' drinking cup and its accessories (lid with spout, trainer lid) (photograph by Albrecht and Elzbieta Lempp)

6.6.1 Development of motor coordination

The natural line in the ontogeny of human feeding emerges earlier, since it is based on the 'natural facilities' that the anatomy and physiology of the developing organism provide. It is built upon the general inclination of infants to transport different objects from their vicinity to their mouth and try to insert them in it. This behavior requires visually guided coordination of the fingers, hand, arm on one side, and the head and mouth of the other. This coordination of the two motor systems—reaching and grasping—develops gradually. These two systems involve different neuro-muscular mechanisms that develop heterochronically in ontogeny. The *grasping*, or manipulation, involves distal joints and muscle groups that are adapted to information about the affordances present in the case of a particular object, whereas the *reaching* part is based on the work of proximal joints in body-centered space (Jeannerod, 1984). Physiologically the reaching component is realized through the work of the extra-pyramidal tract, whereas the grasping part is under the control of the pyramidal pathway (Kuypers, 1962). The former begins to function earlier in ontogeny than the latter, thus in the development of infant behavior it is possible to observe discrepancies in the development of reaching and grasping (see Lockman and Ashmead, 1983). McDonnell's (1979) analysis of research findings on the development of reaching reveals that the reaching in the infants in the first 5 months of life is triggered (but not guided) visually. The arm movements used in such reaching are basically ballistic in nature. The development of visually guided reaching becomes evident at around 5 months of age and peaks at around 7 months. By that time the reaching and grasping systems have become coordinated, so that at the approach to the target object the grasping movements can be proactively prepared for making contact with the object. That coordination, at least in the adult case, is organized by the wrist rotation together with the movement of the reacher's index finger (Wing and Fraser, 1983). The development of grasping of objects of different sizes in infancy has been meticulously recorded by Halverson (1931) and Castner (1932). Halverson found that infants' grasping of a 26 mm cube progressed through a sequence of ten distinctive grasping patterns between the ages of 16 and 52 weeks. These patterns first involved contacting to cube and squeezing it with the whole hand, followed by patterns in which the thumb and the index finger played a more active and precise role in the grasping process. Any particular observed series of stages in the infants' development of grasping patterns is dependent upon the object being grasped. Thus, Castner (1932) who studied infants' grasping of a 7 mm little pellet found that this grasping progressed through four stages. It started from *whole-hand closure* in which the prone hand is brought to a closed fist by simultaneous flexion of the fingers, with the thumb lying alongside the flexed forefinger. This type of closure upon the pellet was the only one observed among 20-week-old infants. This pattern was followed by *palmar prehension* in which fingers flex in such a way as to drag the pellet against the heel of the palm where it can be held. The third stage—*scissors closure*—involves the thumb being drawn in *against the side* of the flexing forefinger so that the pellet is secured between the thumb and the radial side of the forefinger. This movement is conducted in a manner similar to the action of these digits in operating a pair of scissors. This type of closure was observed predominantly at around 36–44 weeks. Finally, Castner observed the emergence of *pincer prehension*—in which the tips of the thumb and forefinger meet to secure the pellet between them. This latter type of prehension was observed in the majority of 52-week-olds, and develops further into the optional opposition of the thumb with digits other than the index figner (see Castner, 1932, pp. 178–179).

Research on infants' reaching and grasping has, in concordance with the meaning of 'reaching', concentrated on the analysis of how the infant's arm/hand system arrives at a target object (e.g. Bower, Broughton, and Moore, 1970; DiFranco, Muir, and Dodwell, 1978; VonHofsten, 1979), rather than on what the infant does *after* the target has been reached. The development of visually guided reaching is a neuro-motor prerequisite for the infant's development of self-feeding behavior. Reaching out for an object, grasping it, and bringing it to the mouth is the complete sequence of behavior that makes self-feeding possible. Exploration of objects by mouth (rather than by hand) is ontogenetically the primary mode by which the infant seeks information about the nature of objects surrounding him. Halverson described the development of infants' mouthing of the cube that he used in his study:

> . . . at 20 weeks, the few infants who secure the cube either push it away or hold it quietly without any further action. At 24 weeks the infants simply hold the cube, bring it to mouth, inspect it, and drop it. At 28 weeks, holding the cube occurs frequently, carrying it to the mouth and inspecting it also occur to a considerable extent. At 32 weeks, holding the cube and carrying it to the mouth are activities of frequent occurrence. These infants often put the cube down, pick it up again, and hold it in both hands. For the three oldest groups the activities are so diversified that none of them are particularly outstanding. However, at 36 weeks, perhaps the most common activities are carrying the cube to mouth, simply holding the cube, dropping and picking it up again, inspecting it, and exchanging hands on it. At 40 weeks the cube is not brought to the mouth as often as at 26 weeks; holding the cube, inspecting it, exchanging hands on it, and banging the table with it are the outstanding activities. At 52 weeks, manipulation of the cube by the fingers is the outstanding activity. (Halverson, 1931, p. 230).

The objects that are taken by the infant and handled one way or another (including mouthing them) are at first individual objects or their parts (e.g. in cases where the child has happened to break an object and bring its pieces into the mouth). The mouthing of such objects is the prerequisite for the natural line in the development of self-feeding in infants: all 'finger feeding' is possible on the basis of reaching for, grasping, and bringing to mouth pieces of food that are of sufficiently small size. The cultural line of self-feeding, however, *requires the infant's capability of synthesizing two objects into a whole (united) object at least for the period of food transport from its original location to the mouth.* The example most obvious in this context is spoon or fork use. In order to self-feed with a spoon, the infant must put together the food-object and the tool-object in a certain way (i.e. taking food into the bowl part of the spoon). He must maintain the unity of the food + spoon whole at least for the time it takes to reach the mouth. After arrival at the destination, the synthesized object is disassembled (as the spoon is taken out of the mouth, leaving the food in the mouth).

The context of infants' eating in contemporary home environments also provides examples where the utensil + food complex object is pre-synthesized by the feeders in order to facilitate the child's self-feeding while at the same time avoiding some side-effects of that act. The example of giving an infant a baby-bottle, or later a cup covered with a special lid, so that he can drink from it himself, is a solution where such pre-synthesis has been provided. The lid (or bottle) decreases the possibility of unwanted side-effects (spilling the liquid) while making it possible for the child to drink independently, once the motor action of lifting the bottle or cup up and holding it is mastered.

The development of the synthesis in infants' handling of objects has been documented in the existing research literature. The logic of the development of the synthesis of different behaviors is made explicit by Gesell and Thompson (1934) who, in accordance with their theoretical interests, attributed causality for that development to maturation:

> Developmentally, combining activity is closely articulated with patterns of individual or discrete activity. Two objects, A and B, lie adjacent. A elicits a discrete attentional-manipulatory response in its own right; so does B; so does A again. At a low stage of maturity these responses are independent events but at higher stages of maturity response B is influenced by stimulus A and tends to have a reference to B. It is not necessary to invoke a law of association or even learning to explain this fact of reference. The phenomenon seems to depend more upon the scope of regard and the range of manipulation and these factors are determined by maturation. (Gesell and Thompson, 1934, pp. 164–165).

The meticulous description of the development of infants' hand movement by Arnold Gesell and his colleagues in the 1920–1930s, which has remained unsurpassed up to the present day in its scientific value, provides ample evidence about the gradual development of synthesizing objects in the process of their manipulation. One of the pairs of objects that was used by Gesell to study the development of coordination of behaving with multiple objects consisted of a cup and a spoon (Gesell and Thompson, 1934, pp. 154–165), which were presented together (in Gesell's standard testing situation) within the subjects' age range of 32 to 56 weeks. Gesell and Thompson describe the development of combining the cup and spoon by the infants, first in their visual regard and secondly in their manipulation of these objects. Their description provides an overview of the richness of behavioral forms that can be observed in the process of establishing synthetic manipulatory behavior (although Gesell and Thompson themselves preferred to abstract away that richness in their summary descriptions of the generic child's development).

The sequence of observable combining of the cup and the spoon involves the following: (a) the child brings the spoon *over* the cup, without dipping it in or letting it fall (observed in some infants at 32 weeks, and in all infants of the sample at 56 weeks); (b) the child places the spoon in the cup, but does not release it (observed at 36 weeks in the earliest, and present in all infants by 56 weeks); and (c) releasing the spoon in the cup after placing it there (observed first at 44 weeks, with 38 per cent of the infants displaying it at the end of the administration of the task at 56 weeks. These three synthetic forms of behavior with cup and spoon were preceded by *combining* them (without putting spoon either on top of, or in cup), as 59 per cent of infants at 32 weeks were observed doing that, with all of them combining the two at 56 weeks (Gesell and Thompson, 1934, p. 157).

6.6.2 Social heterochrony

The precursors of motor behavior with a spoon and a cup in a play (laboratory task) situation serve as the basis onto which the caregivers of the infants build their efforts to socialize the child's developing use of cups and spoons in ways appropriate in the culture. It is possible to view the organization of socialization of children's actions from a perspective of the *principle of social heterochrony*. This principle is introduced here as an extension of the general heterochrony principle of developmental biology. That latter principle describes the emergence of subcomponents of a biological structure at diverse time periods during the organism's development (Anokhin, 1964). The heterochronical nature of biological ontogeny makes the developing organism open to different developmental paths which are decided upon depending on the organism–environment relations at the given time. Heterochrony provides for the plasticity of the organismic structure to become organized in novel complex forms that are built on the basis of the existing subcomponents at the given time. In the case of social heterochrony, these novel complex motor actions in children's development are wrought by caregivers' purposeful canalization of children's actions at a given age, towards learning new skills *on the basis of motor coordinations available to the child at the given time*.

The social extension of heterochrony introduced here is aimed at describing the *variety of possible ways in which a motor functions of a developing child can be socialized through social canalization within the culture.* The beginning of the efforts by 'social others' of the developing child may be located in different places at the age scale. That information is determined by the cultural folk models about 'when is the right time to start' with promoting a new skill to the child, or expecting it to emerge in the child's individual development. This cultural knowledge may be only remotely connected with realistic understanding of the actual developmental courses of motor (or cognitive) capabilities. The content of such cultural models is culture-specific and may fluctuate over time (e.g. Stendler, 1950; Wolfenstein, 1951, 1955; Zahorsky, 1934). The potential lower-age extreme application of the folk models of child socialization corrected by the availability of new developments in the case of children at different ages—by the Zone of Proximal Development. In everyday terms, if a current ethos of infant education in the given culture prescribes a very early effort by adults for the beginning of socialization of a certain function, then all of those efforts would fail, since the given function is still beyond the boundaries of the ZPD. However, under certain conditions—when appropriate teaching methods are used—the results may be attained (for example, see DeVries and DeVries, 1977, on Digo toilet training). The upper-end extremes in the application of folk models of child socialization are compensated for by the children's own learning of acting in culturally acceptable ways in respect to carrying out a given function, using the knowledge acquired by observation in the course of living in their social environments. If children are not instructed in certain motor actions, and these actions are relevant in their lives, then they learn those actions by themselves. Such asymmetry in the process of mapping the cultural planning of children's action socialization on the development of the neuro-muscular body functions in the case of social heterochrony provides for the redundancy in the socialization process, which is necessary for guaranteed success in it. If a child misses being explicitly taught a specially relevant skill, the child may acquire it himself on the basis of observations and trying. If a child is taught it, the skill will be acquired as well. If that teaching starts too early, it will not succeed until the time when it becomes available for the child in the context of ZPD in the teaching–learning situation. In any case, albeit by different routes, the particular important function is acquired by the children in the culture. This view of the role of social heterochrony in child socialization relates to the highly abstract notion of equifinality that is characteristic of all open systems (see 2.1).

6.6.3 Motor skills in the feeding contexts

Despite the long tradition in child psychology of the study of infants' motor behavior, research on children's motor actions within contexts similar to meal settings has been almost non-existent. The single coherent research group in contemporary developmental psychology that has studied the development of motor skills relevant for feeding has done it in conjunction with the issues of the development of children's motor programmes (Connolly, 1970, 1973, 1974, 1975, 1980, 1981; Connolly and Elliott, 1972; Elliott and Connolly, 1974, 1984). This interest involves the conceptual understanding of future-oriented control mechanisms in the organization of motor skills—an idea expressed and elaborated in movement physiology by Nikolai Bernstein (1966). Bernstein's theoretical emphasis is on the active, purposeful functioning of the moving individual who uses a future ideal outcome state as a criterion for adapting the ongoing action to the goal. This perspective fits well with the assumption that the motor skills that emerge in ontogeny become used by the child for some purposes, which in its turn requires integration of knowledge about the environment of the actor, the action means, and the place of action goals in a wider scheme of the child's life-world. The concrete example provided by Connolly (1980) illustrates that issue more realistically:

> Consider the following circumstances, a child aged about 3 (and hence already quite skilled and experienced) is given a boiled egg to eat. The egg sits in an eggcup on a table in front of the child who is provided with a small spoon. The detail of the description of the ensuing encounter of the child and the egg could vary over a wide range, from simply, 'eats with the spoon', to a minute analysis of the postures and movements employed. My purpose, however, is simply to indicate the great complexity of such commonplace actions which we take for granted. In order to solve the problem of eating the egg with the spoon the child must already have a richly developed cognitive system. He must have some idea of what he is aiming at—intention is implied on his part. Further, he must know something of the use and properties of a spoon, in itself a formidable achievement when one is called upon to explain it, which we shall assume. The child must pick up the spoon and hold it both appropriately (correct configuration of the hand on the spoon) and securely. Once this is done the child must take the spoon, correctly orientated, to a specific target location—the egg. The spoon must then be inserted into the egg, which requires postural adjustment of the spoon in the hand itself by the whole upper limb. Inside the egg controlled force must be applied through the spoon, here quite fine tolerance limits apply, too little force and the spoon is not loaded, too much and the egg is destroyed. Once this is done further postural adjustments must be made to extract the loaded spoon from the egg. The final part of the action consists in transporting the loaded spoon (which on the return journey must be managed under a different set of constraints if the egg is to remain on the spoon) to another target, the mouth, and there unloading it. Eating a boiled egg is such a commonplace activity that it causes little amazement and holds no puzzlement for most of us but try and build a machine to do this, or gain some insight into the difficulty by watching the younng child gain a mastery of the task. To master a skill such as this it is necessary first to master certain essential components such as holding a spoon in an adequate stable configuration. Once this is done the spoon can be grasped and used effectively for purposes other than eating boiled eggs. (Reproduced with permission from Connolly, 1980, p. 146).

The essential characteristic of motor skills, according to Connolly (1970), is the flexibility of integrating different subroutines of action into a wide range of possible whole action structures. That flexibility resembles the generative nature of human speech—with the help of its subroutines, ideas ranging from shallow TV commercials to communication of sophisticated feelings and thoughts of poets and writers can all be expressed. Likewise, motor skills, once developed, can be used for acting in very many different environments and in conjunction with an almost infinite variety of objects. On the one hand, the use of a particular motor skills (e.g. child's eating a boiled egg) is highly context specific. However, a skill that has been acquired in a particular specific context may lead to the development of action generation plans that adapt the sub routines of a learned skill to a new conditions, modify them, and unite them into new complex wholes. In all human motor action, the actor–environment relationships provide the context in which any action skill gets developed, and transformed.

Connolly's research on the development of spoon use in children is the part of existing research on motor skill development that is most directly connected with the empirical research described in this chapter. First, Connolly described the form of different grip types that 10–12-month-old infants were observed to use on a spoon when it was given to them (Connolly, 1974, p. 540). Different types of grips are differentially suitable for the use of the spoon in the adult ways. As the infants learn to use the spoon in meal settings, the range of different grip types is narrowed down gradually to retain only those that make the adequate use of the spoon possible. Secondly, the research by Connolly and his colleagues revealed how the structure of the complex motor skill of using a spoon to transport food to mouth developed (Connolly, 1979). The task of spoon use can be divided into different phases (e.g. filling the spoon, lifting and transporting it, emptying it in the mouth, removing it from the mouth). Connolly found that the different parts of the motor skill—its 'subroutines'—were first acquired separately (e.g. the spoon—food manipulation, and mouthing of the spoon), and only later integrated into the full action scheme. Finally, the child develops capabilities to recheck the state of affairs of the spoon and food at different times in the temporal structure of the action. For example, when the child has lifted a semi-filled spoon from the plate, he may return it to the plate to get the spoon full of food before processing to the mouth with it (see Connolly, 1979, p. 248). The particular nicety of the motor skill of spoon use is its relevance in everyday life settings which usually have been left unanalyzed in the research on motor skill development.

6.7 An analysis of the structure of children's meal settings

Children's mealtime in the everyday life of contemporary European or North American middle-class families is a structurally organized setting with usually clear-cut beginning and ending, and with sequential organization the rules of which are introduced by parents and accommodated to the child's behavior. No currently available formal-symbolic methodology is suitable for the description of the structural-dynamic organization of mealtimes (see chapter 5).

Some theoretical analyses in the history of psychology have included passing efforts to explain the psychological side of children's mealtimes. Lewin (1936a) used the example of children's mealtime occasionally as an example of the application of his field theory. Lewin's first example involved the following setting and its interpretation:

> A mother has taken a year-old child away from play and wants to feed him on her lap. He does not want to eat. He is at the moment dominated by the tendency 'away from eating' or 'toward play.' The mother holds the child on her lap and prevents the intended movement 'away from eating.' She puts her arm around him so that he cannot break away. The mother's interference has in this case the character of a barrier [b, in Figure 6.8] between the region of eating (e) and that of play (pl). This barrier at the same time keeps the child (C) from pulling away from the spoon (sp) as it is brought near his mouth. The child now begins to play on the mother's lap. The mother tries to put an end even to this possibility of action and limits the child's space of free movement still further. Thereupon the child tries to widen his region of free movement and begins to struggle with the mother. (Lewin, 1936a, p. 47).

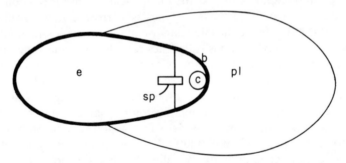

Figure 6.8. Topology of an eating situation—a child is prohibited from leaving for play (from Lewin, 1936, p. 47). Abbreviations: C = child; b = barrier, i.e., mother's interference; e = region of eating; sp = spoon; pl = region of play

The analysis of this episode in terms of the theory presented in this book would reject Lewin's attribution of 'tendencies' ('forces') into the situation, but follows the description of the dynamic nature of the barrier setting (reorganization of the boundary of Zone of Free Movement). The mother's way of getting the task of feeding the child by spoon accomplished is to narrow the child's ZFM down sufficiently so that the feeding can take place. The child may (as in this example), but also need not, attempt to counteract the mother's actions. The dynamics of this example illustrates the process of negotiation that goes on between the mother and child about the boundaries of theZFM in the meal situation.

The other example of mealtime actions of children that Lewin has provided involves the inclusion of objects in the framework of the whole situation. Lewin's example involves analysis of the case where a mother tries to get her child to eat some disliked food:

> . . . one of the most important means by which the adult induces the child to eat an undesired food is to bring him into the 'eating situation.' If a particular kind of food is not desired, the otherwise unified action of eating usually breaks up into a series of separate steps such as: putting the hand on the table (h); taking the spoon (sp); putting the food on the spoon (f); bringing the spoon halfway to the mouth (hw); bringing it to the mouth (m); taking the food into the mouth (i); chewing (ch); swallowing (sw). These steps correspond topologically to a series of regions [see (a) in Figure 6.9.]. The procedure of the adult is sometimes to bring the child (C) step by step through these regions closer to the region of 'real eating' (chewing and swallowing). In doing so he usually meets with increasing resistance in accordance with the fact that with approach to the undesired action the repulsive forces [represented as arrows in Figure 6.9] increase. However, as soon as the food is once in the mouth it is often not spit out, even when the adult has fed the child against its will. Instead the child goes on to chewing and swallowing the food. (Lewin, 1936a, pp. 96–97).

Lewin's example illustrates his observational sensitivity to changes that occur in the situation—the child, after rejecting the parent's pressure towards accepting food, may transform into the state of acceptance of that food, *once* it has reached the mouth. Likewise, the 'breakdown' of a well-established (speedy) action pattern when the child does not like the task is a real enough event in everyday life. Lewin's analysis of the event is likewise dynamic:

> One can show that this change of behavior is brought about essentially by the fact that as the child enters the region of 'real eating' his position and the direction of the field forces are entirely changed. When the child is in one of the preceding regions, for instance, when he holds the spoon halfway to his mouth, then a region of great unpleasantness into which the adult tries to push him, still lies ahead. The adult therefore may have to exert great pressure to induce the child to make a locomotion into the disagreeable region. When the child is once within this region of real eating then the region which lies ahead of him is a more pleasant one of relative freedom [figure 6.9b]. The child therefore often prefers a locomotion in this direction to spitting out, which is a locomotion in the direction of the disagreeable fight with the adult. (Lewin, 1936a, p. 98).

Again, the empirical analysis offered in this book relates closely to Lewin with the exception of the implicit evaluative rationality that is projected into the child in the given example (e.g. a region assumed to be 'more pleasant' by the child than another region). Lewin's use of the term 'region' in this example seems to be synonymous to 'setting' (rule-structured action situation). It is argued by Lewin that once the adult organizes the child's 'move-

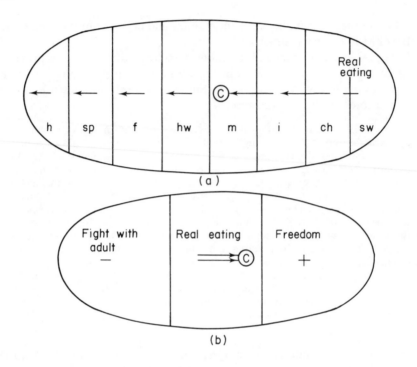

Figure 6.9. Topology of a situation where a child faces disliked food. (a) before entering the region of real eating; (b) after entering the region of real eating (from Lewin, 1936, (p. 97). Abbreviations: force (the direction of the arrow represents the direction of force, its length—the strength of the force, its point—the point of application): locomotion (the point of the arrow designates the place of termination of locomotion, the other end—its departure point); + positive valence; – negative valence. Other abbreviations are similar to those in Figure 6.8

ment' from one well-organized setting to another (e.g. from 'play' to 'real eating'), then the child may accept expectations of the new setting without difficulty, although these same expectations in the previous setting were rejected by the child vehemently. Now, an additional aspect of such 'movement' from one setting to another is the extent to which knowledge about the roles of action within these settings is present in the child's mind. That knowledge emerges in the process of socialization as a result of the child's life history of actions being canalized by the social others in the particular social settings. The knowledge of the rules of the setting is maintained redundantly, both by external and internalized means. Conflict situations tend to occur at the transitions from one setting to another where it is uncertain which rules apply to action regulation (those of the previous, or of the new, setting). This state of uncertainty in the nature of the settings makes it possible for the interactants to *construct new settings* where new sets of rules (which may partially overlap with existing settings) apply. Put another way, the existence of well-structured settings with stable action rules is a means whereby persons try to escape the uncertainty inherent in social situations. When a situation is poorly structured, the actors who are present in that situation construct rules which provide them with a structure (Sherif, 1936). Settings as structured social situations with elaborate scripts for action are socially constructed cultural means for people to lead their lives, rather than rules given to them by some external agent.

What, then, are the implications of this social-constructive view of the ontogeny of mealtime settings? First, *from the perspective of a particular individual child*, the mealtime setting is constructed initially in the context of infant–caregiver–environment transaction *and does ot exist outside of the child's experience*. Secondly, *from the perspective of the caregivers*, the rules of the infant's mealtime exist as *the caregivers' decision about organizing the child's meal setting in accordance with knowledge about the setting in the culture*. The mother knows how to feed the infant, or if she does not know, or is unsure about some aspects of it, she turns to the available cultural sources (her mother, friends, books, etc.) to get information that will enable her to accomplish the task adequately. In that, mothers are helped by their social networks. The ways in which babies are fed (e.g. the basic decision between breast and bottle feeding) is determined not by the mother (and father) of the child by themselves, but under the influence of the whole kinship network within which cultural traditions of child feeding are transferred from generation to generation (Bryant, 1982). In this way it is the mother who translates information present in the culture into the organized setting of *her* child's mealtime. However, the cultural knowledge that she starts from is not abstract but includes the very personal side of being given to her by others who are related to her (her own mother, mother-in-law, aunts, sisters) and whom she may trust. The individuals who provide the particular mother with cultural information usually have their personal modifications added to the information. As a result, no two families within a culture can be expected to organize the child's mealtime in an exactly similar way, since the individual mothers interpret the cultural knowledge differently and construct the mealtime setting for their children in their own ways. However, some basic ultural patterns which are coded in the organization of mealtimes for children in the given (sub) culture are invariably present within the idiosyncratic organizational forms of mealtimes in different households (Lévi-Strauss, 1966; Tambiah, 1969).

6.8 Summary

The physical and cultural structure of children's mealtime contexts was described in chapter 6, together with an overview of psychology's knowhow of infants' and toddlers' motor development. Children's self-feeding actions develop in the mealtime contexts along two lines. The natural developmental line depends upon the child's development of sufficient motor coordination to allow him to accomplish food intake on his own, without any use of cultural utensils. The cultural line—involving the use of food-transport utensils and food containers in culturally prescribed ways—develops under direct canalization by the child's caregivers, and with the help of observational learning by the child.

In chapter 7, observational data on children's development of action in mealtime settings are presented. The children who were observed acted within culturally structured settings that involve high-chairs, Wiggl-Eggs, children's spoons, forks, training cups, and many other highly specialized tools that are used at the present time in child care in American middle-class homes. The ways in which cultural information is coded in the form of such objects was analyzed in chapter 6 as a preview to the presentation of the empirical observations and their analysis.

CHAPTER 7

Cultural regulation of children's action at mealtimes and its development

All the necessary theoretical ground and description of the cultural structure of children's mealtimes is by now completed (chapters 1–6), and it is time to present observational data. The data to be presented in this chapter are derived from videotaped observations of a small number of children from a bigger sample. The way the data will be presented in this chapter follows from the metatheoretical assumptions that were analyzed in chapter 2, and illustrates the application of the theoretical framework (outlined in chapter 4) to the real-life setting of meals. No attempt will be made to introduce formal-structural analysis techniques to the present data, since the epistemological status of the few available techniques of that kind was found to be limited (chapter 5).

7.1 The samples and procedures

The empirical material analyzed here is based on two naturalistic studies of toddlers' mealtimes in contemporary American middle-class families. It started with a study of a cross-section of 34 families when their child was 11–14 months of age. That study was followed by a longitudinal observation of 30 other families in the course of 1.5 years, from the children's age 6–7 months to that of 24–26 months. In both samples, all the families were of high educational background (both mothers' and fathers' education ranged from 12 years to Ph.D. level). The parents of the children were within the age range of 24 to 40 years (mothers: 24 to 40; fathers 27 to 38). The majority of the families were selected on the basis of the local birth records, and contacted first by a letter explaining the aims of the study. If the family was

187

interested in participation, they returned a pre-stamped postcard to the investigator via mail. This contacting procedure serves as an effective filtering device that ensures the inclusion of only those families who are actively interested in research participation, and/or contacting a child psychologist, and who have or develop their own understanding of the relevance of the research. The investigator subsequently visited the family for a brief (30-minute) meeting where he explained the goals of the study and got to know the parents and the children).

The procedure used for home observations of mealtimes was built up around continuous videotaping of the events into which a free-format interview with the caregiver was inserted. At the time previously agreed upon with the parent(s), the investigator arrived in the home with the video equipment and started videotaping the child's behavior, including any behavioral events that the child was involved in and that were accessible to the investigator as allowed to be observed by the parent (e.g. some parents were reluctant to let the investigator videotape their changing the infant's diapers—that reluctance was traced in the parent's actions and the camera was stopped for the time of that event). Otherwise the VCR was kept on recording the unfolding of behavioral events continuously. The videotaped material included some time in the child's behavior before the meal started, the sequence of the whole meal, and some time after the meal had ended. The exact timing of these parts in that sequence of settings depended upon particular circumstances, but in general each home visited produced about an hour's length of videotaped observational material, including semi-structured interviews with parents o their child's recent development that were recorded on the audio channel of the videotape. If the target child had older siblings who were at home during a particular videotaping session, care was taken not to exclude them from the research process—by 'taking pictures' of some activities of theirs, occasionally re-aiming the camera from the target child to the sibling(s).

The interview with parents about the child took place at variable times during the videotaping session. In the beginning of the session, the parents were asked to describe their child's development since the previous home visit. In the middle of the videotaping, at time periods immediately following some action by the child, the parents were asked questions about their previous experience with that (or similar) actions by the child. The possibility of questioning parents immediately after a behavioral event took place in the child's actions made it possible to get information from the parents based on their sharing of the behavioral observation with the investigator, without the need for verbally describing the given behavior pattern from memory. In the end part of the session, immediately after the meal had ended, the parents were queried about how the just observed mealtime was different from other meals, and how the observer's presence influenced the child.

In addition to the videotaped mealtime observations, the parents were asked to fill out a questionnaire at the beginning of the study. The question-naire included questions about the demographic-sociological background of the parents, and their account of their child's development from birth to the time when the study started. Two other questionnaires were administered to parents in the longitudinal sample. These additional questionnaires were administered first when the target children were 14–16 months of age, and secondly at the end of the study at 24–26 months. These questionnaires included information about the child's recent development that was comp-lementary to the interview information recorded on the videotapes.

The research materials collected in this longitudinal study were analyzed as *case histories of individual children's mealtimes in the context of their families*, rather than by aggregating the material into group data. Aggregated data obscure the investigator's picture of psychological phenomena that are structured within, or around, the individual in reality (Valsiner, 1986). There-fore, the structure of mealtime settings and the development of children's self-feeding actions over time in these settings are analyzed here in selected cases of particular families studied. Only a limited number of cases could be included in this book because of space limitations and because of redundancy in the knowledge that emerges from their study. Therefore, the major source of empirical data reported in this chapter comes from longitudinal follow-up of individual cases from the 6–26 month study. During that period of time, the whole structure of children's meal settings underwent substantial change.

7.2 Structural organization of mealtimes and its change

The structural organization of children's mealtimes as observed in the empirical material referred to here provides a good basis for an analysis in terms of the present theoretical concepts. First, the Zone of Free Movement (ZFM—see 4.3.1) of all infants and toddlers is *narrowed down for the purpose of organizing the mealtime*—from the very beginning of the infants' lives until at least by the time when no externally restrictive furniture is used (e.g. infant seat, high-chair). After the external devices of narrowing of the ZFM boundaries are discarded, the child is expected to have internalized certain social rules of acting in the meal setting that carry out the same function. *In general, internalized social norms replace the use of external devices as constraints upon the person's ZFMs in particular situations in ontogeny.* Even with infants and toddlers, in whose case external constraining devices are actively used, additional *behavioral constraints* on children's actions while in the high-chair are applied to narrow the ZFM further. For instance, many parents in our sample did not allow the child to throw objects (food and/or utensils) down on the floor from the high-chair tray. Those who did allow that action usually took some measures to prevent that freedom of the child from spoiling the floor or carpet, by putting plastic covers on the area in which the high-chair was located during the mealtime. Furthermore, a child sitting in the high-chair may be additionally strapped to it (which eliminates the freedom of either standing up in it, or sliding down). During the feeding, the parent is in control of what objects appear within the child's reach (i.e. on the high-chair tray), in which combinations these objects appear, and when they are withdrawn from the tray. *The feeding of infants and toddlers in high-chairs of contemporary middle-class American homes demonstrates all the ambivalence about the child's independence–dependence relationships dialectic of the given society at large*, where almost unlimited freedom of action is provided for individuals in some domains of life, whereas the boundaries of that freedom are strictly controlled by some agent—individual or collective. In the meal situations in the high-chair, the toddlers may have remarkable possibilities of manipulating food objects and utensils in many ways. At the same time, the feeder has full control over the child's freedom of action in the high-chair—when necessary, the ZFM can be further narrowed, leaving the child with very little freedom of action in order to attain a goal of the parent. Likewise, once the particular feeding goals are attained, the boundaries of the ZFM can be restructured to become wider again. The following episode from an observed mealtime provides an example of such purposeful narrowing and subsequent widening of the ZFM. It involves a mother and her toddler son (age 14 months 9 days) at the final minutes of a lunchtime. The child is sitting in a high-chair, manipulating a plastic spoon that the mother had given him to distract him from grabbing her spoon. The mother is facing him and spoon feeding him cottage cheese, episodically explaining her strategies to the videotaping investigator or interacting with older children. The following episode is an example of the restructuring of the ZFM:

CHILD: Drops his plastic spoon on floor.
MOTHER: 'Oh-oh! Did it fall on the floor? Did it fall on the floor? Picks up some spilled cottage cheese from the child's bib with her spoon, saying: 'We are not supposed to leave that, are we?' She approaches the child's mouth with the spoonful of food.
CHILD: Turn his head away, hits the tray with his right arm.
MOTHER: Withdraws the spoon, tries to approach the child's mouth with it again, asking: 'Can you have one more bite?'
CHILD: Turns his head away, starts leaning over the side of the high-chair.
MOTHER: Grabs the child's head with her left hand and turns the child back to face her, saying: 'Come on, pumpkin!' Then grabs the child's chin by her left hand, forcing the child to open his mouth, saying 'One more little bite!'
CHILD: Struggles himself free by kicking his arms in the air and withdrawing the head.
MOTHER: Withdraws spoon, the attempts to approach the child's mouth with the spoon again.
CHILD: Struggles himself free, by kicking arms in the air and withdrawing his head.
MOTHER: Withdraws spoon, asks 'Are you finishing eating?'
CHILD: Hits high-chair tray with his hand.

MOTHER: 'You mean, after all that—you have finally finished eating?' Approaches the child's mouth with spoon again.

CHILD: Turns head away to avoid the food, then turns it back to the central position.

MOTHER: Tries to approach the mouth again with the spoon, *captures the child's right hand with her left*, says to investigator: 'He reaches for me, too.'

CHILD: Frees his hand, kicks with arms in the air.

MOTHER: Withdraws the spoon, then approaches again with it.

CHILD: *Accepts the spoonful, then spits it out immediately.*

MOTHER: Captures with the spoon the food that the child has spat out.

CHILD: Hits the mother's left hand by his right.

MOTHER: *Grasps the child's chin by her left hand, forces the mouth open, puts the food in*, saying: 'Come on, one more little bite, one more little bite!'

CHILD: Kicks with arms in the air, tries to withdraw the head, finally gets free, but *accepts the food*.

This episode illustrates how the mother, having the goal of getting 'one more little bite' of food into the child, first tries to get that bite into the child by recurrent back-and-forth action with the spoon, waiting for the time when the child would be receptive to it. Once this fails, and the mother's immediate goal of getting the bite in remains, she proceeds to narrow the child's ZFM within the existing mealtime situation. First, she takes the child's hand into hers, so that the child's kicking himself free is restricted. As that is not sufficient she grasps the child's face and forces the child to open his mouth and accept the food. In this situation, the child's ZFM is reduced to two options (spit the food back out, or swallow it), the latter of which ends up to be the case in this episode of a mother–child 'fight'.

Situations like the one described here may be rare in the case of generally *laissez-fair* organization of feeding in the families in our sample, and perhaps in the population as a whole. However, certain situations of life (e.g. the necessity of getting the child to accept a certain food, or medicine) may lead parents to occasional extremes of narrowing the ZFM in order to attain their goals. Such ZFM narrowing strategy is effective in general, as it is tested all through the history of child rearing in many cultures.

Beyond the organization of Zones of Free Movement and the regulation of their boundaries dynamically in the context of mealtimes, the Zones of Promoted Action (ZPA—see 4.3.2) are at times used to promote the learning of some new skills. Parents who are feeding their toddler may pursue both immediate (e.g. getting the child fed) and distant goals. The latter may be the reason why ZPAs are introduced, either in the parent–child joint action, or (later) through distal communication between the parents and the self-feeding child. Within ZPAs, certain particular actions that *the child is capable of performing individually, but might decide not to use in the given situation*, can be promoted by parents. If the child, however, does not succumb to the promotion effort, the parents need not force the exercise of the new skill upon him/her. For instance, once a child has learned to use the spoon independently, but reverts to finger feeding herself, the parent may organize the ZPA in different behavioral (by pointing to the spoon, putting the spoon into the child's hand, etc.) or communicative (e.g. telling the child to use the spoon) ways. Here, an important aspect of the ZPA is evident—*the ZPA's function is to promote the further development of some actions that the child has already basically acquired, through the child's own decision to exercise these actions*. For example, a mother may point to a spoon on the tray as part of the ZPA-establishing action *as she knows that the child is already capable of handling it*, and may currently refrain from demonstrating and exercising the skill for some (unspecifiable!) motivational reasons. ZPA is a structure that canalizes the child's own motivation to act, whereas ZFMs canalize the actions themselves without an emphasis on the child's wishes or will. Not surprisingly, ZPAs emerge in the history of child rearing in conjunction with the ideology of thinking about children as independent human beings whose self-worth (or self-esteem) is developed by their own action preferences and (seeming) independence of thinking (see Sunley, 1955, for an account of different ideologies in American child rearing in the nineteenth century).

The actual beginnings of the child's development of new actions are embedded *within adult–child joint action in the Zone of Proximal Development* (ZPD). This structuring of the learning of the new action takes place with the help of setting up a ZFM to organize the new action, starting from its narrowest state, and gradually releasing different parts of the action to be controlled by the child (widening of the given ZFM). the ontogeny of learning the use of spoones provides an example. The adult at first helps the child to use the spoon by accomplishing the whole action (TAKE FOOD FROM CONTAINER ONTO SPOON → PREPARE FOR TRANSPORT (judge the readiness of the child for accepting food) → TRANSPORT→ FOOD RELEASE), which provides the child with perceivable information about the whole action. When the baby starts to grab for the spoon (or when the adult considers it appropriate to involve the child in the action), the organization of action within ZPD begins—the adult gradually relinquishes control over some parts of the action, while retaining control over the others, as well as of the action in its totality. For example, it is usually the HOLDING OF SPOON that is the first part of the whole action into which the child's behavior becomes integrated—the adult puts the spoon into the child's hand, *and controls the movements of the hand + spoon in the process of carrying out the whole action*. The child is kept in the subordinate role with no control over any part of the action, but is being prepared for further learning of it by the adult's guiding the whole motion of the hand + spoon. Next, some parts of the action may become 'liberated' from the adult's control and delegated to the control of the child. For example, the adult may give the spoon to the child *and let him dip it into the container with food*, after which the adult helps the child to get food onto the spoon, withdraw the spoonful of food from the container, take the hand + spoon + food to the child's mouth, and release the food. Likewise, the pre-final part of the action (hand + spoond + food reaching the child's mouth) may be delegated to the child—the spoon is filled under adult's control, and set into a starting position for the journey towards the mouth by the adult. Now, the adult guides the child's hand + spoon + food half-way towards the child's mouth, releases it, and lets the child complete the transport part of the action. Then, again, the adult may regain control over the spoon and help the child to release the food in the mouth and return the spoon. Further development of the action leads to even less control on behalf of the adult, where the child is alotted control over different parts of the action, reaching full control over all components of the action at last. In order to be successful in teaching the child the new skill, the process of guiding the learning of the skill by structuring (and restructuring) its emergence through ZFMs has to be coordinated with the ZPD of the particular child (with his previous life experience, up to the given time). If the ZFM is set so that it allows the child to control a part of the action that he still cannnot master, the ZFM has to be reset in a way that takes care of that part, until the child is ready to learn it. *The dynamic restructing of ZFM in the context of learning a particular type of action canalizes the emergence of that action so that it provides the child with selective learning experience for some of the parts of the action earlier than others, in correspondence with what is empirically (by trying, not succeeding, and trying again) found to be available to the child within the ZPD.*

7.3 Analysis of individual case histories of the canalization of mealtime actions in infants and toddlers

From all the theoretical consierations outlined at length in the present book it follows that the most appropriate strategy for developmental research is the analysis of the process of development by looking at individual developing systems longitudinally over a period of time, and interdependently with the contexts of their existence at every available step. The following sections include the presentation of research materials on three children from the longitudinal (6–7 to 24–26 months of age) sample. All these cases are analyzed along similar lines. First, some background information about the child and his/her family is given. That is followed by a quantitative analysis of the amounts of time spent by the child and parent(s) during each of the mealtimes studied on one or another kind of self- or other-feeding activity or merely in contact with food. This information provides the background for the most central topic of the empirical analyses—the structural description of the canalization process that is represented by narrative descriptions of the sequence of events within the mealtimes that were observed, and by more specific analyses of sequences of particular child–parent–environment transaction episodes that occurred in one or another 'crucial' moment during a particular meal. These 'crucial' episodes are usually not the most frequent ones when viewed within the quantitative domain. It is usually some single, rare episodic events that are more informative than the dominant recurrent of well-mastered actions.

Finally, it will be very obvious that all three cases presented here happen to be those of female toddlers. This clear dominance of one sex in the data is of no importance here, since the study is cast in the individual-socioecological reference frame, rather than the usual (inter-individual) one. In the latter case, the issue of 'sex differences' would be of interest, but given the emphasis on the former frame it is of no relevance for the empirical analysis that is outlined in this chapter.

7.4 The case of Laura

7.4.1 Family background

Laura is the first child of a college graduate mother (26 years of age at the time of the child's birth) who works as a technical secretary, and a dental technician father (also 26 years of age). Laura was born healthy ($^1/_5$ minute Apgar rating $^8/_9$ at birth), after a pregnancy without medical complications of psychological difficulties. The parents were involved in Lamaze preparations for childbirth. The mother reported some 'post-partum blues', which disappeared after a few weeks. Laura was given her own room (next to parents' bedroom) for sleeping from the first day at home. Her health between birth and the beginning of participation in our study was reported to have been very good (parents reported one virus infection and two colds for that period).

Laura's mealtimes were observed seven times, at her ages (months: days): (1) 6:27, (2) 9:01, (3) 13:19, (4) 15:08, (5) 18:03, (6) 21:03, and (7) 25:17. The feeding was usually organized by her mother, with the father being present on some occasions and helping the mother in her work. Due to an equipment failure, the fifth videotaping session did not cover the whole meal, but only the end part of it.

7.4.2 The time distribution of food-contact activites

The data on time distribution of Laura's food-contact actions (feeding or otherwise, by herself, her mother, or by both herself and the mother) are presented in Table 7.1. As is evident from that Table, Laura's general (summary, percentagewise) spending of time in contact with food changed dramatically over the 19-month period.

As expected, the dominant (100 per cent time) way of getting fed at 6:27—the mother spoon feeding Laura—was gradually substituted by, first, the dominance of the child's self-feeding with the use of her hands (e.g. at

Table 7.1. Developmental changes in mealtime food-contact time allocations between different child-centered actions (case: Laura).

| Action category | Observed mealtimes at child's age: | | | | | | | | | | | | | |
| | 6:27 | | 9:01 | | 13:19 | | 15:08 | | 18:03 | | 21:03 | | 25:17 | |
	f	%	f	%	f	%	f	%	f	%	f	%	f	%
M spoon feeds CH	574	100.0	367	55.9	70	6.0	128	12.8	—	—	—	—	—	—
M finger feeds CH	—	—	7	1.1	—	—	—	—	—	—	—	—	—	—
CH finger feeds	—	—	282	43.0	1074	91.6	729	73.0	34	7.9	168	22.5	117	21.5
CH drinks from cup with lid	—	—	—	—	29	2.4	136	13.6	—	—	80	10.7	—	—
M–CH joint action with spoon	—	—	—	—	—	—	6	0.6	15	3.5	—	—	—	—
CH plays with food or utensil	—	—	—	—	—	—	—	—	373	86.1	69	9.2	—	—
CH spoon feeds herself	—	—	—	—	—	—	—	—	11	2.5	407	54.6	428	78.5
M–CH joint action with regular glass	—	—	—	—	—	—	—	—	—	—	22	3.0	—	—
TOTAL	574		656		1173		999		433		746		545	

M= mother; CH = child, f = frequency of 1-second time units

13:19 that method occupied 91.6 per cent of time). Later on, Laura was seen to use the spoon—first, predominantly for handling the foods on the high-chair tray (dipping the spoon into food, trying to get food onto spoon, banging with spoon on tray and food, etc.—anything except transporting food to the mouth region). At the end of our observations she spent most of the time spoon feeding herself adequately, with occasional (21.5 per cent of all the time of the meal spent in contact with food) use of finger feeding herself. This wide general picture of the basic change in Laura's mealtime towards utensil-mediated self-feeding proves that the child's eating habits became culturally organized during the period of our observations. More interestingly, certain events that were observed only rarely and proved to be transitory in the bigger quantitative picture of the mealtime events provide more direct and structured information about the process of mother–child interaction. These include the mother–child joint action with the spoon in the process of feeding (observed at 15:08 and 18:03) and their joint action in the process of drinking from a regular glass (observed at 21:03).

7.4.3 Changes in the mealtime setting and the development of utensil use

The view upon the sequence of events during the observed mealtimes provides better information about the process of child feeding and its socialization than the summary 'time budgets'. At age 6:27, Laura's mealtime had a very simple sequential structure. After the child was set ready for the meal (by being put into an infant seat located on a table, and attaching bib to the child), the mother proceeded to spoon feed her without interruption for 6 minutes 19 seconds. The first time Laura was observed to turn her head away from the approaching spoon with food was at 4.50 (4 minutes, 50 seconds) into the meal, which was followed by mother's recurrent attempts to get the spoonful of food into her mouth (L turns head away→M withdraws spoon→ L turns head back → M approaches with spoon again → L either accepts the food now, or turns head away again, with repetition of the subsequent maternal effort). There was an 8-second pause (from 6.30 to 6.38) in the meal, followed by continuous spoon feeding in the course of which the child continued to display head-turn away at times. This led the mother to ask (at 7.50). 'Are you through?', adjust the child's position in the seat (8.18–8.25), and continue spoonfeeding until 9.00. That was followed by a period of waiting to see whether the child might accept some more food, tickling her, wiping her mouth and face, and cleaning off the dipped food from the bib. After that (at 10.40 into feeding) Laura was removed from the infant seat. This marked the end of the mealtime. At no time was Laura attempting to touch the spoon, the movement of her limbs was characterized by non-specific activation (kicking feet and extending arms back and forth, being practically in a semi-reclining position in the seat). On no occasion did the mother attempt to get her to touch either the food, its container, or the spoon.

The sequential picture of Laura's mealtime at 9:01 is already different. The child is put into the high-chair. Maternal spoon feeding is still prevailing (mother feeds her uninterruptedly from 0.03 to 6.10 of the mealtime). At 6.00 the mother asked, referring to Laura's refusal to accept food, 'Is that all?' The child's mouth and hands are subsequently wiped, after which the mother offers Laura a cracker *which the latter accepts by hand*. The acceptance of the cracker is followed by a long (from 7.05 to 11.47) period of Laura's bimanual and unimanual manipulation of the cracker, and mouthing it (together with eating it). The mother observes Laura finger feeding herself, once helping her daughter by putting a piece of cracker into her mouth by her (mother's) fingers (11.47–11.50). After that, Laura drops the cracker on the floor (where the dog gets it). Laura continues to sit in the high-chair without food until 13.18, after which the mother wipes the child's mouth, face, and hands and cleans up the tray, Laura gets into fussing, and by 14.19 the meal is over as she is taken down from the high-chair.

This second observed mealtime involved mother–daughter exchange of food (cracker) *from hand to hand* and the subsequent finger feeding by the child. Laura's finger feeding during this mealtime could not be characterized as an efficient action, since it involved excessive manipulation of the food together with mouthing/eating it. The mother essentially provided Laura with a two-course meal—feeding her semi-liquid food with the spoon herself, then cleaning up the child, followed by the second course of 'finger-food'. Again, no opportunity was given to the child to manipulate any of the feeding utensils, and neither was Laura observed to try to grab the spoon during the first course of the meal.

Laura's third observed mealtime (at 13:19) includes the appearance of new forms of meal organization. Although spoon feeding by mother was still present, it was not organized into long time periods, but present intermittently with the provision of finger-foods for the child for self-feeding (putting pieces of ham *on the tray, rather than into the child's hands*). The presence of a drinking cup (with a lid with spout) was evident episodically. Laura indicated her wish to drink by a gesture (arms raised at the level of shoulders, pointing towards mother, sometimes accompanied by a vocalization). *After the child displayed that gesture, the mother immediately gave Laura the cup into her hands*, and she raised the cup bimanually to drink. After drinking was accomplished, *the mother immediately removed the cup from the child's reach (i.e. the tray)*, until the child displayed the gesture again. The child was not given access to the cup other than when drinking, which was communicated by the child and immediately understood by the mother who provided the cup. No use of spoon, nor grabbing of it, was observed among the child's actions during this observed meal.

The novel action type of *the mother and child cooperating in handling the spoon* was first observed in Laura's case during the fourth session (at 15:08). After the usual preparations for the feeding (until 0.38 into the mealtime) the mother proceeded to provide food for the child's finger feeding, intermittently with spoon feeding by the mother, until 5.14 of the mealtime. The first episode of mother–child joint action with the spoon was observed between 5.14 and 5.20: the mother gave the spoon (with food on it) to the child, who accepted it with her left hand. Mother did not release the spoon, but guided the child's hand (with the spoon) to the mouth. After that episode, the mealtime proceeded by the child's finger feeding or drinking (the cup, as previously, was given to the child on demand and removed after the child had drunk and released the cup). The mother also tried to continue to spoon feed Laura, with greater refusal efforts on behalf of the child towards the end of the meal (at 24.46).

A qualitatively new picture of the child's actions at mealtime, mediated by the use of utensils, was observed at 18:03 (unfortunately this was the case where equipment failure made it impossible to record the whole meal, so only the final 7.20 of that meal constitute the observational basis here). The qualitative novelty of action during that observation session is evident even from Table 7.1—most of Laura's food-contacting time was spent *using the spoon while manipulating food*. The child acted with the spoon in different ways, mostly dipping it into the plate (with some solid food—like cheesecake—in it), hit the food by spoon, took some food from the plate and put it on the tray. Actual self-feeding with spoon (i.e. food transport from plate or tray to mouth) was observed only occasionally, and mother–child joint feeding with spoon only twice. Child's finger feeding was likewise rare, although the nature of the food (solid cake) and the location of its pieces (both on the plate and on tray) made it possible to finger feed.

Laura's next meal was observed at 21:03. At that observation the structure of the mealtime had reached a state where Laura fed herself most of the time with the spoon, and mother–child joint action while spoon feeding was not observed. However, when Laura abandoned the spoon for some time, the mother reminded her of it. The following summary of events from the end of the seventh to that of tenth minute of the meal provides the action sequence:

6.58–7.54—Laura uses spoon to feed herself.
7.54–8.00—Quits feeding, bangs with spoon on the lid of the cup on the tray.
8.00–9.01—the child continues with finger feeding. AT 8.39 MOTHER INTERVENES VERBALLY, SAYING: 'You are supposed to be using your spoon.' Laura continues to finger feed, mother does not repeat her reminder.
9.01–9.12—Mother cleans the tray and wipes Laura's face and hands.
9.12–9.26—Laura grabs the spoon from tray, manipulates it. MOTHER COMMENTS: 'That's right, use your spoon.' Laura proceeds to spoon feed herself, and drops the spoon on the floor at the end of the time period.
9.26–9.42—Mother wipes the tray, Laura talks to the mother.

This action sequence illustrates the reality of the ZPA as it is ontogenetic-ally transformed from the sphere of joint action to communication—the use of the spoon is promoted (verbally) when the child temorarily abandons the use of the spoon and reverts to finger feeding.

Another important novelty in the way the child drank from the cup (with lid) was observed: after the child had asked for the cup, the cup was given *and not taken away after Laura had drunk*, but was left on the tray. Laura was observed to handle the cup for the first time unimanually (as well as continuing the bimanual hold of the cup sometimes). The mother did not help the child to act with the cup, but *on the one occasion when she offered Laura a drink from a regular glass she held the glass herself, letting Laura hold it bimanually, and helped the child to lift the glass for drinking*, not releasing the glass.

Laura's coordination of the actions of the left and right hands in the self-feeding context was observed particularly in the final half of the meal, when the mother gave her a spoon and a jar with some semi-liquid prune purée (10.43–14.28). The jar and the spoon were put *on the tray* (rather than either of these into the child's hands). Previously the child had been given a cookie which she continued to handle when the jar and spoon were given to her. At first, Laura used the cookie as a dipping tool to get the food from the jar and carry the food + cookie to the mouth, intermittently with manipu-lation of the spoon, jam, and the cookie on the tray. Between 12.40 and 12.50 of the mealtime, an interesting novel form of inter-limb coordination in this action context was observed: Laura *took the jar into her left hand* and raised the jar approximately 4–5 cm from the tray, and then *took the spoon into her right hand* and spoon fed herself from the jar. The importance of this observation lies in the child's reconstruction of the eating setting by her non-use of the available support (the tray) for the jar, and in the coordination of manual handling of both tools involved—the container and the food-transport instrument.

The final observation of Laura's mealtime (at 25:17) revealed general consolidation of the self-feeding with spoon. This took the form of *exchange of hands* while spoon feeding herself. During the first 6.11 of the mealtime Laura was observed to feed herself with the spoon in her left hand (intermit-tently with finger feeding for which the right hand was used). Then the spoon was changed from the left to the right hand, and used by that hand until 10.42, when it was changed back to the left (until 10.51, after which the meal moved into its end phase). In terms of frequencies, the spoon was used approximately equally by the left (20 self-feeds) and the right (19 self-feeds) hands during the meal. However, the use of the two hands was not 'random', but involved longer sequences of the use first of one, and then the other, hand.

Another important observation during this mealtime was the child's action (at 4.48–4.58) where, *holding the spoon in her left hand, Laura used her right hand to take some food by her fingers, put it on the spoon, and then transport the spoon + food to her mouth.* This structure of action was observed twice in a row. It illustrates the integration of the 'natural' and 'cultural' lines in the ontogeny of self-feeding.

7.5 The case of Sophie

7.5.1 Family background

Sophie was born as the second child into a family where the mother (aged 29 at the child's brith, secondary education) is from Africa and the father American (38 years of age, Ph.D.-level education). The family's first child (daughter) was 8 years old when Sophie was born.

Sophie's mealtimes were videotaped five times, at the following ages: (1) 8:05, (2) 12:10), (3) 15:13, (4) 17—10, and (5) 25:00 months. All mealtimes were recorded at lunchtimes, around noon.

7.5.2 The time distribution of food-contact activities

The data on the distribution of time that Sophie spent in contact with food at each of the longitudinally observed mealtimes are presented in Table 7.2.

These summary data are instructive in two respects. First, they replicate the finding of the role of child's play with food and utensils (see Table 7.1) as an immediate concomitant of the development of both Laura's and Sophie's self-feeding actions in mealtime contexts. By the end of the first year of life, Sophie's mother had reversed her strategy of *not* giving the child the opportunity to manipulate utensils and food. Since that manipulation thus occurred in the ZFM of Sophie's actions in the immediate environment (high-chair tray), both the manipulation of food and utensils and finger feeding herself became possible. The food and utensil play that was first observed at 12 months subsequently declined in its quantitative share of the mealtime, as the child's self-feeding actions (both with fingers/hands and utensils) became more skillful.

The second useful piece of information that data in this table denote is the *dependence of the particular actions on the structural conditions set for the meal setting by the mother.* The mother has full control over the way she structures the mealtime setting. The child may (and indeed—was observed to) demand one or another alteration in the ZPA/ZFM structure that the mother had set up, and the mother may (and did) 'give in' on the issues that the child tried to change, but the ultimate control over the whole situation remained in the mother's hands. She made the decision to provide the child with fork and not with spoon—thus resulting in non-occurrence of child's spoon feeding herself during the observed mealtimes. She made it possible for the child to play the game of feeding another person—initiating the

Table 7.2. Developmental changes in mealtime food-contact time allocations between different actions of the child (case: Sophie).

Action category					Observed mealtimes at child's age:					
	8:06		12:10		15:13		17:10		25:00	
	f	%	f	%	f	%	f	%	f	%
M spoon feeds CH	270	39.1	—	—	—	—	—	—	—	—
M fork feeds CH	—	—	—	—	—	—	38	6.2	—	—
M gives drink	25	3.6	—	—	—	—	—	—	—	—
CH plays with food and utensils	395	57.3	398	31.4	133	38.7	77	12.7	—	—
CH finger feeds (= hand feeds)	—	—	604	47.7	112	32.5	112	18.4	420	67.8
CH spoon feeds	—	—	—	—	—	—	—	—	—	—
CH fork feeds	—	—	—	—	47	13.7	209	34.4	110	17.8
CH drinks herself	—	—	84	6.7	52	15.1	48	7.9	65	10.5
M—CH joint action:										
with fork	—	—	—	—	—	—	43	7.1	—	—
with cup/glass	—	—	—	—	—	—	20	3.3	—	—
CH feeds other actor (mother, father, doll)	—	—	180	14.2	—	—	61	10.0	24	3.9
TOTAL			1266		344		608		619	

M = mother; CH = child; f = frequency of 1-second time units period at 12:10 where Sophie was observed finger feeding the mother. She provided the soft-animal-toy for the child in high-chair at 17:10 which Sophie subsequently 'fed'. The mother's decision to give the child a sandwich at 25:00 resulted in the extensive hand feeding by the child during the meal observed at that age.

7.5.3 Changes in the mealtime setting and the development of utensil use

As is evident from the summary data in Table 7.2, the longitudinal course of Sophie's mealtime organization progressed towards greater differentiation of the action repertoires that could be observed. At 8:06, the child is confined in the high-chair and no food is made constantly available to child. This is evidenced in the mother's keeping the food container (a child's three-partition feeding plate) not on the high-chair tray but on the table next to it, out of the reach of the child. The mother explicitly acknowledges that she does not give to the child any utensil except the cup to handle during the meal. The course of the meal at that age verifies that strategy—the mother spends the first 2.05 of the meal spoon feeding the child. At some spoon-feeding cases the mother opens her mouth widely at the time that she expects the child to do likewise (1.29), and withdraws spoon with food when the child occasionally refuses to open the mouth. The cup emerges in the situation at 2.05 to 2.30 feeding time. The mother gives the child a cup (with a lid and spout), by putting it onto the tray in front of the child. The child looks at it and examines by her right hand, pushing it off onto its side. The mother lifts it back up. The child pushes the cup around on the tray, the mother intervenes (at 2.26) and puts it back up in front of the child. This episode of negotiation of ZFM boundary (child playing with cup, mother taking it and setting it upright) is followed by *the mother giving the drink from the cup without releasing control over it*. Once the child has finished drinking, the mother retrieves the cup and puts it on the table out of the child's reach, but in her visual field. The next longer period of time (2.38–4.53) during that meal is again spent by the mother's spoon feeding the child (at 3.54 an example of mother's mouth opening occurs; at 4.17–4.31 the mother tires to spoon feed twice with no effect until getting the food to the child on the third try). After a brief side-oriented activity (interaction with father), the mother's spoon feeding of the child continues until 6.08.

The events of the meal continue: the mother tries to give the child an apple (putting it onto the tray) but the child shows no interest, after which the apple is retrieved to starting position (plate). After wiping the child's mouth, the mother offers her drink from the cup (by putting the cup on the tray), but the child does not take it. The mother proceeds to give the child a drink from the cup herself; child drinks with arms stretched out in air at shoulder level, making no attempt to grab the cup. After drinking is finished, the mother leaves the cup on tray. Child at first watches it, then proceeds to grab the cup by handles bimanually, then releases right hand and keeps only left, mouthes the spout, seems to drink. The mother takes the cup away from the child and gives her a piece of apple. The rest of the meal is spent by Sophie's mouthing of the piece of apple.

The second mealtime that was observed in the study took place at Sophie's age 12:10. The mother's strategy of organizing the mealtime is quite different from the previous session—instead of keeping utensils and food (except for the cup with lid) away from the high-chair tray, now the mother *gives different utensils to the child and puts food onto the tray*, thus creating the possibility (ZFM) for the child to manipulate the food and utensils, and promotes the child's acting with food in particular ways (ZPA). The latter is evident in the mother's triggering of the 'child-feeds-mother' game (see below).

The actual structure of the second mealtime starts from a relatively lengthy preparatory phase—the mother prepares food and brings it to Sophie while the child is ready in the high-chair, with bib attached, ready to eat. At 1.31 the mother puts the child's three-section feeding plate *onto the high-chair tray* (a qualitative change from the previous observation session), while continuing to mix the food in the different sections of the plate, explaining to the child: 'That's hot' a number of times. Child proceeds to manipulate the food by hands, and then starts finger feeding herself with the right hand.

At 2.46 the mother gives the child a plastic spoon (with twisted handle, similar to that in Figure 6.5) *in a way that forces the child to accept it by her right hand* (i.e. keeping the handle of the spoon to the right from the child's point of view). The child accepts the spoon by handle using her right hand, brings to contact with food, but proceeds to put it down on tray. Mother takes it away and puts it back on tray (on the child's right side) immediately. The child uses right hand to manipulate it on tray. At 3.28, another similar plastic spoon is given to the child's left hand. It is accepted by the child, who then puts both spoons down onto the plate. The mother acts to adjust one of the two for right-hand use and withdraws the other (3.38). The child uses the spoon to touch food, manipulates the spoon, at 4.10 points towards the other spoon (on table outside child's reach but in the visual field) which the mother gives to her, after which the child continues to manipulate the two spoons on tray and plate, making no effort to bring either of them close to mouth or into it, with or without food. This is followed by a relatively long period (4.23–7.39) of finger feeding (using the right hand). The mother takes away both spoons.

A drinking episode follows at 7.39. The child vocalizes and points in the direction of the cup (with lid and spout, but no handles) that is on the adjacent table out of child's reach. Mother gives the cup—*by putting it on the tray in front of the child*, from where the child lifts it bimanually and drinks. After the child has finished drinking and puts the cup down on the tray, the mother leaves the cup there (rather than removing it to the adjacent table) while the child proceeds to finger feed herself. At 8.58 the mother gives the child a plastic fork, which is accepted by the left hand. After some manipulation, the child puts it into her right hand, contacts food with it, and abandons it on tray, resuming finger feeding.

An episode concerning the attempts to cross ZFM boundaries in respect to actions with utensils followed at 9.48–12.53 of the meal:

CHILD: Takes fork into right hand, touches food, manipulates it with fork, vocalizes and points with left hand towards other utensils on the table.
MOTHER: Gives a plastic spoon into her left hand.
CHILD: Manipulates both fork and spoon on the plate, in contact with food, but no self-feeding effort with these utensils is observed. At 11.25 gets a piece of food onto spoon and transports to the edge of the tray, and releases the food overboard.
MOTHER: Catches the piece of food by her hand.
CHILD: Fusses, gives the spoon to mother, continues to manipulate with the fork.
MOTHER: Accepts the spoon.
CHILD: Continues manipulation of fork, at 12.28 for the first time puts the fork in mouth in adequate way (handling it with left hand) but with no food on it, keeps mouthing it (until 12.51).

This episode illustrates the boundary condition of the ZFM being located at the subset of actions involving the throwing of objects (here—food) over the edge of the tray onto the floor. The child is allowed to play with food and utensils on the tray, and is not pushed to use the utensils in a particular way (although the utensil use is promoted—by the mother's returning of utensils to child from time to time).

This episode is followed by another drinking episode that was observed to include some important novel aspect (at 12.53–13.14). The child takes the cup from tray bimanually and drinks, then puts it back onto plate, where it loses balance and falls onto its side. *The child proceeds to adjust it*—first by trying to set it upright on the food in the plate, with no success. She then puts it down upright in the place from where she had taken it when she started to drink (left of plate on far end of tray). She then proceeds to manipulate the fork. At 13.14–14.10 an effort towards getting the fork into a piece of food is observed: the child holds the fork in her right hand and adjusts a piece of food in plate with her left hand. That action fails, since she uses the whole right arm, which is unsteady, to aim the fork at the food.

At the fifteenth minute, the mother introduces new food on a different plate. In the process of that introduction, the boundary of ZFM is again observable. When the mother puts a new (round, regular) plate with food on the tray the child makes an effort to lift the plate from the tray, which is counteracted by the mother who pushes the plate back onto the tray surface. The child proceeds to manipulate the food by fingers, and to finger feed herself.

At 19.05 the investigator triggers a demonstration of the child's feeding the mother. The mother asks the child to feed her, makes herself available for that, and the child proceeds to finger feed the mother (during the period 19.20–21.28). A couple of minutes later (at 23.55–24.47), and after finger feeding herself, the child initiates feeding the mother—starting from high-pitch vocalization and holding up right arm/hand with food. When the mother comes, the child puts food in her mouth. At the second time the child begins to play approach/withdrawal game with mother—when the mother approaches child withdraws her hand with food, leading to the mother's withdrawal, after which the child then approaches the mother's mouth with her hand again. The most interesting observation occurred when the child's hand was arriving at the mother's mouth—while putting the food into the mother's mouth the child opened *her own* mouth wide.

The *actual use of a utensil for transport of food to mouth* was observed starting from our third videotaping session (at 15:13). That session began with the child sitting in the high-chair, having the (three-sectional) plate and cup (with lid and spout) on the tray and a fork in her right hand. The child mouthes the fork, and at 1.19 uses the operation of her left hand to *dip the fork in food and bring the fork with some food to the mouth*, after which she continues mouthing the fork. This event is repeated at 2.12.

Between 2.52 and 3.18 another action version with fork takes place: the child while holding the fork in her left hand gets some food onto the fork (some of it is in-between the fork's tines). Then, using her right (free) hand, she takes the food from the fork and puts it into her mouth in the regular fashion of finger feeding. The importance of this little episode lies in the demonstration of flexibility in the child's actions—once the utensil use has emerged ontogenetically in the social context, the child continues to have the freedom to decide when *not* to use the utensil but revert to using the hand pure and simple. The cultural organisation of mealtimes generates *redundancy in action possibilities* which affords an increased number of different possible ways to solve the food transport problem. However, such shifting back and forth between utensil and hand use may be seen in actual mealtime practices only in early ontogeny—later, when the structure of mealtime settings becomes internalized, it takes an adult quite a bit of courage to grasp food by hand during some formal dinner party when the luxurious situation has furnished the person with a set of forks or spoons.

Sophie's third mealtime session proceeds with mouthing the fork and playing with the food on the tray. At 4.05 the child starts to push the plate away from the tray, the mother takes it away,and new food (banana) is given to the child (4.54). The rest of the mealtime (until it ends at 9.09) is spent by the child finger feeding herself banana pieces, drinking from the cup, and occasionally interacting with the mother in a manner not related to eating.

The fourth observed mealtime (at age 17:10) includes some further novelties in its structure. First, a regular (metal instead of plastic) fork is given to the child. Secondly, for the first time in the course of observations the cup used for drinking lacks the lid (with spout), and is thus an equivalent for a regular cup (with the handle).

The session begins with the mother putting the child in the high-chair and lowering the tray. The mother then puts the plate (three-section) on tray, uses steel fork to stir some food, leaves it all for child, who is engaged in finger feeding herself. At 0.40–1.07 the child takes fork with her right hand and *adequately transpots food to mouth*. She does not release the whole forkload but only part of it, withdraws the fork with the rest of the load to the plate, and then advances to the mouth again with the same load and releases all of it in the mouth. This is the first episode where the child was observed to use the fork independently in ways that guaranteed adequate food transport, which in this case was related to withdrawal of some of the food on fork and using it at the next action.

The session proceeds with the child finger feeding, then playing with fork and food (holding the fork by all five fingers at the very end of the handle, dipping it into the food), drinking from cup, finger feeding again, mouthing fork. At 4.56 an episode of mother–child joint action starts. The mother says 'Let me help you' to which the child answers with a 'No!'. Nevertheless the mother takes some food onto the fork, gives it to child to be accepted by the right hand, and the child finishes the action by accepting the fork + food from mother and taking it to the mouth with the final releasing of it in mouth (5.38). After a period of child feeding herself with the fork, a similar episode of joint action occurs, after the child begins to play (pointing to a drawing on the side of the cup on the tray, with fork). That episode again is connected with the issue of ZFM boundary regulation:

> MOTHER: Takes the fork, prepares its foodload, and puts the fork + food on tray so that the handle is on the child's right side.
> CHILD: Picks up the fork by the right hand, manipulates it, tries to take load off the fork with her left hand.
> MOTHER: Says: 'No, that's ok.'
> CHILD: Finally transports the fork + food to mouth, helps with her left hand to keep food in mouth when withdrawing the fork with the right hand. Goes on to hit the plate with the fork, then tries to dip the fork into the cup.
> MOTHER: Interrupts the dipping action and redirects child's hand with fork.
> CHILD: Tries again to dip the fork in the cup.
> MOTHER: Takes away cup.
> CHILD: Throws fork down onto the floor, bangs on tray with the right hand.
> MOTHER: Picks up the fork, wipes it clean, and gives it back to the child.
> CHOLD: Uses the regained fork to hit the tray.
> MOTHER: 'No!'
> CHILD: Throws the fork down on the tray.
> MOTHER: Takes the fork away.
> CHILD: Bangs on the tray with hand, reaches out towards mother.
> MOTHER: Remains inactive, asks 'Eat more!'
> CHILD: 'No'.

This episode ends as the child switches into finger feeding herself. The negotiation involved in the episode illustrates the ways in which the ZFM for acting with the fork during the meal is negotiated. The mother excludes the banging on tray with fork, throwing it (or other objects) overboard onto floor, from ZFM. The child, however, begins to display these actions and persists in doing so (e.g. after the mother eturns the fork). The boundary is reinstated by eliminating the fork from the situation and suggesting (ZPA) that the child continue eating more without the fork (i.e. the child's reaching out towards the mother at the end of the episode may have been a gesture to get the fork back).

After some time of the child's finger feeding, the mother returns the fork into the situation (at 7.43)—again by getting a load of food onto it herself first. Then she puts the fork on the plate so that it is ready for right-hand use. The child who has been episodically interested in the camera then takes fork + food and transports it to the mouth, after which the child continues using the fork to feed herself. Suddenly she gives the fork to the mother, who collects a forkload and tries to feed the child using the fork herself. The child refuses (by withdrawing head), the mother abandons the feeding effort and puts the fork on the plate ready for right-hand use. The child pays no attention to the food—sits, looks at mother, points at camera, no food-related action. Only 20 seconds later does the child take the fork, manipulate it, and proceed to use it to feed herself. After putting the food in the mouth with it, she puts fork back in plate. The mother takes the fork, again collects food onto it, gives fork + food to the child, who takes it, first *offers to feed the mother*, then transports it to her own mouth.

The next minute of the mealtime (9.40–10.36) is spent in occasional joint action of the mother and child around drinking from the cup, and using the fork again. An interesting episode starts at the end of this period when the child requests a soft toy (Kitty-cat) which is located on the table next to the high-chair. The mother puts the kitty-cat to sit next to the child in the high-chair, on the left side of the child. The presence of the toy animal in the structure of the meal creates new possibilities for the child's actions and for the mother's regulation of these actions. At 10.36–10.47 the child grasps the cup with her right hand only (as her left arm is around the kitty-cat). The mother immediately says: 'Two hands! Two hands only!' The child releases Kitty-cat, and the mother adjusts it in the sitting position, saying 'Kitty-cat, she sits there'. The child proceeds to take the cup with both hands and drinks. This little episode illustrates how the addition of a new object into the situation triggers the canalization effort of otherwise well-established action—the child had been seen previously many times to lift the cup bimanually, but tried to do it unimanually since her left hand was not available. Immediately the mother intervenes to reinstate the ZFM boundary condition.

The following period (10.47–11.50) is spent in the mother's fork feeding the child while the latter is playing with the toy—e.g. lowering the Kitty-cat to 'eat' from the plate. As a result the toy gets dirty with ketchup, the mother retrieves and cleans it, then returns it to the position in the high-chair. At 11.50 the next interesting episode begins. The mother prepares a forkload and gives it to the child, who accepts it by right hand. She then starts to 'feed' the Kitty-cat with the fork and then transports the forkload into her own mouth. This action sequence is repeated, until at 12.35 the mother prepares a forkload and attempts to fork feed the child, who refuses and plays with Kitty-cat, adjusts it in high-chair. The action then proceeds to eating broccoli—the mother takes a piece of broccoli by her hand and gives it into the child's right hand. The child tries to feed it to the Kitty-cat by her hand, then transports broccoli into her own mouth. The child is observed finger feeding the Kitty-cat repeatedly, with no maternal intervention. This, however, ceases to be the case when the child takes the cup and tries to give the Kitty-cat a drink (14.19–14.35)—the mother intercepts the child's hands with cup when she predicts that the next thing the child is going to do is to raise it in front of Kitty-cat's nose. She also verbally reminds the child: 'Not kitty! No!' the child gives in, and the mother proceeds to clean the tray while the child remains inactive. After some efforts by the mother to fork feed the child and to offer more food (refused by the child), the mother proceeds to end up the mealtime (16.05).

The fifth observed mealtime in this case took place at the child's age of 25:00 and was characterized by a number of previously unobserved novelties. First, the child is no longer *put* into the mealtime position—sitting in the high-chair by the mother but is urged by her to climb into the high-chair (and down from it at the end of the meal) 'all by herself', which she does. Secondly, the high-chair is used as an equivalent of an ordinary chair—instead of lowering the tray to confine the child after she has climbed into the sitting position, the mother pushes the whole chair with the child to a position at the regular table. Thirdly, the mother uses a regular plate as the food container, putting it together with a regular fork in front of the child. The fork, not coincidentally, is placed on the child's right side of the plate. A napkin is also provided within the distance of the child's reach.

The child at first hand feeds (sandwich) with her right hand, then (at 0.33) fork feeds holding the fork by the very end of the handle in her right hand. This is followed by the child's wiping her own mouth/nose with napkin (takes from table). The meal proceeds with the child hand feeding, drinking from the open (no lid) cup, using the fork to manipulate food; at 7.25 the child says 'Okey' and stands up on the chair, calling 'Mommy!'. The mother takes away the plate, the child sits down, and the mother brings another plate with new food.

The child proceeds to hand feed herself. In the period 9.58–10.22 the father appears episodically in the situation, insisting that the child feed him. The child feeds the father by hand, and then comments 'He took a bite' pointing towards him by finger. The rest of the meal is uneventful (from the perspective of the present investigator, of course): the child hand feeds herself by left hand (10.22–12.20), talks, says her name at mother's insistence and talks about a recent visit to the zoo, while holding food in the left hand but not acting with it (12.20–14.00). She then proceeds to hand feed and talk intermittently (14.00–15.48), after which demands 'Down!' which leads to the mother's cleaning of her mouth and moving away the chair from the table, so that the child can get down—by herself.

7.6 The case of Sarah

7.6.1 Family background

Sarah was born as the second child of educated parents (mother's age 31, nurse by professional training, father's age 30 at the time of Sarah's birth, occupation—pediatrician). The mother's pregnancy was medically uneventual, and Sarah's condition immediately after delivery very good ($1/5$ minute Apgar ratings 9 and 9). Her health from birth until the beginning of the participation in this study had been generally good—the mother reported only occasions of jaundice on the fourth and fifth days of life, and otitis media at the sixth month. Sarah's older sister Emily was 2 years old when Sarah was born. The older sister was psychologically prepared for the birth of the sibling during the mother's pregnancy, and according to the mother's report she was 'excited initially and then began sharing in caring routine' after Sarah was born. In the first 6 weeks of life Sarah was sleeping in her parents' bedroom, after which she began to share the older sister's bedroom. At the beginning of the study Sarah was still nursing, although the mother reported that she had just started her on solid foods.

Sarah's actions in the home environment were videotaped seven times. The first videotaping session (at child's age 6:07) did not include any episodes of feeding. The data reported in this section are derived from the remaining six sessions that occurred at the following ages: (2) 8:01, (3) 12:11, (4) 14:26, (5) 17:02, (6) 19:02, and (7) 21:28. After the seventh videotaping session the following of Sarah's development was ended because of the family's relocation from the area.

7.6.2 The time distribution of food-contact activities

As for the previously presented two longitudinal cases, the quantitative information relating to the child's time spent in different versions of contact with food in summarized in a table format (see Table 7.3).

Similarly to the other two cases, longitudinal observations at Sarah's mealtime reveal a pattern of change from mother-controlled feeding, and child-controlled feeding without the use of utensils, to the child's feeding herself independently with a utensil, sometimes reverting back to the use of fingers and hands. Like in the other cases, the time spent in mother–child joint

Table 7.3. Developmental changes in mealtime food-contact time allocations between different child-centered actions (case: Sarah).

| Action category | Observed mealtimes at child's ages: | | | | | | | | | | | |
| | 8:01 | | 12:11 | | 14:26 | | 17:02 | | 19:02 | | 21:28 | |
	f	%	f	%	f	%	f	%	f	%	f	%
M spoon feeds CH	150	27.3	—	—	—	—	—	—	—	—	—	—
M nurses CH	163	29.6	—	—	—	—	—	—	—	—	—	—
CH finger feeds	—	—	48	23.4	43	12.4	53	19.9	255	36.4	39	9.3
CH drinks (open cup)	—	—	—	—	97	28.0	94	35.2	69	9.8	49	11.7
CH fork feeds	—	—	3	1.5	—	—	85	31.8	191	27.3	—	—
CH spoon feeds	—	—	—	—	57	16.4	—	—	—	—	185	44.0
CH plays with food or utensils	237	43.1	121	59.0	138	39.8	28	10.5	160	22.9	131	31.2
M-CH joint action on food and utensil	—	—	33	16.1	12	3.4	7	2.6	25	3.6	16	3.8
TOTAL	550		205		347		267		700		420	

M = mother; CH = child; f = frequency of 1-second time units action upon feeding with a utensil (fork, spoon, or cup) occurs infrequently in general. The frequency of joint action can be seen to decline after the control over utensils is delegated to the child. Differently from the other presented cases, Sarah's mother was observed to nurse her at the earliest age (8:01) when Sarah's mealtime was videotaped. On the child's side, the fluctuations over time in the percentages of time spent in different food-contact actions reveal the relevance of situational specificity of the time allocation. When a spoon was made available (at 14:26 and 21:28), it was used in conjunction with finger feeding. Likewise, when the meal included a fork to be used (12:11, 17:02, and 19:02), that utensil was used in conjunction with finger feeding. Remembering that the form of forks given to toddlers makes them functionally similar to spoons, the motor skills used by the child while using either of those utensils can be observed to demonstrate similarity. However, what remains to be stressed in respect to the quantitative overview of the time allocation at mealtimes is the co-presence of utensil-mediated and utensil-non-mediated feeding actions, together with a substantial amount of time spent on manipulation of the food, the utensil, or both of those.

7.6.3 Changes in the mealtime setting and the development of utensil use

The longitudinal observation of Sarah's mealtimes revealed a general developmental pattern similar to that observed in the other two cases. However, the practical arrangements of Sarah's mealtimes excluded the usual framing device used in other families—during the videotaped observations Sarah was not observed to be put into the high-chair (although the interview with the mother revealed that they sometimes do use the high-chair—on those occasions when the family is having dinner together and they want to include Sarah). The rare use of high-chair, however, was supplemented by active use of other furniture or human child-restraining devices. Thus, the setting at session 2 (at 8:01) was organized by the mother's holding of the child on her lap, while spoon feeding was performed. During sessions 3 (age 12:11) and 4 (14:26) the child was observed sitting in a small wooden chair (with arm restraints) that was drawn close to the low table. This organization of the setting is functionally very similar to the high-chair. During the remaining three sessions the child was observed to sit on a plastic chair (with no arm supports) at a plastic round children's table. This arrangement made it possible for the child to move out, and back into, the chair without the help of the others. As will be evident from the description of the child's actions that follows, Sarah made use of that freedom of action repeatedly during the mealtimes.

7.6.4 The description of actions at mealtime

Session 2 took place in the morning, beginning at 9 o'clock, when Sarah was 8:01, and involves the mother's feeding yoghurt to the child who is sitting on the left side of mother's lap, being constrained by the mother's left arm. The first two minutes of the mealtime (from 0.00 to 2.09) are filled by mother's spoon feeding the child, and adjusting the child. The mother is talking with the investigator about Sarah's behavior. The child is not observed to try to catch the spoon.

At 2.09, the first observed episode of the transfer of the spoon from mother to the child is observed. The mother puts a plastic spoon (which she had been using for the feeding) into the child's left hand. The child transports the spoon's handle to her mouth, sucks the handle, then takes the handle out of her mouth, manipulates the spoon bimanually. She then puts the spoon into her right hand, and mouthes the bowl part of the spoon, takes the spoon out of her mouth, manipulates it, mouthes the bowl part again. She then arches her back while the mother is adjusting ther shoes, fusses; mother wipes child's mouth with a cloth.

This episode is following by the mother carrying the child to the kitchen (on her arm), washing an apple, and returning to the table. When the child is again sitting on the mother's lap at the table, the apple is given to her to mouthe upon. At 4.39–4.49 the mother attempts to resume spoon-feeding, but the child holds the apple in such a way that it blocks the approach of the spoon. The mother abandons spoon feeding attempts, and the child's mouthing of the apple continues, until at 5.15 the apple gets loose from the child's hands and falls onto the floow. Between 5.15 and 5.31 the mother responds to the situation—she holds the child under her left arm, stands up and takes the fallen apple from the floor, carries it to kitchen, washes it, returns to the table and gives the apple back to the child. The child continues to mouthe the apple. However, now the mother's right hand supports the apple, preventing it from falling.

At 6.20 the mother takes the apple away from the child and puts it on the table. The child fusses. Mother resumes spoon feeding. By the end of the period (at 6.54) the child refuses to get another spoonful. The mother responds by returning the apple to the child. The child holds and mouthes it, while the mother assists with her right hand. Finally the child releases the apple, the mother holds it and tries to get the child to take more of it, which the child does not.

The session then proceeds into non-meal activity (at 7.42 the mother puts the child down onto floor). After the child fusses and does not take interest in objects promoted by the mother, she is picked up again (at 8.12) and set to nurse (at 8.33). The nursing (at the table) lasts until 11.16. It is followed by another episode with the apple involved. The mother removes the child from the breast, holds her on her arm, prepares food with the other hand.

At 11.41 sits down at table, still holding the child on her arm. The child reaches out for the apple that is on the table, at 12.23 gets hold of it, but it drops onto the floor. Mother retrieves it from the floor and offers to child, who continues to handle the apple and mouthe it, while the mother's right hand supports the apple. The meal ends at 12.29.

The data reported here are particularly interesting from the perspective of the beginning of the socialization of the child for accepting the adults' cultural meaning of 'dirty'. The two episodes in which the apple is dropped to the floor—at 5.15 to 5.31, and at 12.23 to 12.29—with the subsequent varied action by the mother are relevant in this case. In the first instance, the mother changes the whole situation (i.e. carrying the child to the kitchen sink while she is washing the fallen apple) in order to resume the previous activity state of the child (mouthing the apple). Note that the mother's hand after the fall of the apple is used to protect the apple from falling again. In the second episode, the mother is inconsistent with the first episode in her action—no washing 'ritual' is organized when the apple falls again. Nevertheless, the mother proceeds to use her right hand to prevent further drop of the apple.

The third videotaped meal session took place when Sarah was 12:11. The mealtime lasted for 4 minutes 40 seconds, and was videotaped during the midday. The child is sitting at a low table in a chair (which is moved to the table so that she can't fall—practically a substitute of high-chair). Food is located in front of the child on a plate (special 'warming'-plate, with three sections). The child holds a fork in her right hand, while she finger feeds herself banana pieces by the left. The older sister is sitting in a similar chair at the same low table, facing Sarah.

At 0.35, the mother adds some banana pieces onto plate. The child uses fork in her right hand to mash them in the plate. At 0.51 the fork is transferred from the right to the left hand, and the child continues to manipulate food by her right hand. Thus far, the child's feeding process has been that of self-feeding. However, the situation changes into an episode of mother–child joint action. During the period 1.12–1.39 the mother intervenes, puts fork into child's right hand, and helps the child's hand with fork to get food onto it. The mother then leaves it up to the child to finish the transport of food to mouth. However, the child continues to manipulate food with the fork. The mother intervenes again, guiding the child's hand with fork to get some food and guides the hand + fork to child's mouth. Following the success, the child is left to her own resources again, and continues to manipulate food on plate with fork. The mother intervenes again to help the child to get food onto the fork, leaving it to her to finish food transport—she, however, does not use the fork, switching to finger feeding with left hand while holding food on fork in her right hand up in the air above the level of her right ear.

This episode of mother–child joint action about the use of the fork in feeding is interesting as an example of mother's promotion of the fork use (by setting up a ZPA) that persists over the period of the episode. In this episode, the joint action occurs three times in a row—as the first 'help' by the mother (reducing the child's freedom of movement with hand to using fork) is not followed by the child's independent completion of the food-transport task, the mother intervenes again *and guides the child's hand with fork to the mouth*. In the present terminology, the mother decreased the ZFM in the context of the child's action of food transport by eliminating alternative actions other than straight food-to-mouth transfer by her guiding of the child's action. However, immediately after that the ZFM boundaries are rearranged again towards leaving greater degrees of freedom to the child's action—in the third joint action occasion described in this episode the mother again only helped the child to get food onto the fork, leaving it up to the child to finish the action. Despite the fact that the child did not proceed along the expected way (and reverted to finger feeding with her left hand while holding the fork up in the air by the right), the mother did not intervene another time.

The meal continues with the child's individual actions—she finger feeds, then manipulates food with fork, finger feeds again. Following an episode of the child's banging on the table with the fork, a brief (from 2.24 to 2.27) effort by the mother to guide the child to use the fork is then recorded again: she takes child's right hand (which already is holding the fork) and guides it back to the plate towards food, releasing it there. The child continues to manipulate food on plate using both the right hand with fork and the left hand. Finger feeding is resumed by the child, and then she manipulates food on the plate with the fork.

At 3.15 the child tries to slide her body down under the table. The mother comes and adjusts her back into a sitting position on the chair. The mother talks to the older child, while the child slides herself again under the table. The mother takes her from the chair, sets her to stand on floor, asks 'Are you all done?', 'All done?' (sets the plate on table further away from the edge of the table). The child moves towards the table looking at the plate, grabs it with her left hand by edge, the mother sets the child back onto the chair in sitting position, brings the plate closer, and assists the child's right hand with fork to get some food. The child's hand is then released. She goes on to manipulate food on the plate with fork held in right hand. At the brief period of 3.53 to 3.56, the child is observed to transport fork with some food to mouth on her own, with the right hand.

The end of the meal period is initiated by the child. At 3.56 she starts to slide down under the table. The mother comes and sets her to stand on the floor, removing chair further from the table. The child goes back to the chair and climbs up on it, while the older sister comes over to the chair and assists her. The childs stands briefly up on the chair, looking at the plate on the table. The table is moved away from the chair (at 4.40)—which serves as the actual event that marks the end of the meal. The child turns around and starts climbing down from the chair, with mother's assistance.

The theoretically most interesting aspect of the observed actions at session 3 was the episodic organization of the mother–child joint action. It was only occasionally that the mother intervened to promote the use of the fork, and to assist the child in fork use by jointly performing a subpart of the action. It is clear that the child *can* accomplish the food transport with a fork at this age (as is evidenced by the single self-feeding instance with the fork at 3.53–3.56). It is equally clear that the mother is trying to promote the use of the fork more often than the child actually ends up using it. However, the mother's fork-promotion efforts were triggered under some specific conditions that occurred in the feeding situation. These conditions included the child's manipulation of food by fork (before the first joint-action episode that started at 1.12), beating on the table with the fork (before the second episode), and child's general body-position readjustment in the chair. Following these diversions from the feeding activity that were wrought by the child's actions, the mother tried to guide the child towards the use of the fork in the context of her self-feeding action. However, the mother's guidance was not persistent in two of the three episodes, and in the third case she quitted her instruction efforts after three repetitions of the joint-action sequences with the fork.

The episodic nature of parent–child joint action that serves the promotion of new cultural motor (or cognitive) skills may be a general characteristic of child socialization processes in any culture. There is no time-urgency involved in parent's efforts to get their children to master new skills excessively quickly. Instead, the parents may only episodically, on some (but not many) occasions, direct their children's actions towards the desired end results. Time and cultural organization of the children's environments make such episodic guidance efforts functional, since the development of utensil use while eating is redundantly organized. If the parents do not guide their child to the use of the spoon or fork, but provide an example of the utensil use in their own everyday actions at mealtimes, the child will eventually be canalized into the use of these implements anyway.

The next videotaped meal session (4) took place at a lunchtime when Sarah was 14:26. Like in the previous session, the child was sitting at a small table on a small chair, holding a spoon in her left hand. The same 'warming-plate' that was seen in the previous time is in front of the child on the table. From the very beginning of the meal, the child is observed to spoon feed herself. The mother occasionally adjusts the plate (to bring it closer to the child on the table) and says 'M-mm' when child's food transpofrt to mouth succeeds. After the initial 39 seconds of the mealtime, the child proceeds to manipulate the food on the plate with spoon in left hand. She then drops the spoon on the plate and proceeds to finger feed with her left hand. During 0.47 to 1.01 the mother takes the spoon and rearranges the food on the plate. This is followed by a promotion effort. The mother takes the child's left hand, saying 'Here . . . ,' and puts the spoon in her left hand, releasing the hand then. The child proceeds to manipulate food on plate with spoon for 7 seconds, after which she resumes spoon feeding herself for 6 seconds. This is followed by unhurried eating efforts—the child sits with the spoon in her left hand, watching around. She then tries to get food from the corner of the plate with the spoon, no success, switches to getting it with fingers of her right hand, succeeds, and then transports the piece of food to her mouth with her right hand. The mother re-enters the situation, adjusts the plate, while the child drops spoon in plate.

At 1.56 a drinking episode starts (which lasts until 3.18). The child reaches out for the cup (no lid, standing on the left side—from child's perspective—of the plate). The mother puts out her hand to safeguard the cup on its way to the child's mouth, then withdraws hand. Child handles the cup by the left hand, holding it by the rim, then utilizes bimanual grip to drink. Drinks.

Following the drinking episode, the mother adjusts the plate, then puts the spoon in the child's right hand. After that the child spoon feeds herself, and the mother vocalizes 'M-mm!' after each successful food-transport action. The child tries to get food on the spoon, then loses some that falls onto the table. The child picks it up with left-hand fingers and takes to mouth. The meal proceeds by food manipulation by the child with spoon, mother's adjusting of the cup and plate, child's independent drinking and playing with cup.

At 5.09 an interesting encounter between the mother and the child begins. The child takes a piece of food from the plate with her left hand and puts it into her mouth. She then takes another piece from the plate and drops it into the cup. The mother immediately interferes saying 'No!' and moving cup further away on the table from the child, after rescuing the piece of food from the cup. The child draws the cup closer by hand, and looks for the piece of food in it. She then takes the spoon from the plate by left hand, looks at it, holds it up in air, and drops it—it falls onto the floor. Child looks after it, mother picks it up and puts it back onto the plate, turning the plate so that spoon's handle is close to child.

During the time 5.39 to 6.10, the child grabs the spoon and bangs with it on plate, then takes a piece of food from plate by left hand and puts it into mouth, continues banging on plate with spoon in right hand, moves on to bang on table. The mother intervenes when banging is extended to the table and redirects child's hand-with-spoon back to plate. The child continues to bang with spoon on plate, then again on table. Finally abandons spoon onto plate, and finger feeds. At 6.20 she turns to her left side and looks down over the side of the chair, sliding (climbing) down from the chair. The mother moves in to safeguard, then picks her up and sets her down to stand on the floor. The child walks away to the living room, and the meal is over.

The description of the session 4 reveals that by this time the child has become of the habit of using the implement (this time—spoon) on her own. The mother's efforts to promote the child's actions have also been transformed. Whereas some episodes similar in structure to those in session 3 (e.g. putting the utensil into the child's hand) could be observed, no longer was there any recurrency of these efforts, nor active help to the child in getting food onto the utensil, observed. It is quite reasonable to expect that this feature of no-help in action depends strongly upon conditions (e.g. nature of food, child's activity level, the utensil used), so generalizations about absolute change of maternal guidance strategies may be unwarranted here.

Session 5 took place at morning breakfast time when Sarah was 17:02. She is sitting at a little children's table made of plastic. This is a new table that has not been seen before (was purchased only recently). More importantly, she also is sitting on a new plastic children's chair. This chair has no armrests and therefore does not constrain the child to stay at the table, but allows getting down/up easily. The food is in the warming-plate in front of the child on the table. She manipulates food on plate with fork (in right hand), and with the left hand.

The observation of session 5 is interesting in the sense of actions relating to the event of dropping food onto the floor. The first episode of that kind takes place at 0.22–0.44. Apparently some food has fallen onto the floor, so the child looks down and slides down from the chair to stand. The mother comes to her, picks up the food *and puts it back onto the plate*.

The second episode of a similar kind follows suit. Between 0.44 and 1.10 the child picks food onto fork (in her right hand), and starts to transport it towards her mouth. The mouth opens in expectation of getting the food. The food, however, falls from the fork onto the floor. The child slides herself down onto the floor, picks up the food from the floor by her left hand, and puts it into her mouth. (The older sister comments: 'Yucky.') The child returns to sit in the chair. The mother did not intervene in this episode.

The child continues to sit, manipulate food with fork, fork feed, and look around. The third episode involving the food dropped onto the floor begins at 1.43. The child slides herself down from the chair to stand on the floor. Picks up some food from the floor with her left hand, puts it into her mouth. (At the same time the mther passes by to bring a cup to the older sister at the table and puts it on table.) The child looks at the mother, runs away from the table and ends up sitting on the floor at the refrigerator (about 2 m from the table). Gets up, runs back to the table: mother helps her to sit down on the chair, sets a plastic cup (no handle, no lid) on the left from the plate (child's perspective), saing 'Here we go'. The child drinks from cup, using bimanual hold. Puts cup back on table where it was. Plays with cup on table.

The period from 2.51 to 4.16 included child's feeding herself with fork, finger feeding, food manipulation, and banging on the plate with her right hand. The fourth episode of handling the food dropped onto the floor emerges from the child's self-feeding efforts and is characterized by the following course of events:

> 4.16–4.36—The child takes food by fingers of right hand, manipulates food in hand, transports part of it to the mouth. Some food remains in hand when it is withdrawn from the mouth, gets loose and falls onto floor.
> 4.36–5.38—The child looks down at the fallen food. Slides down from chair, and while standing starts to push the fallen food with her foot, looking in the direction of the mother. Mother: 'What are you doing there?' The child keeps pushing food on floor. The mother intervenes, saying 'Aeh-aeh! Pick it up and put in the garbage, O.K.!' Child picks the food up. Mother: 'Put in the garbage.' The child turns to the table and tries to put the picked-up food onto the plate. Mother intervenes: 'No, aah-aah! Nn-nh!', picks the pieces that the child had put back onto plate up again and puts them into child's right hand, directing child towards the garbage can. Child toddles over to the garbage can, opens it, throws the food into the can, and lets the garbage can cover fall down to close the can. Then opens the cover again, and begins to take something out from it (5.20). The mother intervenes, saying 'Yakky', taking the objects/ substance from child's hands and throwing it back into the can. At 5.27 picks up the child and takes her to the kitchen sink, where she washes the child's hands. Then puts the child back onto the floor.

This episode is followed by the child returning to the door, resuming self-feeding and drinking, looking around. Another episode involving the garbage can follows beginning at 7.28 (which is the actual end point of the meal). The child sits idle, then slides herself onto the floor and toddles to the garbage can (at 7.39). Opens the cover, looks inside, grasps something (which turns out to be a big piece of cardboard inside, takes it out. Mother shouts: 'Sarah!', rushes to the child, takes the object from her hands and throws it back into the can, saying 'No!'. The mother closes the lid, takes the child, goes to the kitchen sink and washes her hands there, then puts the child down.

The four episodes observed in this session that involves the child's handling of food that had fallen onto the floor constitute an interesting case that allows us to trace the process of canalization of the child's actions with food in conjunction with the cultural meaning of 'dirty'. A certain variability in the mother's actions in the four episodes is evident. In the first episode, the mother herself returned the fallen piece of food onto the child's plate. In the second episode, the child picked up the food and put it into her mouth. This recurs during the third episode, during which the mother also does not intervene. Finally, it is only during the fourth episode that the handling of the food from the floor as edible is moved beyond the ZFM boundary. The child—similarly to how the mother acted in the first episode: tried to return the piece of food that she had picked up to the plate. However, the mother had already cognitively restructured the ZFM in the situation (evident in the verbal direction given to the child to take the piece to the garbage). Thus, an action that previously had been within ZFM (returning food onto the plate, and/or eating it) was now outside the ZFM, while the mother set up the ZPA for getting the child to throw the food into the garbage. The child indeed acts as the mother wants her to—by going over to the garbage can and putting the piece of food in it. However, this action is followed by a separate action *concerning garbage*—the child opens the can again and starts to manipulate its content. The mother intervenes, and at the end of *both* of the episodes involving garbage the child is taken to the kitchen sink for washing her hands.

It is interesting to note the episodic nature of the mother's structuring of the situations where food is picked up from the floor. At times the child can experience no change (the food is still edible after being on the floor), but at other times she is subjected to active and extensive coding of the cultural meaning of 'dirty' in a similar context. Paradoxically it is the *child* in episode 4 who behaves in a consistent manner (by trying to put the food back onto the plate—like she could observe the mother doing during episode 1!). In the given observational context this is not surprising—the mother's task of taking care of two children, doing things in the kitchen, and interacting with the investigator make it only very natural that her observations of the child do not include all the occasions when some food falls onto the floor and the child picks it up. In contrast, the child in the meal setting is in a position to have a fuller observational experience of these situations. From the child's perspective, the mother's non-interference in some, and active interference in other cases, create the demand of decision making under conditions of uncertainty.

Videotaping of Sarah's mealtime at session 6 took place at the child's age of 19:02 and included a midday meal. Sarah was observed sitting at the same plastic children's table as during session 5. An ordinary (adult) plate with food is in front of the child on the table. The mother says: 'Here's your fork' and puts it into the child's right hand. The child proceeds by sucking her fingers, holding the fork up in the air with the right hand, looking at the camera. At 0.36 tries to manipulate food on plate with fingers of the left hand, holding the fork up in the air with her right. Mother: 'Can you use your fork? Use your fork, please!' The child looks in the direction of the mother and continues to manipulate food on plate with her left hand. Then proceeds to finger feed with the left hand, while holding the fork in her right hand in the air. Reaches back with left hand for more food. Mother comes close, points to the fork in the child's right hand, says: 'Use the fork, please!' Mother guides the child's right hand + fork to get some food onto the fork, then releases the child's hand. The child proceeds to use the fork in the right hand to transport food to the mouth. Then sits, idle. Continues intermittent finger feeding of pieces of cheese and meatballs for the next 2 minutes (1.20–3.21).

The next joint-action episode takes place at 3.21–3.31. The child picks up a meatball by her left hand, looks in the direction of the mother. The mother comes and takes hold of the child's right hand (which holds the fork). She guides child's left and right hands so that the fork in the right hand enters the meatball in the child's left hand. The mother then guides the child's right hand with fork + meatball to child's mouth. The meatball is swallowed by the child. The mother guides child's right hand-with-fork back to the plate. This is followed (during 3.31–4.30) by child's independent actions. She picks up food with fork (in her right hand), transports half-way to mouth, keeps fork up in air, then proceeds to mouth + swallow the food. Fork feeding is repeated, accompanied by looking in the direction of the mother. At 4.30 a brief episode of food-drop and retrieval is observed. A piece of food falls from child's fork onto floor. The mother comes, picks it up, and returns to the child's plate. The child uses the fork to feed herself.

An episode of drinking follows (at 4.42–5.15). The child puts the fork from right hand to left hand, reaches out in the direction of the mother with her right hand (towards her right). Vocalizes. Mother: 'Juice, please?' and gives a plastic open cup into the child's right hand. The child takes the cup, proceeds to drink from it unimanually (right hand). After drinking, stretches the right hand with cup towards the mother, who takes the cup.

An episode of complex motor action involving food and utensil follows immediately after the drinking episode (during 5.15 to 5.51). The child takes a meatball from the plate by her right hand, manipulates it. Then exchanges hands: the fork from the left hand is put into the right, and the meatball into the left. Holding the meatball steady in the left hand, tries to push the fork with the right to get it into the meatball (all this happens in the air, above the plate). Does not succeed, ends up transporting the meatball to mouth with her left hand, while holding the fork in her right hand up in the air. Mouthes the meatball but cannot be seen to bite it, takes it out of mouth with the left hand and resumes the effort by the right hand to get the fork into the meatball (held again up in air by the left, then the left hand is lowered to the table and gets support from it). In this way, succeeds in getting the fork into the meatball, and then transports it to the mouth with the fork + right hand. Mouthes the meatball-on-fork, bites, takes into mouth, removes fork from mouth.

The meal proceeds by the child's manipulation of the fork and food, looking around, feeding herself by hand, and by fork. At 8.55 takes a big piece of food onto fork with right hand, transports to mouth, and mouthes. Mother: 'You can use your fingers with that.' The child puts food from mouth back onto plate, uses left hand to get the piece off from fork on the plate. Mother: 'Here you go.' Child looks at mother. Mother: 'You can pick that up with your fingers.' Looks at the mother. Mother: 'Use your hand.' The child takes the piece again onto fork. Mother: 'You don't have to use fork for that.' The child transports the piece to mouth with fork and puts it *all* in mouth. The mother intervenes immediately, calling out 'Oh, oh! Here!' and takes the piece out from child's mouth. She then cuts it up on the child's plate. Then sets one small piece onto fork, puts it into child's hand, and releases hand + fork + food. The child proceeds to take an additional piece onto fork, transports towards mouth, but part of its falls down on its way. The child looks down while mouthing fork. The mother comes, picks up the fallen piece, puts it back onto plate. Child continues to mouthe the fork, then goes on to feed herself with the fork, manipulate food, looking around, and hitting the plate with the fork. This continues intermittently until 11.46 when the child gets down from the chair. The mother comes and wipes her hands and mouth. The child then gets the cup from the mother. Mother says: 'Use both hands!' while giving the cup to her. The child drinks while standing on the floor. The meal is over at 13.10.

The observations at session 6 are noteworthy in two respects. First, developmentally the transition of the mother's action promotion efforts from direct joint action with the child to distal communication to verbal means is nicely demonstrated. The mother was observed giving verbal suggestions from the distance, and intervening only when the child happened to act in a potentially dangerous way (putting an excessively big piece of food into the mouth). Secondly, the child (at 5.15–5.51) displayed a sequence of complex motor actions of a synthetic kind, relating the utensil to the food under difficult problem-solving conditions that required precise dosage of force applied bimanually on the fork and the food.

The last session (7) when Sarah was videotaped during a mealtime took place at her age of 21:28 and involved a morning meal. The child is again at the small plastic table (as in sessions 5 and 6); in front of her is a big soup plate (with cereal), spoon in plate (ready for right-hand grasp). The child holds a blanket by both hands, and pulls it up to cover her lap.

At 0.08 the child takes spoon by right hand, while the mother assists by drawing the plate closer to the child on the table. The child spoon feeds. Then proceeds to hold the spoon in right hand up in the air at shoulder level. Looks at camera and in the direction of mother, no action. Shen then proceeds with intermittent spoon feeding, finger feeding, looking around, mouthing her hand, and manipulating food on the plate.

At 4.00 an episode of food-drop begins. The child spoon feeds with right hand. Some cereal falls onto her shirt. The child abandons the spoon on plate, and raises her shirt with both hands, exposing breast region, vocalizes, looks around, mouthes left hand. The mother brings a napkin, gives it into child's right hand, adjusts food on plate with spoon, sets spoon onto plate. The child wipes table on both sides of the plate with the napkin (which is in right hand), while holding the left hand in mouth, then looks at camera. Stretches out right hand with napkin in the direction of mother. The mother comes, takes the napkin, wipes child's face, child coughs, looks at her left hand, gives it to mother who wipes it, examines it after wiping. Mother proceeds to wipe child's lap, while the child watches. The episode is over by 6.00, when the child grabs the spoon by right hand, spoon feeds, older sister sings, child looks around holding spoon in mid-air. This is followed by sitting (holding spoon in mid-air with the right hand), looking around, spoon feeding, mouthing the spoon, stirring in plate with the spoon.

At 8.26 she has difficulty getting more food onto the spoon. Proceeds to abandon the spoon on table on the right side, uses both hands to lift the plate to the mouth and drink. Puts plate back on table. Then mouthes both hands, and at 9.00 resumes spoon feeding.

Another episode relating to cleaning starts at 9.24. The mother comes and wipes the child's mouth with a napkin. The child looks in mother's direction, stretches out right hand with spoon, vocalizes. Mother takes the spoon, puts it into plate, and hands a napkin into child's right hand. The child wipes mouth herself, then abandons napkin on the table, and proceeds to drink (getting the cup from the mother at 9.58).

The child's actions at the table come to a close at 10.25. She gets down, holding cup in right hand, and drags the blanket along with left hand. Walks over to kitchen oven. Stands in front of the mother, who wipes her mouth/ face. The meal is over at 10.52.

7.7 Conclusions: the longitudinal analysis of individual children's actions at mealtimes

The three longitudinal cases analyzed in this chapter revealed quite clearly both the general direction in the development of independent self-feeding (shared in all of the cases), and the idiosyncratic particular joint-action forms that were observed at different mealtimes and that changed over time. The quantitative analyses of the time that each of the three children spent in contact with food revealed a fact that at the first instance may seem paradoxical—the adult–child joint action in meal settings that is related to the children's learning of the use of culture-given utensils *is a remarkably rare phenomenon during everyday meals*, at least in the cases described. Nevertheless, the same impression also emerges from other cases (not reported here) of contemporary American children of middle-class backgrounds. However, the quantitative time distribution data are illusionary in a very informative way—demonstrating again the notion that was well understood by Lewin (1931)—*it may be the rare (rather than frequent) structured psychological phenomena that are of decisive relevance for children's development.* During mealtimes at any age (e.g. see Newson and Newson, 1968) the children's ZFM may include the use of hands and fingers which are perfectly sufficient for transporting food to mouth. The extension of the hand by attaching to it a utensil provided by the culture is part of the socialization of children that is redundantly guaranteed by the universal use of these utensils in the society. As a result, the task of canalizing children towards utensil use takes the form of *episodic direction* of the child's action by an adult (or older sibling), rather than that of an intensive instruction session. The conditions for triggering the adults' episodic acting in the ZPA of utensil use can be highly variable, relating both to the child's action at the time (e.g. a child banging on the tray with spoon, followed by mother's redirection of hand + spoon to food on plate) and to the adult's goals and time resources (e.g. a mother in a hurry in the morning has simply no time to promote spoon use to her toddler and knows well indeed that the child can learn to use the spoon if given time). This episodic nature of canalization of child development in real-life settings may seem to lead to inconsistency in parental child-oriented actions and is definitely different from the picture of children's learning process that is presented by the majority of learning theorists. These theorists, however, may have been looking at the phenomena as those are reduced to their elements. They have tried to find explanations for children's development in particular and frequently occurring behavior-reinforcement adjacencies in which the structured and culturally meaningful nature of the contexts in which behavior occurs have been overlooked. In contrast, cultural canalization of child development may be adequately described by a sequence of variable and largely non-repetitive events that take place in the child's life and which provide impetus for further individual action of the child within the culturally set constraints that make up the structure of the settings. That is how rare but subjectively important events in humans' lives may have longer-term impact upon their future lives, whereas the majority of high frequency recurrent behaviors or life events become automatic and lose their canalizing relevance for a person's development.

7.8 Summary

The present chapter provided the link of the theoretical system outlined in previous chapters with one particular example of empirical investigation—a longitudinal study of infants' and toddlers' action development in their everyday meal situations. Meal situations are a good example of settings that are socially organized so as to attain both immediate (e.g. getting the child fed) and longer-term goals (e.g. canalizing the child towards culturally appropriate ways of acting with food and utensils used to keep or transport the food).

The empirical longitudinal case observations of the mealtime situation give evidence for the gradual transition from fully parent-controlled feeding (the most extreme example of that would be the parent's spoon feeding of the infant thrugh the whole meal) to fully child-controlled actions with the relevant utensils for feeding. The general control of the mealtime organization remains with the parent—she decides what food is given, when, in conjunction with what utensils, and how the child's demands are to be reacted to. The children's actions—which sometimes leave the impression of being unconstrained—remain independently dependent (see 4.1.3) upon the structure of the setting that the parent has constructed in accordance with the parental goals and cultural knowledge. Parental active participation in canalization of children's actions in a structured setting like mealtime is often a rare occasion that emerges when necessary—that is, at times when the child may cross a Zone of Free Movement boundary or try to renegotiate it, or when the parent sets herself the goal of promoting a particular new action to the child (Zone of Promoted Action). As was evident from the longitudinal description of the mealtimes in individual cases, the particular forms of parent–child–environment relationships can be highly variable dependent upon the circumstances, whereas the general process by which the parents regulate child–environment relationships and canalize their future development in some (again—variable in their particulars) directions is built along similar lines. The empirical analyses presented in chapter 7 provide one (but not the only) possible way in which the relatively abstract ideas of cultural-historical thinking in psychology can be transposed from the level of theory to the domain of direct empirical work at deriving meaningful data from the richness and fluidity of phenomenology of child development.

CHAPTER 8

Conclusions: cultural constraining of children's developing action structures

The elegance of child development is in its complex organization which is so closely intertwined with the cultural environment that it easily remains unaffected by the occasional fads in education and child psychology. It is that robust reality of child–environment relationships that guarantees sufficiently adequate socialization of children in the majority of cultures and at any historical period.

Furthermore, ideas *about* children's development have themselves emerged in cultural-historical contexts. Therefore, any theoretical explanation of children's development is a by-product of human cultural history. It is a constructed explanatory system—created by adults who have been curious about the children for one or another reason. Ideas that have enjoyed wide popularity among child psychologists and educators at different times have happened to match with the cultural background of adults in the first place. Only as a result of purposeful socialization of children under the guidance of adults do these ideas become transferred to those whom they are thought to represent—the children themselves. Children within a culture are socialized to become adults within that culture. If the science of psychology, including child psychology, is a differentiated part of the adults' culture, children are socialized to accept it as such. That socialization may involve both the conceptual (e.g. what kinds of ideas 'make sense' when used as explanations in psychology) and applied aspects. In the latter case, former children are socialized towards asking child psychologists certain kinds of questions, and refraining from expecting answers to other questions from these specialists.

Undoubtedly there exist vastly different ways in which child psychologists

226

have become part of their cultures in different areas of the world. In some, child psychologists may enjoy the status of 'experts' in the eyes of parents who may turn to them for advice in many cases—often to find out that their questions have no simple answers. In others, psychologists may be in the process of establishing their 'expert' role in fierce competition with the knowhow of folk psychology of children that is available to parents through the mothers' social networks and the availability of folk remedies and curers. Whatever is the status of child psychology in a particular society at the time, child psychologists are involved in the complicated societal discourse about their own role in the culture. Quite often, psychologists' thinking is carried away by that (undoubtedly important) participation in such discourse, and the more fundamental scientific foundations of their views of child development are not analyzed in sufficient depth by them.

It was the goal of this author, pursued all through this book, to make available to the interested reader an analysis of the process of child development that recognizes the inevitable dependence of that process on the one hand, and is general enough to transcend the limits of any particular culture of the other. This goal made it necessary to address issues at different levels of generality, ranging from the most abstract (philosophical) axioms (labeled 'basic assumptions' in this book) to a detailed presentation of empirical observations from a very limited action context (children's mealtimes) and age range (toddlerhood) in a cultural context (that of the contemporary middle class in the United States of America) which is highly atypical as compared with the majority of cultures around the world.

8.1 Context-bound nature of psychological explanations

The first conclusion from the ideas expressed in the book is relevant for the conceptual-methodological side of psychological thinking. Every step in the scientific analysis of developmental phenomena in psychology involves the inevitable and necessary consideration of all mutually related levels of inquiry, from the phenomena studied to the most abstract theoretical ideas and their cultural backgrounds ('basic assumptions'), and back to the construction of empirical and formal-mathematical tools that are applied in the process of psychological research. This conclusions, of course, has relevance well beyond the boundaries of developmental psychology in particular and perhaps psychology in general. It is applicable in any area of science that at a certain point is felt to be in a 'crisis' because it has either lost contact with the reality of the phenomena which is studies, or has become excessively devoted to the empirical manipulation of that reality so that the general epistemological function of the science is lost. As must be evident to the reader who labored through the pages of this monograph, developmental psychology can be considered to suffer from both of these problems. Its research traditions over the recent decades have facilitated the increasing disinterest in the real-life (and complex) phenomena of child development. When these phenomena are mentioned in the scientific researcy literature, the contemporary authors may feel obligated to include an assurance in the text that this mentioning of 'anecdotal evidence' is not considered by them to be 'scientifically valid' datum. In conjunction with such apologies for occasional 'softness' in breaking away from the standards of 'hard' science as applied to psychological phenomena, researchers work hard to make inferences of relevance to some real-world issues from quantified data of various kinds. The latter need no longer adequately represent the psychological phenomena from which they were derived. However, the mismatch between the data and the phenomena they are claimed to represent is usually not noticed. At the same time, the questions of handling the data are given excessive attention by the researchers.

Such a situation, if it occurs in any science, 'hard' or 'soft' alike, can be dangerous to its actual progress. First, the loss of contact with the reality of phenomena makes it possible to elevate a certain constructed entity into the status of criterion of the truthfulness of research. This can happen in the realm of abstract theories. For instance, in some cases a particular theory of a certain influential psychologist may be considered to be 'the true one' on the grounds of its notable influence, popularity among psychologists (= consensual validation), intuitive acceptability by laypersons, or for any other reason that excludes the psychological phenomena themselves as at least part of the criterion. Likewise, a certain method of study, or of data analysis, may be endowed with the status of 'objectivity' in the research process, and thus expected to result in 'truth' with greater ease.

In both cases, the given science can easily become an exercise in loyalty to one or another implicitly accepted belief, rather than a process whereby new knowledge is created. Such a change can easily be hidden behind a consensus among the members of the scientific community that differentiates 'right' from 'wrong' ways of thinking in science on some abstract-evaluative basis, rather than in conjunction with the object of investigation.

In the behavioral sciences, it has been the voiced concern of ethologically minded investigators that over the past decades have called for investigators' greater familiarity with the phenomenology they claim that they study. However, mere intimate contact with such phenomenology is not sufficient in itself. It should alert the psychologist to the way in which the phenomenon seems to be organized. That can subsequently lead to research using hypotheses that are adequate for the phenomena, rather than taken from the investigator's socialized common sense on some *ad hoc* basis. A scrutiny of the psychologist's thinking at different levels of abstraction is necesary to grant the consistency of the scientific thought and avoid eclectic thinking in the theoretical side of psychological investigations.

8.2 Developmental psychology and the conceptualization of processes of development

Despite the frequent use of the label 'developmental psychology' in contemporary literature on child psychology, little explicit interest in the theoretical analysis of development as a process seems to be widespread in contemporary psychology. The earlier theoretical efforts to analyze development as process—by James Mark Baldwin, Jean Piaget, Lev Vygotsky, Mikhail Basov, Heinz Werner, and others—have either been largely forgotten, or transformed into an interest in the outcomes of development.

The reason why such loss of interest in the process of development has pervaded stems from the application of non-developmental data-derivation techniques to developmental phenomena. This has become an established practice in child psychology. As a result, it is the domain of developmental psychology, first and foremost, where Wittgenstein's observation of 'the problems and methods passing one another by' is especially true as a description of the contemporary affairs in that discipline. The habitual use of theterm 'the scientific method' in child psychology in the sense of the Baconian ideology (rather than the systems approach of natural philosophies) has led psychologists either to avoid asking (and thus, answering) developmental questions in child psychology; or, in case some developmental questions are asked, they are answered in ways that do not represent the developmental phenomena in the area of empirical data derivation and analysis.

8.3 Development as a structurally organized process with inherent unpredictability

Starting from the state of affairs in contemporary developmental psychology in which issues of development are rarely addressed (see also Benigni and Valsiner, 1985), a theoretical system that helps to explicate the organization of child socialization processes was proposed. That system is explicitly directed towards *the study of the process of development* (see 1.1) rather than its outcomes. The process of child development is embedded within the structurally organized environment which is interconnected with the system of *cultural meanings* of the society a child is born into, and whose member the child eventually becomes. Furthermore, the culturally structured environment of a developing child is also *dynamic*. It undergoes constant changes, only some of which are produced by the child's own acting upon it. The environment can be changed by the actions of the other people among whom the child develops. In this respect, purposeful actions by parents, older siblings, or teachers organize many sides of a child's environment in order to attain *their* goals in respect to the child's development. The environment may also change due to the actions of social groups in a given society which the particular child and his immediate social network have minimal or no influence upon. For example, a war between rival political groupings in a country restructures the whole environment of families (and developing children within those families) in drastic ways. From those conditions, there is often no way out other than adaptation to the circumstances with as little loss as possible. Finally, all the environment of human beings is vulnerable to changes that nobody can directly control once they happen, or can even prevent from happening (e.g. natural disasters).

All these four major kinds of environmental change create a situation where the environmental dynamics are unpredictable in principle already to their own nature. The process of child development that takes place under such conditions has to cope with such environmental uncertainty in ways that guarantee a satisfactory result of the process. This can be possible under conditions of high flexibility in the ways in which the developing child interacts with his environment. Also, the developing psychological processes of the child are to be buffered against occasionally excessive fluctuations in the environmental conditions. Such buffering can be achieved by the child's active role in his relations with the environment. The environment does not have a direct and long-lasting 'molding' effect on the child. Instead, the child's own activity determines which particular aspects of the environmental input become influential. This perspective is the core of Piaget's 'constructivist' perspective which has been widely known in psychology. However, its actual implications in the form of the study of the assimilation–accommodation system as a process has largely evaded further development and concretization in developmental psychology.

Developmental phenomena represent an open-systems process in which the exact predictability of outcomes is impossible, because these outcomes are constructed over time in the process of organism–environment transaction. However, thinking about the processes of development is usually oriented to the task of trying to predict future outcomes. Possibly that is the case for the very reason that the uncertainty of future development needs to be reduced at a given time at least in the thinker's mind—all the more on those occasions when it is the least realistic. At different times and across all cultural conditions in human history, fortune tellers, priests, and psychologists have been asked to reduce the uncertainties about the future by providing people with ways of thinking that help them to construct at least some (be it oftentimes illusionary) certainty about the relative stability of things, organisms, and persons.

The Western culture-based common sense has largely guided theoretical endeavors in child psychology, canalizing it in ways congenial with laypersons' ideologies. Laypersons may be asking developmental psychologists questions about the relative stability of the development of particular children in order to reduce the excessive uncertainty that is hidden in the future. These questions are regularly answered as part of applied (and necessary) social-cognitive support to the laypersons in their practical efforts and concerns.

However, these answers cannot adequately represent the reality of developmental processes since these, as open-systems phenomena, are in principle unpredictable in any exact way.

8.4 Epistemological background of the theory

A theoretical analysis of child development has to accept the unpredictable nature of development. One possible way of conceptualization of the developmental process is represented by the theoretical stance in this book, which is based on the idea of the *bounded (limited, constrained) nature of organisms' actions within their environments*. This perspective affords at most the prediction of some general directions of the future developmental processes.

The present theoretical system is built on a number of 'basic assumptions'. These basic assumptions are axioms constructed in the course of cultural history to structure the way in which people think about the world. Chapter 2 outlined a number of these basic assumptions. The present theory is constructed on the purposeful selection of some of these assumptions. First, it starts by assuming that child development is characterized by the *inclusive* (as contrasted to exclusive) *separation* of the developing child and its environment (see 2.1). Secondly, the *dynamic* aspects of the developmental processes (rather than the relatively stable nature of outcomes of these processes—see 2.2) is the target of the present theoretical analysis. Thirdly, the theory assumes the existence of variability between children in their development, and within the development of any particular child. This acceptance of variability in its different forms as the phenomenon of central importance for development finds its expression in the assertion that *generality is evidenced in variability, rather than uniformity, of behavior and thinking* (see 2.3). The open-systems nature of developing organisms makes it obligatory to view development from the standpoint of structural wholism rather than additive elementarism (2.4), and to expect the developmental processes to be organized in a satisficing (rather than maximizing) manner (see 2.5). Every individual developing child is an organism interrelated with his environment, and is thus lawful in himself (see 2.6). That lawfulness is organized by systemic (rather than elementaristic) ways of looking at causality, and may be expected to require catalyzing conditions in the organism or environment to help the causal system maintain or facilitate development (2.7).

It must be pointed out that each of the basic assumptions used as the basis for the present theory happens to be the one (of the respective options) which is habitually rejected both by the laypersons' thinking about children, and by the majority of child psychologists (who have followed the laypersons' common sense). Furthermore, the present framework is built up within the individual–socioecological frame of reference, whereas the majority of psychological theories are constructed from the perspective of the inter-individual reference system (3.1).

8.5 Summary of the theory and its historical antecedents

The present theoretical system relies on different aspects of earlier theoretical systems in psychology. It follows James Mark Baldwin, Jean Piaget, and Lev Vygotsky in their emphasis on the active nature of the developing child in the process of development. It uses Piaget's notion of 'progressing equilibration' (3.2.2) in conjunction with the notion of *increasing disequilibration* borrowed from the thinking currently used in contemporary thermodynamics (3.2.4). However, the present theoretical system goes beyond Piaget's traditions of empirical study of children's actions within environments, the structure of which is not explicitly studied in most of Piagetian research. This task is accomplished here by looking at the ways in which caregivers structure the child's environment in various concrete ways. In this respect the present system relates to Kurt Lewin's thinking about the structure of psychological field and its change (3.6). However, the present author stops short of accepting Lewin's major domain of interests—projection of the causality for happenings in the psychological field to different 'field forces'. Instead, the developing child and his caregivers are viewed as being engaged in constant negotiation and renegotiation processes involving different 'boundaries' in their relationships with one another and the environment at large. These boundary conditions define (and redefine) the structured nature of the child–environment relationships, which (following Vygotsky's key idea of internalization of external experience—3.5.1) is gradually carried over from the realm of child's (externally constrained) actions on the environment into his internally constrained thinking, feeling, and programming of actions. The process of socio-cultural constraining of child development is referred to by the use of the term 'canalization' that has been used in theoretical biology (Waddington, 1942, 1966). However, Waddington's original notion of 'canalization' is used here in an altered meaning. In this context the term refers to the directive, but not determinative, role of structurally organized child–environment relationships, rather than to the presence of strictly determined developmental pathways among which the organism at times may choose but which the organism cannot participate in constructing by its own actions (4.1.4).

The theoretical system outlined in this book was built around three abstract concepts of *zones* that are applicable to real phenomenology in concrete ways. First, the *Zone of Free Movement* (ZFM) characterizes the set of what is available (in terms of areas of environment, objects in those areas, and ways of acting upon these objects' to the child's acting in the particular environmental setting at a given time. The ZFM is a functional structure, it is constantly generated and regenerated as the child and the caregiver move from one environmental setting to another and from seeking one set of goals to trying to attain other ends. Thus, the structure of ZFM is dynamic; given the change in goals or conditions, the boundaries of ZFM are constantly being reorganized. That reorganization may be initiated by either the child or caregivers, or by all of them at the same time. The ZFM is also episodic. Any particular ZFM is constructed in accordance with the local conditions of the environment and the child and adult(s) and serves its purposes under these conditions. Once no longer functional, a particular ZFM can be abandoned, replaced by another, or gradually transformed into another. Thirdly, the ZFM is exclusive. It delineates the domains of children's actions that the caregivers do not let the child get involved in.

The second zone-concept used in the theory is the *Zone of Promoted Action* (ZPA). This, in contrast to ZFM, is an *inclusive* concept. It illustrates the directed effort of the people around the child to guide his actions in one, rather than another, direction. ZPA, like the Zone of Free Movement, is also episodic (it is set up in particular situations, and can be abandoned later) and dynamic. It works in conjunction with the ZFM, and the way child development is culturally canalized can be characterized by the relationships the particular ZFM and ZPA have with each other. For example, a narrow Zone of Free Movement (i.e. one that allows the child to act only in one way), when paired with a Zone of Promoted Action that matches the ZFM, leads to the most controllable situation one can think of in parent–child relationships: the child *can* act in only one way, the parent urges or commands the child to act in that way, and the child can either revolt (refuse to act in that way), or will act in the expected way. The latter is particularly the case if the only action in ZFM is not only promoted but strictly required—without an acceptance of the no-action solution (see 4.3.3). It is not surprising that the social institution of military discipline makes efficient and purposeful use of the case of narrow ZFMs paired with strictly required ZPAs.

In the other extreme, the provision of a 'wide' Zone of Free Movement with a 'narrow' Zone of Promoted Action in it creates situations where seemingly the children are given a very great freedom for the development of their 'selves'. The child has a large number of possible actions available to him in the given setting, and very few of those are supported by active promotion on behalf of the caregivers. The latter may act with the belief, based on an ideology prominent in the culture, that children need a wide margin of freedom to develop in the best possible ways, and that constraining them may hamper their 'natural' development. The actual development of children under such conditions may lead them to choose a pathway of development on their own. That pathway might not please their parents, though. Not all actual uses by children when a wide range of freedom is provided for them will lead to outcomes that are to the liking of the freedom-providers. In this sense, the parents may facilitate the potential future development of their children in *both* 'positive' and 'negative' directions (as those are viewed by the parents). Such arrangements logically lead to the socialization of children towards becoming 'free-willed' individuals, in concordance with the complex expectations that are accepted in the culture. In the interaction between 'free-willed' individuals, however, 'clashing of wills' is a frequent and expected phenomenon.

The use of zone terminology makes it possible to conceptualize some aspects of child rearing which at a first glance seem to be irreconcilable opposites. For example, the opposition between 'strict' versus 'permissive' parenting styles disappears when viewed from the perspective of ZFM/ZPA complexes. The 'strict' version of parenting involves setting up ZFM and ZPA so that the latter covers most (or all) of the former, and so that parental 'promotion' of actions in the Zone of Promoted Action approaches the conditions of 'requiring' them. The 'permissive' version of parenting involves relatively loosely defined ZPAs in conjunction with wide ZFMs. In that case the child is left to his own devices to make decisions about actions. Both these versions of parenting can be described by the same system of concepts (ZFM/ZPA). Furthermore, this unitary explanation allows one to understand how sometimes 'permissive' parents become 'strict' with their children, or vice versa. Instead of describing the 'style' of parenting that is attributable to the parents' personalities, the zoniferous view of the process of development affords description of conditions in parent–child–environment relationships that are interpreted in everyday language in the terminology of the static qualities of 'permissiveness' or 'restrictivenss'.

The ZFM/ZPA system is not yet sufficient to explain the progression involved in development. Even if parents very much want to make a good piano-player out of their infant child by limiting the child's freedom of action (e.g. imagine a Zone of Free Movement that includes only the 'manipulation' of piano keys while the infant is held at the piano) and strictly demanding the desired action (e.g. ZPA=ZFM: parent 'pushing' the infant's touching of the piano keys), the child need not become a great pianist. Instead, the ZPA/ZFM system that is set up in ways that do not take into account what is possible for a child at a particular age,and on the basis of his particular developmental history, fails in its function. The third core concept of the theoretical system is taken from Vygotsky's contribution to psychology, and redefined here to fit the basic idea of selective limitation of variability as the mechanism of development. It functions to determine when the ZPA/ZFM system can fulfill its expected function. This is the *Zone of Proximal Development* (ZPD)—the set of actions that the child can perform when helped by another person, but which are not yet available to the child in his individual acting. The ZPD is the zone within which promotion efforts of the caregivers (ZPA) can lead to the accomplishment of the particular actions by the child jointly with adult, whereas these actions are not yet observed among the child's actions within the non-ZPA portion of the Zone of Free Movement.

8.6 The theory and problems of its formalization

It is clear that a theoretical system at one time or another becomes dependent upon some formalized language that could make its explanations more rigorous to those who understand them, and at least give the appearance of mathematical rigor for those who are unfamiliar with its content. Given the structural-dynamic nature of the ZPA/ZFM/ZPD system, the traditional formalizations using assumptions of the statistical world view are inappropriate for any formalization effort of the system. Instead, a mathematical-symbolic system that could be evoked for formalizing the present theory has to retain the structured nature of developmental reality and describe the process of transformation of the structures. Chapter 5 included a brief critical account of a selection of existing formalisms that have voiced claims to being adequate for the description of processes of development. This consideration led to a conclusion that was essentially negative. Despite the applicability of some of these formalisms to certain developmental phenomena, none of them was adequate for the reality of the development of children's actions. All of the systems mentioned are thus poor candidates for the complex role of a formal system that could model such a basic everyday happening as the adults' organizing of their children's relationships with their environments. Mathematical concepts play a very curious epistemological role in science. They may profoundly improve the thinking of investigators in a certain field, if the concepts that are applied fit the phenomena under study. Equally easily these may lead to an increasing confusion in those areas of science where their appication helps to change some essential aspects of the phenomena which are being studied. Developmental psychology was shown to be in a particularly vulnerable situation in this respect. Both key issues of development—change of complex systems over time, and the dependence of that change on relationships with structured environments—are ill-treated by the branches of contemporary mathematics which are available for developmental psychologists.

8.7 An empirical application: child socialization at mealtimes

Finally, the highly abstract theoretical system was brought down to the realm of empirical research in chapters 6 and 7. These chapters illustrate a possible use of the theoretical system in the case of a very limited, although culturally highly important, setting of child socialization. In line with the context-sensitive nature of the theory, the culturally organized structure of the meal-time setting and the necessary development of infants' motor skills were analyzed in chapter 6. That was followed by presentation of individual case histories of three toddlers and their parents at mealtimes from 6–7 to 24–26 months of age.

The mealtime context includes cultural expectations that are coded into fixed-feature objects that surround the child in this context. Some of these objects are directly usable by the child, others serve to make up the structural context for the development of new actions. The cultural canalization of children's actions thus starts from the structuring of the setting for those actions. For example, if a mother sits a toddler in a high-chair, and provides him with food and feeding utensils (by putting them on the tray), subsequently leaving the child to its own resources eating, the child's *behaviorally individual* process of self-feeding is still canalized socially *since the action context and action tools carry the cultural canalization function.* Furthermore, in the majority of cases observed the mother remained neither an impartial observer of the self-feeding toddler, nor a domineering feeder. The mother provided the child with help *at points of acting where it was considered necessary*, but not all the time. Once a child had acquired the basic skills of handling of feeding utensils, the mother would let the child act without assistance unless s/he started to act in ways going beyond the Zone of Free Movement established at the given time. The children were consistently helped when the actions they tried to perform were not yet fully established in the children's action repertoires. However, the caregivers gradually started to delegate control over parts of the developing action sequence to the children, retaining their helping role in the case of other parts. The adult–child *joint action* in these situations created the system of zones (involving ZPA and ZFM) for the acquisition of particular motor skills (e.g. use of spoon, fork, or cup). Once the particular action sequence had been securely established in the child's motor repertoire, the caregivers allowed it to be exercised further already in the course of children's individual acting, providing help only when it was perceived to be necessary or when the acquisition of a new skill began. The 'informal education' of toddlers' actions at mealtimes was observed to take place in a low-key manner. Toddlers were observed to eat largely by themselves, alternating between hand and utensil use. They were often given ample time to feed themselves. However, the whole setting of mealtimes was fully under the organizational control of the caregiver, who could intervene by restricting some action by the child, or promoting utensil use, at times that she termed necessary. No highly 'economical' picture of children's mealtimes emerged in the course of this author's empirical observations. The children were not trying to act in ways that would 'maximize' some aspects of the eating process while 'minimizing' some 'costs'. For example, they could proceed to take time off eating to play with the food and the utensil, or they could revert to finger feeding themselves long after their handling of spoons or forks had become well-established. The mothers were not observed to try to make their children eat quicker, or excessively, or with less 'mess', despite the fact that the method of collection of empirical materials (videotaping in homes) facilitated the 'showing-off' of the children to the eyes (and videocamera) of the investigator. Instead, the mothers seemed to organize the children's mealtimes in accordance with the nutritional needs of the children at the time, and by pursuing culturally given socialization goals the attainment of which was expected to be an event of the future. The mealtimes gave evidence for the use of the principle of satisficing. That basic principle is found to be the foundation of most of human problem-solving in complex real-life situations (Simon, 1956).

8.8 The principle of satisficing

The principle of satisficing has been only rarely used in psychological research. An emphasis on that principle in psychological thought makes it possible to consider a range of versions of a particular phenomenon *equally sufficient* for fulfilling a certain function that is essential to the organism and its development. The principle of equifinality, which consitutes the core of the open systems theory, is closely linked to satisficing.

The unstructed mixture of frames of reference that have been used in psychology has facilitated the forgetting of the principle of satisficing in the majority of theoretical accounts of development. For example, when the inter-individual reference frame is used to consider examples of 'equally sufficient' actions or cognitive strategies, that frame of reference prescribes the result that some of these end up considered to be 'better' than others. Much of psychological theorizing has in fact equated the status of 'the best' specimen of a class of phenomena with 'the adequate' one, thus approaching the study of psychological phenomena from the perspective of a maximizing ethos. That emphasis leads the investigators to discarding many different aspects of the phenomena under study (which are sufficient, although not 'the best', for a certain purpose) as 'non-optimal'. Along such lines, psychologists often consider the formal model which gives 'the best fit' with some empirical data (when compared with alternative models) to be *the* 'true' model of the given data. The two alternatives—(a) that the model may fit the data best, but some other ones may also fit them sufficiently well and be realistic and (b) that even the best model (and all the others compared) may have no connection with reality—are seldom given much theoretical consideration. In contrast, a satisficing perspective affords theoretical explanations in psychology the adequate character of conceptualizing a variety of qualitatively different ways of organizing the same function in different particular instances.

8.9 The theory and its range of potential usefulness

Turning to other empirical phenomena in developmental pscyhology, it must be emphasized that the present theoretical system is not limited to the particular kind of phenomenology that was used as the example of the empirical elaboration of the theory. Besides mealtimes, many other domains of child socialization where goal-directed actions take place would fit as empirical grounds on which specific propositions stemming from the present theory can be tested. For instance, the way infants are dressed (see Benigni and Valsiner, 1984; Brackbill, 1971; Mead, 1954) in accordance with the historical traditions set limits on their motor activity while they are not yet ready to locomote themselves. Furthermore, when they begin to creep or crawl (McSwain, 1981), and walk in two- or three-dimensional space (i.e. climb— Valsiner and Mackie, 1985), their actions are selectively restricted by purposeful organization of child–environment relationships by the caregivers. All these phenomena have the same functional organization in common, although the particular details of actions and the environments differ a great deal.

This invariant basic organization has been the topic of this book. The caregivers set limits on the general *range* of children's action opportunities, rather than determine the 'prototypic' actions that the child can perform. Determination of the exact typical form of actions is practically impossible in reality, since the contexts in which a given action can occur are highly variable, and in each particular case the action is adapted to the context which is the only way in which the developing child can not only survive but develop further.

There exist, of course, psychological phenomena to which the theoretical system presented in this book is *not* applicable in any conceivably fruitful ways. These phenomena are characterized by either an absence of environmental or person-based structural organization or where the structural organization is highly complicated (e.g. in the case of the presence of a variety of partially conflicting goals of the persons involved in a situation). The theoretical system assumes that the reality is structurally organized, and is built upon this assumption. Any phenomena in the case of which the structural organization cannot be assumed (e.g. subjects' responses to a set of randomly presented stimuli) are uninteresting for empirical research that is based on the theoretical framework outlined in this book.

8.10 The final point: *limited* indeterminacy of development

Aside from treating the material in this book as an example of construction of a context-sensitive theory in developmental psychology, what else can we learn from this excursion into the world of toddlers, and their eating under confinement in high-chairs? Hidden in the theory that was presented in this book is an effort to solve the philosophical controversy between deterministic and indeterministic views on child development. Usually, psychologists adopt either one, or the other, perspective on child development. The deterministic view of child development is evidenced in beliefs in both nativistic and extremely environmentalistic views on what determines child development. It also submerges in empirical child psychologists' efforts to discover predictability of behavior later in children's age from some behavioral indicators earlier in ontogeny. In contrast, investigators who adopt the indeterministic stance emphasize the child–environment transaction, often to excess.

The perspective emerging from the thinking behind the present theory differs from both of these extremes of the old philosophical controversy. Instead of solving that problem by taking either the 'determinist' or 'indeterminist' positions in looking at psychological phenomena, the present theoretical system is based on the idea of of determinacy when the outcomes as well as the general direction of cultural socialization of children's action are concerned. However, the particular ways of acting by children and adults are not determined in any strict way *within* the constraints that are set up to canalize their development. Within the constrained structure of child–environment relationships indeterminacy of particular actions is rampant, but the construction of the constraints that set the boundary conditions for children's action development is a deterministic and goals-oriented process. In sum, psychological development, both in ontogeny and in history, can be considered deterministically indeterministic. This deterministic (bounded) indeterminacy guarantees the developing organism the possibility of developing novel ways of acting *within a strictly determined range of options* at every time in development. The flexibility of the developing organism within that constrained range of possibilities may be of crucial significance in situations where the organism has to continue existing under changing environmental conditions. After all, the development of children's actions has to afford novelties that the parental generation lacked or could not create. Under these conditions, human progress can proceed in its curious ways, with advances and drawbacks, and result in the myriad of the never-ending activities of ordinary human beings within their culturally structured life environments.

References

Abelson, R. P. (1981), Psychological status of the script concept. *American Psychologist*, **36**, 7, 715–729.

Allen, P. M. (1981). The evolutionary paradigm of dissipative structures. In E. Jantsch (ed.), *The evolutionary vision: toward a unifying paradigm of physical, biological, and sociocultural evolution* (pp. 25–72). Boulder, CO: Westview Press.

Allen, P. M. (1982). Self-organization in the urban system. In W. C. Schieve and P. M. Allen (eds), *Self-organization and dissipative structures: applications in the physical and social sciences* (pp. 132–158). Austin: University of Texas Press.

Allen, P. M., and Sanglier, M. (1980). Order by fluctuation and the urban system. In M. Zeleny (ed.), *Autopoiesis, dissipative structures, and spontaneous social orders* (pp. 109–132). Boulder, CO: Westview Press.

Allport, G. W. (1942). *The use of personal documents in psychological science*. New York: Social Science Research Council.

Anokhin, P. K. (1964). Systemogenesis as a general regulator of brain development. In W. A. Himwich and H. E. Himwich (eds), *Progress in brain research*, vol. 9 (pp. 54–86). Amsterdam: Elsevier.

Anzai, Y., and Simon, H. (1979). The theory of learning by doing. *Psychological Review*, **86**, 124–140.

Baldwin, A. L. (1940). The statistical analysis of the structure of a single personality. *Psychological Bulletin*, **37**, 518–519.

Baldwin, A. L. (1942). Personal structure analysis: a statistical method for investigating single personality. *Journal of Abnormal and Social Psychology*, **37**, 163–183.

Baldwin, A. L. (1944). An analysis of children's eating habits. *Journal of Pediatrics*, **25**, 71–78.

Baldwin, A. L. (1946). The study of individual personality by means of the intraindividual correlation. *Journal of Personality*, **14**, 151–168.

Baldwin, J. M. (1892). Origin of volition in childhood. *Science*, **20**, 286–287.

Baldwin, J. M. (1896). Consciousness and evolution. *Psychological Review*, **3**, 300–309.

Baldwin, J. M. (1902). *Social and ethical interpretations in mental development*, 3rd edn. New York: Macmillan.

Baldwin, J. M. (1906). *Thought and things: a study of the development and meaning of thought*, vol. 1. London: Swan Sonnenschein & Co.

239

Baldwin, J. M. (1930). James Mark Baldwin. In C. Murchison (ed.), *A history of psychology in autobiography*, vol. 1 (pp. 1–30). New York: Russell & Russell.

Bandura, A. (1983). Temporal dynamics and decomposition of reciprocal determinism: A reply to Phillips and Orton. *Psychological Review*, **30**, 166–170.

Barker, R., Dembo, T., and Lewin, K. (1941). Frustration and regression: an experiment with young children. *University of Iowa Studies in Child Welfare*, **18**, 1, 1–312.

Bartlett, F. C. (1932). *Remembering*. Cambridge: Cambridge University Press.

Basar, T., and Oldser, G. J. (1982). *Dynamic noncooperative game theory*. London Academic Press.

Basov, M. (1929). Structural analysis in psychology from the standpoint of behavior. *Journal of Genetic Psychology*, **36**, 267–290.

Basov, M. (1931). *Obshchie osnovy pedologii*, Moscow and Leningrad: Gosizdat (In Russian, English title: *General foundations of pedology*).

Bateson, G. (1972). *Steps to an ecology of mind*. New York: Ballantine.

Bem, D., and Allen, A. (1974). On predicting some of the people some of the time: the search for cross-situational consistencies in behavior. *Psychological Review*, **81**, 506–520.

Bem, D., and Funder, D. C. (1978). Predicting more of the people more of the time: assessing the personality of situations. *Psychological Review*, **85**, 485–501.

Benigni, L. (1974). Dipendenza alimentare e sviluppo communicativo nel primo anno di vita. Paper presented at the 8th Congress of the Societa Italiana di Neuropsichiatria Infantile, Taormina, 9–12. October.

Benigni, L., and Valsiner, J. (1984). Il corpo del neonato i suoi confini sociali. In L. Gandini (ed.). *Dimmi come lo vesti* (pp. 89–135). Milano: Emme Edizioni.

Benigni, L., and Valsiner, J. (1985). Developmental psychology without the study of developmental processes? *ISSBD Newsletter*, no. 1.

Bennett, P. G., and Dando, M. R. (1979). Complex strategic analysis: hypergame study of the fall of France. *Journal of the Operations Research Society*, **30**, 1, 23–32.

Bernstein, N. A. (1966). *Ocherki po fiziologii dvizheniya i fiziologii aktivnosti*. Moscow: Meditsina. (In Russian, English title: *Studies in the physiology of movement and physiology of activity*).

Berresford, A., and Dando, M. R. (1978). Operational research for strategic decision-making: the role of world-view. *Journal of the Operational Research Society*, **29**, 2, 137–146.

Berry, R. S., and Andresen, B. (1982). Thermodynamic constraints in economic analysis. In W. C. Schieve and P. M. Allen (eds.), *Self-organization and dissipative structures: applications in the physical and social sciences* (pp. 323–338). Austin: University of Texas Press.

Bertalanffy, L. von (1950). The theory of open systems in physics and biology. *Science*, **111**, 23–29.

Bertalanffy, L. von (1960). Principles and theory of growth. In W. W. Nowinski (ed.), *Fundamental aspects of normal and malignant growth* (pp. 137–259). Amsterdam: Elsevier.

Bertalanffy, L. von (1981). *A systems view of man* Boulder, CO: Westview Press.

Bohm, D. (1980). *Wholeness and implicate order*. London: Routledge & Kegan Paul.

Boole, G. (1854). *An investigation of the laws of thought, on which are founded the mathematical theories of logic and probability*. London: Walton & Maberly.

Bossard, J. H. S. (1948). *The sociology of child development*. New York: Harper & Brothers.

Bower, T. G. R., Broughton, J. M., and Moore, M. K. (1970). Demonstration of intention in the reaching behavior of neonate humans. *Nature*, **228**, 679–681.

Brackbill, Y. (1971). Cumulative effects of continuous stimulation on arousal level in infants. *Child Development*, **42**, 17–26.

Brandt, L.W. (1973). The physics of the physicist and the physics of the psychologist. *International Journal of Psychology*, **8**, 1, 61–72.

Braudel, F. (1973). *Capitalism and material life 1400–1800*. New York: Harper & Row.

Brent, S. (1984). *Psychological and social structures*. Hillsdale, NJ: Erlbaum.

Brown, R., and Fish, D. (1983). The psychological causality implicit in language. *Cognition*, **14**, 237–273.

Bruner, J. S. (1960). *The process of education*. Cambridge, MA: Harvard University Press.

Bruner, J. S. (1972). The nature and uses of immaturity. *American Psychologist*, **27**, 1–22.

Bruner, J. S. (1975). The ontogenesis of speech acts. *Journal of Child Language*, **2**, 1–19.

Bruner. J. S: (1976). From communication to language—a psychological perspective. *Cognition*, **3**, 155–187.

Bruner, J. S. (1978). Acquiring the uses of language. *Canadian Journal of Psychology*, **32**, 202–218.

Bruner, J. S. (1981). The organization of action and the nature of adult–infant transaction. In G. D'Ydewalle and W. Lens (eds.), *Cognition in human motivation and learning* (pp. 1–13). Hillsdale, NJ: Erlbaum and Leuven University Press.

Bruner, J. S. (1983). *In search of mind: essays in autobiography*. New York: Harper & Row.

Bruner, J. S. (1984). Vygotsky's zone of proximal development: the hidden agenda. *New directions for child development*, no. 23, 93–97.

Bruner, J. S., and Sherwood, V. (1976). Early rule structure: the case of 'peekaboo'. In R. Harré (ed.), *Life sentences* (pp. 57–62). London: Wiley.

Bryant, C. A. (1982). The impact of kin, friend and neighbour networks on infant feeding practices. *Social Science and Medicine*, **16**, 1757–1765.

Bush, R. R. and Mosteller, F. (1955). *Stochastic models for learning*. New York: Wiley.

Buss, A. (1978). The structure of psychological revolutions. *Journal of the History of the Behavioral Sciences*, **14**, 57–64.

Buss, A. (1979). The historical context of differential psychology and eugenics. In A. Buss, *A dialectical psychology* (pp. 27–42). New York: Irvington Publishers.

Cairns, R. B. (1983). The emergence of developmental psychology. In W. Kessen (ed.), *Carmichael's handbook of child psychology*, 4th ed., vol. 1: *History, theory, and methods* (pp. 41–102). New York: Wiley.

Cairns, R. B., and Ornstein, P. A. (1979). Developmental psychology. In E. Hearst (Ed.), *The first century of experimental psychology*, Hillsdale, N. J.: Erlbaum.

Cairns, R. B. and Valsiner, J. (1982). The cultural context of developmental psychology. Paper presented at the 90th APA Convention, Washington DC.

Cairns, R. B., and Valsiner, J. (1984). Child psychology. *Annual Review of Psychology*, **35**, 553–577.

Castner, B. M. (1932). The development of fine prehension in infancy. *Genetic Psychology Monographs*, **12**, 2, 105–193.

Cattell, R. B. (1944). Psychological measurement: normative, ipsative, interactive. *Psychological Review*, **51**, 292–303.

Cazden, C. (1983). Peekaboo as an instructional model: discourse development at home and at school. In B. Bain (ed.), *The sociogenesis of language and human conduct* (pp. 33–58). New York: Plenum.

242

Chapman, M. (1982). Action and interactions: the study of social cognition in Germany and the United States. *Human Development*, **25**, 295–302.

Chomsky, N. (1959). A note on phrase structure grammars. *Information and Control*, **2**, 393–395.

Chomsky, N. (1966). *Topics in the theory of generative grammar*. The Hague: Mouton.

Chomskey, N. (1976). On the biological basis of language capacities. In R. W. Rieber (ed.), *The neuropsychology of language* (pp. 1–24). New York: Plenum.

Chomsky, N. (1980a). On cognitive structures and their development: a reply to Piaget. In M. Piatelli-Palmarini (ed.), *Language and learning: the debate between Jean Piaget and Noam Chomsky* (pp. 35–52). Cambridge, MA: Harvard University Press.

Chomsky, N. (1980b). *Rules and representations*. New York: Columbia University Press.

Cole, P. M. (1985). Display rules and the socialization of affective displays. In G. Zivin (ed.), *The development of expressive behavior: biology–environment interactions* (pp. 269–290). Orlando, FL: Academic Press.

Connolly, K. J. (1970). Skill development: problems and plans. In K. J. Connolly (ed.), *Mechanisms of motor skill development* (pp. 3–21). London: Academic Press.

Connolly, K. J. (1973). Factors influencing the learning of manual skills by young children. In R. Hinde and J. Stevenson-Hinde (eds), *Constraints on learning* (pp. 337–363). London: Academic Press.

Connolly, K. J. (1974). The development of skill. *New Scientist*, **62** (900), 537–540.

Connolly, K. J. (1975). Movement, action and skill. In K. S. Holt (ed.), *Movement and child development* (pp. 102–110). London: Heinemann.

Connolly, K. J. (1979). The development of competence in motor skills. In C. H. Nadeau, W. R. Halliwell, K. M. Newell, and G. C. Roberts (eds), *Psychology of motor behavior and sport* (pp. 229–252). Champaign, IL: Human Kinietics Publishers.

Connolly, K. J. (1980). Motor development and motor disability. In M. Rutter (ed.), *Developmental psychiatry* (pp. 138–153). London: Heinemann.

Connolly, K. J. (1981). Maturation and the ontogeny of motor skills. In K. J. Connolly and H. F. R. Prechtl (eds), *Maturation and development: biological and psychological perspectives* (pp. 216–230). London: Heinemann.

Connolly, K. J. and Elliott, J. (1972). The evolution and ontogeny of hand function. In N. G. Blurton Jones (ed.), *Ethological studies of child behavior* (pp. 329–383). London: Cambridge University Press.

Coulter, N. A. (1973). Contributions to a mathematical theory of synergic systems. In A. Locker (ed.), *Biogenesis, evolution, homeostasis* (pp. 57–61). New York and Heidelberg: Springer.

Curran, V. H. (ed.) (1984). *Nigerian children: Developmental perspectives*. London: Routledge & Kegan Paul.

Czikszentmihalyi, M., and Rochberg-Halton, E. (1981). *The meaning of things*. Cambridge: Cambridge University Press.

Davis, K. (1938). Mental hygiene and the class structure. *Psychiatry*, **1**, 55–65.

Davydov, V., and Radzikhovskii, L. A. (1980). Vygotsky's theory and the activity principle in psychology, I. *Voprosy Psikhologii*, No. 6, 48–59.

Davydov, V., and Radzikhovskii, L. A. (1981). Vygotsky's theory and the activity principle in psychology, II. *Voprosy Psikhologii*, No. 1, 67–80.

DeVries, M. W., and DeVries, M. R. (1977). Cultural relativity of toilet-training readiness: a perspective from East Africa. *Pediatrics*, **60**, 2, 170–177.

Diepold, B. (1983). Essstörungen bei Kindern und Jugendlichen. *Praxis der Kinderpsychologie und Kinderpsychiatrie*, **32**, 8, 298–304.

DiFranco, D., Muir, D., and Dodwell, P. (1978). Reaching in very young infants. *Perception*, **7**, 385–392.

Dolby, R. G. A. (1977). The transmission of two new scientific disciplines from Europe to North America in the late 19th century. *Annals of Science*, **34**, 287–310.

Douglas, M. (1975). Deciphering a meal. In M. Douglas, *Purity and danger*. London: Routledge & Kegan Paul.

Douglas, M., and Gross, J. (1981). Food and culture: measuring the intimacy of rule systems. *Social Science Information*, **20**, 1, 1–35.

Draguns, J. G. (1984). Microgenesis by any other name. . . . In W. D. Froehlich, G. Smith, J. G. Draguns, and U. Hentschel (eds), *Psychological processes in cognition and personality* (pp. 3–17). Washington DC: Hemisphere Publishing Co.

Dreyer, C. A., and Dryer, A. S. (1973). Family dinner as a unique behavior habitat. *Family Process*, **12**, 291–301.

Duncker, K. (1938). Experimental modification of children's food preferences through social suggestion. *Journal of Abnormal and Social Psychology*, **33**, 489–507.

Duncker, K. (1945). On problem-solving. *Psychological Monographs*, **58**, 5, 1–112.

Ekman, P., Friesen, W. V., and Ellsworth, P. (1972). *Emotion in the human face*, New York: Pergamon.

Elias, N. (1978). *The civilizing process: the development of manners*, New York: Urizen Books.

Elliott, J., and Connolly, K. J. (1974). Hierarchical structure in skill development. In K. J. Connolly and J. Bruner (eds), *The growth of competence* (pp. 135–168). London: Academic Press.

Elliott, J., and Connolly, K. J. (1984). A classification of manipulative hand movements. *Developmental Medicine and Child Neurology*, **26**, 283–296.

Erikson, E. H. (1963). *Childhood and society*. New York: W. W. Norton.

Eysenck, H. J. (1985). The place of theory in the world of facts. In K. B. Madsen and L. P. Mos (eds), *Annals of theoretical psychology*, vol. 3 (pp. 103–114). New York: Plenum.

Festinger, L., Riecken, H. W., and Schachter, S. (1956). *When prophecy fails*. Minneapolis: University of Minnesota Press.

Flanagan, O. (1981). Psychology, progress and the problem of reflexivity: a study in the epistemological foundations of psychology. *Journal of the History of the Behavioral Sciences*, **17**, 375–386.

Fortes, M., and Fortes, S. L. (1936). Food in the domestic economy of the Tallensi. *Africa*, **9**, 237–276.

Franck, I. (1982). Psychology as science: resolving the idiographic–nomothetic controversy. *Journal for the Theory of Social Behavior*, **12**, 1, 1–20.

Fraser, N. M. and Hipel, K. W. (1979). Solving complex conflicts. *IEEE Transactions on Systems, Man, and Cybernetics*, smc–9, 12, 805–810.

Freud, A. (1963). The concept of developmental lines. *The Psychoanalytic Study of the Child*, **18**, 245–265.

Fu, K. S. (1970). Learning control systems—a review and outlook. *IEEE transactions on automatic control*, **15**, 210–221.

Fu, K. S. (1974). *Syntactic methods in pattern recognition*. New York: Academic Press.

Galton, F. (1904). Eugenics: its definition, scope and aim. *Nature*, **70**, 1804, 82.

Garfinkel, P., Moldofsky, H., and Garner, D. (1980). The heterogeneity of anorexia nervosa. *Archives of General Psychiatry*, **37**, 1036–1040.

Gärling, T., and Valsiner, J. (eds) (1985). *Children within environments: towards a psychology of accident prevention*. New York: Plenum.

Gauld, A., and Shotter, J. (1977). *Human action and its psychological investigation.* London: Routledge & Kegan Paul.

Gesall, A., and Ilg, F. L. (1937). *Feeding behavior of infants.* Philadelphia: Lippincott.

Gesell, A., and Thompson, H. (1934). *Infant behavior: its genesis and growth.* Westport, CT: Greenwood Press.

Gilmore, R. (1981). *Catastrophe theory for scientists and engineers.* New York: Wiley.

Golinkoff, R. M. (1983). The preverbal negotiation of failed messages: insights into the transition period. In R. M. Golinkoff (ed.), *The transition from prelinguistic to linguistic communication* (pp. 57–78). Hillsdale, NJ: Erlbaum.

Goody, J. (1982). *Cooking, cuisine and class.* Cambridge: Cambridge University Press.

Gottlieb, G. (1976). The roles of experience in the development of behavior and the nervous system. In G. Gottlieb (ed.), *Neural and behavioral specificity* (pp. 25–54). New York: Academic Press.

Graves, N. B., and Graves, T. D. (1978). The impact of modernization on the personality of a Polynesian people. *Human Organization,* **37**, 2, 115–135.

Greenfield, P. (1984). A theory of the teacher in the learning activities of everyday life. In B. Rogoff and J. Lave (eds), *Everyday cognition: its development in social context* (pp. 117–138). Cambridge, MA: Harvard University Press.

Greenfield, P., and Lave, J. (1982). Cognitive aspects of informal education. In D. Wagner and H. Stevenson (eds), *Cultural perspectives on child development* (pp. 181–207). San Francisco: W. H. Freeman.

Grossmann, K. (1986). From idiographic approaches to nomothetic hypotheses: Stern, Allport, and biology of knowledge, exemplified by an exploration of sibling relationships. In J. Valsiner (ed.), *The individual subject and scientific psychology:* (pp. 37–69). New York: Plenum.

Guckenheimer, J. (1978). Comments on catastrophe and chaos. *Lectures on mathematics in the life sciences,* **10**, 1–47.

Halverson, H. M. (1931). An experimental study of prehension in infants by means of systematic cinema records. *Genetic Psychology Monographs,* **10**, 2–3, 107–286.

Hardie, R. P., and Gaye, R. K. (1930). *Aristotle's Physica.* Oxford: Clarendon Press.

Harkness, S., and Super, C. (1983). The cultural construction of child development. *Ethos,* **11**, 4, 221–231.

Harré, R. (1980). *Social being: a theory for social psychology,* Totowa, N. J.: Rowman & Littlefield.

Harré, R. (1981). Rituals, rhetoric and social cognition. In J. P. Forgas (ed.), *Social cognition* (pp. 211–224). London: Academic Press.

Harré, R., and Secord, P. F. (1972). *The explanation of social behavior.* Oxford: Blackwell.

Harsanyi, J. C. (1982). *Papers in game theory.* Dordrecht: Reidel.

Haslerud, G. M. (1979). Which paradigm is both relevant to concerns of psychologists and also scientifically feasible? *Psychologia,* **22**, 177–188.

Henle, M. (1977). The influence of Gestalt psychology in America. *Annals of the New York Academy of Sciences,* 291, 3–12.

Henle, M. (1978). Kurt Lewin as a metatheorist. *Journal of the History of the Behavioral Sciences,* **14**, 233–237.

Herzog, W. (1984). *Modell and Theorie in der Psychologie.* Göttingen: C. J. Hogrefe.

Holden, G. H. (1985). How parents create a social environment via proactive behavior. In T. Gärling and J. Valsiner (eds.). *Children within environments: toward a psychology of accident prevention* (pp. 193–215). New York: Plenum.

245

Holland, D. C., the Quinn, N. (eds). (1987). *Cultural models in language and thought.* Cambridge: Cambridge University Press.

Holy, L., and Stuchlik, M. (1981). *The structure of folk models.* New York: Academic Press.

Hoppe, F. (1930). Erfolg and Misserfolg. *Psychologische Forschrung,* **14,** 1–62.

Horton, R. (1967). African traditional thought and Western science. *Africa,* **37,** 50–71 and 155–187.

Howard, N. (1971). *Paradoxes of rationality: theory of metagames and political behavior,* Cambridge, MA: MIT Press.

Howard, N. (1974). 'General' metagames: an extension of the metagame concept. In Anatol Rapoport (ed.), *Game theory as a theory of conflict resolution* (pp. 261–283). Dordrecht: Reidel.

Hume, D. (1854). *Philosophical works of David Hume,* Vol. 1. Boston, MA: Little, Brown, & Co.

Hutchinson, G. E. (1948). Circular causal systems in ecology. *Annals of the N.Y. Academy of Science,* **50,** 221–246.

Inhelder, B., Garcia, R., and Voneche, J. (eds) (1976). *Épistémologie génétique et équilibration.* Neuchâtel: Delacjaux & Niestle.

Isaac, G. (1978). The food-sharing behavior of protohuman hominids. *Scientific American,* **238,** 4, 90–109.

Jantsch, E. (1980). *The self-organizing universe.* Oxford: Pergamon.

Jeannerod, M. (1984). The timing of natural prehension movements. *Journal of Motor Behavior,* **16,** 3, 235–254.

Jevons, W. S. (1873). *The principles of science.* London. (New York: Dover, 1958 reprint).

Jürgensen, H. (1976). Probabilistic L-systems. In A. Lindenmayer and G. Rozenberg (eds), *Automata, languages, development* (pp. 211–225). Amsterdam: North Holland.

Kasai, T. (1970). An hierarchy between context-free and context-sensitive languages. *Journal of Computer and System Science,* **4,** 492–508.

Katz, D. (1928). La Psychologie de la faim et de l'appétit, en particular chez l'enfant. *Journal de Psychologie,* **25,** 165–180.

Keats, D. M. (1982). Cultural bases of concepts of intelligence: a Chinese versus Australian comparison. Paper presented at the 2nd Asian Workshop on Child and Adolescent Development, Bangkok.

Kelly, G. A. (1955). *The psychology of personal constructs,* vol. 1. *A theory of personality.* New York: Norton.

Kelso, J. A. S., Holt, K. G., Rubin, P., and Kugler, P. (1981). Patterns of human interlimb coordination emerge from the properties of non-linear, limit cycle oscillatory processes. *Journal of Motor Behavior,* **13,** 4, 226–261.

Kindermann, T. (1985). A learning theoretical perspective on dependent and independent behaviors in children. Paper presented at 8th Biennial Meetings of the International Society for the Study of Behavioural Development, Tours, 6–10 July.

Kindermann, T. (1986). Entwicklungsbedingungen selbständigen und unselbständigen Verhaltens in der fruehen Kindheit. Unpublished doctoral dissertation, Free University of Berlin.

Kitahara-Frisch, J., and Norikoshi, K. (1982). Spontaneous sponge-making in captive chimpanzees. *Journal of Human Evolution,* **11,** 41–47.

Köhler, W. (1925). *The mentality of apes.* New York: Liveright (reprinted 1976).

Konner, M. (1976). Maternal care, infant behavior and development among the 'Kung. In R. B. Lee and I. DeVore (eds), *Kalahari hunters-gatherers* (pp. 218–245). Cambridge, MA: Harvard University Press.

Kozulin, A. (1984). *Psychology in utopia*. Cambridge, MA: MIT Press.

Kugler, P. N., Kelso, J. A. S., Turvey, M. T. (1982). On the control and coordination of naturally developing systems. In J. A. S. Kelso and J. E. Clark (eds), *The development of movement control and co-ordination* (pp. 5–78). Chichester: Wiley.

Kugler, P. N., Turvey, M. T., and Shaw, R. (1982). Is the 'cognitive penetrability' criterion invalidated by contemporary physics? *Behavioral and Brain Sciences*, **5**, 2, 303–306.

Kuhn, J. R. D., Hipel, K., and Fraser, N. (1983). A coalition analysis algorithm with application to the Zimbabwe conflict. *IEEE Transactions on Systems, Man, and Cybernetics*, **smc–13**, 3, 338–352.

Kuhn, T. S. (1970). *The structure of scientific revolutions*, 2nd edn. Chicago: University of Chicago Press.

Kuhn, T. S. (1977). Objectivity, value judgement, and theory choice. In T. S. Kuhn, *The essential tension; selected studies in scientific tradition and change*. Chicago: University of Chicago Press.

Kuipers, B. (1984). Commonsense reasoning about causality: deriving behavior from structure. *Artificial Intelligence*, **24**, 169–203.

Kuipers, B., and Kassirer, J. P. (1984). Causal reasoning in medicine: analysis of a protocol. *Cognitive Science*, **8**, 363–385.

Kumarin, V. (1976). *Anton Makarenko: his life and his work in education*. Moscow: Progress (in English).

Kurzweil, E. (1980). *The age of structuralism: Lévi-Strauss to Foucault*. New York: Columbia University Press.

Kuypers, H. G. (1962). Corticospinal connections: postnatal development in rhesus monkeys. *Science*, **138**, 678–680.

Lakshmivarahan, S., and Thathachar, M. A. L. (1973). Absolutely expedient learning algorithms for stochastic automata. *IEEE Transactions on Systems, Man, and Cybernetics*, **smc-3**, 3, 281–286.

Lancy, D. (1975). The social organization of learning initiation rituals and public schools. *Human Organization*, **34**, 4, 371–380

Leenders, F. H. R. (1983). Responsivity during lunch of mothers and their 3-to-4 year old children as a function of child's behavioral style. Paper presented at the 7th Biennial Meetings of the International Society for the Study of Behavioural Development, München.

Leont'ev, A. N. (1975). *Deyatel'nost', soznanie, lichnost'*. Moscow: Izdatel'stvo Politicheskoi Literatury. (In Russian, English title: *Acitivity, consciousness, personality*).

Lerner, R., and Busch-Rossnagel, N. (eds) (1981). *Individuals as producers of their development*, New York: Academic Press.

Lévi-Strauss, C. (1963). *Structural anthropology*, New York: Basic Books.

Lévi-Strauss, C. (1966). The culinary triangle. *Partisan Review*, **33**, 586–595.

Lewin, K. (1917). Kriegeslandschaft. *Zeitschrift für angewandte Psychologie*, **12**, 440–447.

Lewin, K. (1931). The conflict between Aristotelian and Galileian modes of thought in contemporary psychology. *Journal of General Psychology*, **5**, 141–177.

Lewin, K. (1933). Environmental forces. In C. Murchison (ed.), *A handbook of child psychology*, 2nd end (pp. 590–625). Worcester, MA: Clark University Press.

Lewin, K. (1935a). *A dynamic theory of personality*. New York: McGraw-Hill.

Lewin, K. (1935b). Psycho-sociological problems of a minority group. *Character and Personality*, **3**, 175–187.

Lewin, K. (1936a). *Principles of topological psychology*. New York: McGraw-Hill.

Lewin, K. (1936b). Some social-psychological differences between the United States and Germany. *Character and Personality,* **4**, 265–293.

Lewin, K. (1938). *The conceptual representation and the measurement of psychological forces.* Durham, NC: Duke University Press.

Lewin, K. (1939). Field theory and experiment in social psychology: concepts and methods. *American Journal of Sociology,* **44**, 868–896.

Lewin, K. (1942). Field theory and learning. In N. B. Henry (ed.), *The forty-first yearbook of the National Society for the Study of Education.* Part II. *The psychology of learning* (pp. 215–242). Bloomington, IL: Public School Publishing Co.

Lewin, K. (1943a). Defining the 'field at a given time'. *Psychological Review,* **50**, 292–310.

Lewin, K. (1943b). Cultural reconstruction. *Journal of Abnormal and Social Psychology,* **38**, 166–173.

Lewin, K. (1943c). The special case of Germany. *Public Opinion Quarterly,* **7**, 555–566.

Lewin, K. (1948). *Resolving social conflicts.* New York: Harper & Brothers.

Lewin, K. (1951). *Field theory in social science.* New York: Harper & Brothers.

Lewin, K., Lippitt, R., and Escalona, S. K. (1940). Studies in topological and vector psychology 1. *University of Iowa Studies in Child Welfare,* **16**, 3.

Lewin, K., Lippitt, R., and White, R. (1939). Patterns of aggressive behavior in experimentally created 'social climtes'. *Journal of Social Psychology,* **10**, 271–299.

Lewin, R. (1984). Why is development so illogical? *Science,* **224**, 1327–1329.

Lewontin, R. C. (1978). Adaptation. *Scientific American,* **239**, 157–168.

Lewontin, R. C. (1981). On constraints and adaptation. *Behavioral and Brain Sciences,* **4**, 244–245.

Lindenmayer, A. (1968). Mathematical models for cellular interactions in development. *Journal of Theoretical Biology,* **18**, 280–299 (a) and 300–315(b).

Lindenmayer, A. (1975). Developmental algorithms for multicellular organisms: a survey of L-systems. *Journal of Theoretical Biology,* **54**, 3–22.

Lindenmayer, A. (1978). Algorithms for plant morphogenesis. In R. Sattler (ed.), *Theoretical plant morphology* (pp. 37–81). The Hague: Leiden University Press.

Lindenmayer, A., and Rozenberg, G. (eds) (1976). *Automata, languages, development.* Amsterdam: North Holland.

Lockman, J. J., and Ashmead, D. (1983). Asynchronies in the development of manual behavior. In L. P. Lipsitt and C. Rovee-Collier (eds), *Advances in infancy,* vol. 2. (pp. 113–136). Norwood, NJ: Ablex.

London, I. (1944). Psychologists' misuse of the auxiliary concepts of physics and mathematics. *Psychological Review,* **51**, 266–291.

London, I. (1949). The development of person as a joint function of convergence and divergence. *Journal of Social Psychology,* **40**, 219–228.

London, I., and Thorngate, W. (1981). Divergent amplification and social behavior: some methodological considerations. *Psychological Reports,* **48**, 203–228.

Luria, A. R. (1979). *Iazyk i soznanie.* Moscow: Moscow State University Press.

Luria, A. R., and Artemieva, E. (1970). On two ways of achieving the validity of psychological investigation. *Voprosy psichologii,* no. 3, 106–112.

Lutz, C. (1983). Parental goals, ethnopsychology, and the development of emotional meaning. *Ethos,* **11**, 4, 246–362.

McCall, R. (1977). Challenges to a science of developmental psychology. *Child Development,* **48**, 333–344.

MacDonald, N. (1983). *Trees and networks in biological models.* Chichester: Wiley.

McDonnell, P. M. (1979). Patterns of eye-hand coordination in the first year of life. *Canadian Journal of Psychology,* **33**, 4, 253–267.

McGrew, W. C. (1977). Socialization and object manipulation of wild chimpanzees. In S. Chevalier-Skolnikoff and F. Poirier (eds), *Primate bio-social development: biological, social, and ecological determinants.* New York–London: Garland Press.

McGrew, W. C., Tutin, C., and Baldwin, P. J. (1979). Chimpanzees, tools, and termites: cross-cultural comparisons of Senegal, Tanzania, and Rio Muni. *Man,* **14**, 185–214.

McSwain, R. (1981). Care and conflict in infant development: an East-Timorese and Papua New Guinean comparison. *Infant Behavior and Development,* **4**, 225–246.

Mark, L. C., and Todd, J. T. (1983). The perception of growth in three dimensions. *Perception and Psychophysics,* **33**, 2, 193–196.

Mark, L. S., Todd, J. T., and Shaw, R. E. (1981). Perception of growth: a geometric analysis of how different styles of change are distinguished. *Journal of Experimental Psychology: Human Perception and Performance,* **7**, 855–868.

Maruyama, M. (1963). The second cybernetics: deviation-amplifying mutual causal processes. *American Scientist,* **51**, 164–179.

Maruyama, M. (1982). Four different causal metatypes in biological and social sciences. In W. C. Schieve and P. M. Allen (eds), *Self-organization and dissipative structures: applications in the physical and social sciences* (pp. 354–361). Austin: University of Texas Press.

Mead, M. (1954). The swaddling hypothesis: its reception. *American Anthropologist,* **56**, 395–409.

Merton, R. K. (1936). Puritanism, pietism, and science. *Sociological Review,* **28**, 1–30.

Miller, G. D. (1977). Classroom 19: a study of behavior in a classroom of a Moroccan primary school. In L. C. Brown and N. Itzkowitz (eds), *Psychological dimensions in Near-Eastern Studies.* Princeton, NJ: Darwin Press.

Minsky, M. (1982). A framework for representing knowledge. In Y.-H. Pao and G. W. Ernst (eds), *Tutorial: context-directed pattern recognition and machine intelligence techniques for information processing* (pp. 339–419). Piscataway, N.J.: IEEE Computer Society.

Minuchin, S., Rosman, B. L., and Baker, L., (1978). *Psychosomatic families: anorexia nervosa in context.* Cambridge, MA: Harvard University Press.

Mitroff, I. (1974). Norms and counter-norms in a select group of Apollo moon scientists: a case study of the ambivalence of scientists. *American Sociological Review,* **39**, 579–596.

Mitroff, I. I., and Featheringham, T. R. (1974). On systemic problem solving and the error of the third kind. *Behavioral Science,* **19**, 383–393.

Monberg, T. (1975). Fathers were not genitors. *Man,* **10**, 1, 34–40.

Moscovici, S. (1961). *La Psychoanalyse: son image et son public.* Paris: PUF.

Moscovici, S. (1984). The phenomenon of social representations. In R. Farr and S. Moscovici (eds), *Social representations* (pp. 3–69). Cambridge: Cambridge University Press.

Narendra, K. S., Thathchar, M. A. L. (1974). Learning automata—a survey. *IEEE Transactions on Systems, Man and Cybernetics, smc-4,* **4**, 323, 334–.

Nelson, K. (1981). Social cognition in a script framework. In J. H. Flavell and L. Ross (eds), *Social cognitive development* (pp. 97–118). Cambridge: Cambridge University Press.

Newson, J. (1974). Towards a theory of infant understanding. *Bulletin of the British Psychological Society,* **27**, 251–257.

Newson, J., and Newson, E. (1963). *Infant care in an urban community,* London: Allen and Unwin.

Newson, J., and Newson, E. (1968). *Four years old in an urban community*, Chicago: Aldine.

Newson, J., and Newson, E. (1975). Intersubjectivity and the transmission of culture: on the social origins of symbolic functioning. *Bulletin of the British Psychological Society*, **28**, 437–446.

Newson, J., and Newson, E. (1976). *Seven years old in the home environment*. New York: Wiley.

Nicolis, G., and Prigogine, I. (1977). *Self-organization in nonequilibrium systems*. New York: Wiley.

Ninio, A., and Bruner, J. (1978). The achievement and antecedents of labelling. *Journal of Child Language*, **5**, 1–15.

Nixon, J., and Pearn, J. (1977). Emotional sequelae of parents and sibs following the drowning or near-drowning of a child. *Australian and N. Z. Journal of Psychology*, **11**, 265–268.

Ochs, E. (1982). Talking to children in Western Samoa. *Language and Society*, **11**, 77–104.

Ozment, S. (1983). *When fathers ruled: family life in reformation Europe*. Cambridge, MA: Harvard University Press.

Pankow, W. (1976). Openness as self-transcendence. In E. Jantsch and C. H. Waddington (eds), *Evolution and consciousness: human systems in transition* (pp. 16–36). Reading, MA: Addison-Wesley.

Pastore, N. (1949). *The nature-nurture controversy*. New York: King's Crown Press.

Pattee, H. H. (1971). Physical theories of biological co-ordination. *Quarterly Review of Biophysics*, **4**, 2–3, 255–276.

Pattee, H. H. (1972). Laws and constraints, symbols and languages. In C. H. Waddington (ed.), *Towards a theoretical biology*, vol. 4 (pp. 248–258). Chicago: Aldine.

Pattee, H. H. (1973). Physical problems of the origin of natural controls. In A. Locker (ed.), *Biogenesis, evolution, homeostasis* (pp. 41–49). New York–Heidelberg: Spriner.

Paulhan, F. (1928). Qu'est-ce que le sens des mots? *Journal de Psychologie*, **25**, 289–329.

Pearn, J., and Nixon, J. (1977). Bathtub immersion accidents involving children. *Medical Journal of Australia*, **1**, 211–213.

Piaget, J. (1970a). Piaget's theory. In P. H. Mussen (ed.), *Carmichael's manual of child psychology*, 3rd ed, vol. 1 (pp. 703–732). New York: Wiley.

Piaget, J. (1970b). *Structuralism*. New York: Basic Books.

Piaget, J. (1971a). *Insights and illusions of philosophy*. London: Routledge & Kegan Paul.

Piaget, J. (1971b). *Biology and knowledge*. Chicago: University of Chicago Press.

Piaget, J.)1972). *The principles of genetic epistemology*, New York: Basic Books.

Piaget, J. (1977). *The development of thought: equilibration of cognitive structures*. New York: Viking.

Piaget, J. (1980). Reply to Thom. In M. Piatelli-Palmarini (ed.), *Language and learning: the debate between Jean Piaget and Noam Chomsky* (pp. 368–370). Cambridge, MA; Harvard University Press.

Polanyi, M. (1958). *Personal knowledge*, London: Routledge & Kegan Paul.

Prigogine, I. (1973). Irreversibility as a symmetry-breaking process. *Nature*, **246**, 67–71.

Prigogine, I. (1976a). Genèse des structures en physico-chime. In B. Inhelder, R. Garica, and J. Voneche (eds), *Épistémologie génétique et équilibration* (pp. 29–38). Neuchâtel: Delachaux & Niestle.

Prigogine, I. (1976b). Order through fluctuation: self organization and social system. In E. Jantsch and C. H. Waddington (eds), *Evolution and consciousness: human systems in transition*, Reading, MA: Addison-Wesley.

Prigogine, I. (1982) Dialogue avec Piaget sur l'irréversible. *Archives de Psychologie*, **50**, 7–16.

Prigogine, I., and Nicolis, G. (1971). Biological order, structure, and instabilities. *Quarterly Journal of Biophysics*, **4**, 107–148.

Raikov, B. (1961). *Karl Baer: his life and works*, Moscow–Leningrad: Izdatel'stvo Akademii Nauk SSSR (in Russian).

Rapoport, Anatol (1974). Prisoner's dilemma—recollections and observations. In A. Rapoport (ed.), *Game theory as a theory of conflict resolution* (pp. 17–34). Dordrecht: Reidel.

Richards, A. I. (1939). *Land, labour and diet in Northern Rhodesia*, London: International Institute of African Languages and Cultures.

Richards, A. I., and Widdowson, E. M. (1936). A dietary study in North-Eastern Rhodesia. *Africa*, **9**, 166–196.

Rogoff, B., and Gardner, W. (1984). Adult guidance of cognitive development. In B. Rogoff and J. Lave (eds), *Everyday cognition: its development in social context* (pp. 95–116). Cambridge, MA: Harvard University Press.

Rogoff, B., Malkin, C., and Gilbride, K. (1984). Children's learning in the 'zone of proximal development'. *New Directions for Child Development*, **23**, 31–44.

Rogoff, B., and Wertsch, J. (Eds.) (1984). Children's learning in the 'zone of proximal development', *New Directions for Child Development*, **23**.

Rosenkrantz, D. J. (1969). Programmed grammars and classes of formal languages. *Journal of the Association of Computing Machines*, **16**, 107–131.

Rothbaum, F., Weisz, J. R., and Snyder, S. S. (1982). Changing the world and changing the self: a two-process model of perceived control. *Journal of Personality and Social Psychology*, **42**, 1, 5–37.

Saxe, G., Gearhart, M., and Guberman, S. R. (1984). The social organization of early number development. *New Directions for Child Development*, **23**, 19–30.

Schank, R., and Abelson, R. (1977). *Scripts, plans, goals, and understanding*. Hillsdale, NJ: Erlbaum.

Schwartz, D. M., Thompson, M. G., and Johnson, C. L. (1982). Anorexia nervosa and bulimia: the socio-cultural context. *International Journal of Eating Disorders*, **1**, 3, 20–36.

Shaw, R. E., and Pittenger, J. (1977). Perceiving the face of change in changing faces: implications for a theory of object perception. In R. Shaw and J. Bransford (eds), *Perceiving, acting, and knowing (pp. 103–132)*. Hillsdale, NJ: Erlbaum.

Sherif, M. (1936). *The psychology of social norms*. New York: Harper & Brothers.

Shotter, J. (1975). *Images of man in psychological research*. London: Methuen.

Shotter, J. (1983). 'Duality of structure' and 'intentionality' in an ecological psychology. *Journal for the Theory of Social Behaviour*, **13**, 19–43.

Shotter, J. (1984). *Social accountability and selfhood*. Oxford: Basil Blackwell.

Shotter, J., and Newson, J. (1982). An ecological approach to cognitive development: implicate orders, joint action, and intentionality. In G. Butterworth and P. Light (eds), *Social cognition: studies of the development of understanding* (pp. 32–52). Chicago: University of Chicago Press.

Simon, H. A. (1956). Rational choice and the sturcture of the environment. *Psychological Review*, **63**, 2, 129–138.

Simon, H. A. (1957). *Models of man*. New York: Wiley.

Simon, H. A. and Rescher, N. (1966). Cause and counterfactual. *Philosophy of Science*, **33**, 323–340.

Slade, P. D., and Russell, G. F. M. (1973). Awareness of body dimensions in anorexia nervosa: cross-sectional and longitudinal studies. *Psychological Medicine*, **3**, 188–199.

Smedslund, J. (1978). Bandura's theory of self-efficacy: a set of common sense theorems. *Scandinavian Journal of Psychology*, **19**, 1–14.

Smedslund, J. (1980). Analyzing the primary code: from empiricism to apriorism. In D. Olson (ed.), *The social foundations of language and thought* (pp. 47–73). New York: Norton.

Smith, J. A., and Ross, W. D. (1908). *The works of Aristotle*, vol. 8. *Metaphysica*. Oxford: Clarendon Press.

Smollett, E. (1975). Differential enculturation and social class in Canadian schools. In T. R. Williams (ed.), *Socialization and communication in primary groups* (pp. 221–231). The Hague: Mouton.

Sommerville, C. J. (1983). The distinction between indoctrination and education in England, 1549–1719. *Journal of the History of Ideas*, **44**, 3, 387–406.

Sorokin, P. (1956). *Fads and foibles in modern sociology and related sciences*. Chicago: Regner.

Stendler, C. B. (1950). Sixty years of child training practices. *Journal of Pediatrics*, **36**, 122–134.

Stent, G. (1981). Strength and weakness of the genetic approach to the development of the nervous system. *Annual Review of Neuroscience*, **4**, 163–194.

Stern, D. (1974). The goal and structure of mother–infant play. *Journal of the American Academy of Child Psychiatry*, **13**, 3, 402–422.

Sunley, R. (1955). Early 19th century American liteature on child rearing. In M. Mead and M. Wolfenstein (eds), *Childhood in contemporary cultures*. Chicago: University of Chicago Press.

Super, C., and Harkness, S. (1981). Figure, ground, and gestalt: the cultural context of the active individual. In R. Lerner and N. Busch-Rossnagel (eds), *Individuals as producers of their development*. New York: Academic Press.

Tambiah, S. J. (1969). Animals are good to think and good to prohibit. *Ethnology*, **8**, 423–459.

Tawney, R. (1926). *Religion and the rise of capitalism*. New York: Harcourt, Brace, & Co.

Teigen, K.-H. (1984). A note on the origin of the term 'nature and nurture': not Shakespeare and Galton but Mulcaster. *Journal of the History of the Behavioural Sciences*, **20**, 363–364.

Thathachar, M. A. L., and Ramakrishnan, K. R. (1981a). An automation model of a hierarchical learning system. In H. Akashi (ed.), *Control science and technology for the progress of society* (pp. 1065–1071). Oxford: Pergamon.

Thathachar, M. A. L., and Ramakrishnan, K. R. (1981b). A hierarchical system of learning automata. *IEEE Transaction on Systems, Man, and Cybernetics*, **11**, 3, 236–240.

Thelen, E. (1983). Learning to walk: ecological demands and phylogenetic constraints. In L. P. Lipsitt and C. Rovee-Collier (eds), *Advances in infancy research* (pp. 213–249). Norwood, NJ: Ablex.

Thelen, E., and Fogel, A. (1986). Toward an action-based theory of infant development. In J. Lockman and N. Hazen (eds), *Action in social context: perspectives on early development*. New York: Plenum.

Thom, R. (1973). A global dynamical scheme for vertebrate embryology. *Lectures on mathematics in the life sciences*, **5**, 3–45.

Thom, R. (1975). *Structural stability and morphogenesis: an outline of a general theory of models*. Reading, MA: Benjamin/Cummings.

Thom, R. (1976). The two-fold way of catastrophe theory. In A. Dold and B. Eckmann (eds), *Structural stability, the theory of catastrophes, and applications in the sciences,* Vol. 525 of *Lecture notes in mathematics* (pp. 235–252). Berlin–New York: Springer.

Thom, R. (1980). The genesis of representational space according to Piaget. In M. Piatelli-Palmarini (ed.), *Language and learning: the debate between Jean Piaget and Noam Chomsky* (pp. 361–368). Cambridge, MA: Harvard University Press.

Thompson, D'Arcy (1942). *On growth and form,* 2nd edn. Cambridge: Cambridge University Press. 1st edn published 1917.

Thorngate, W. (1986). The production, detection, and explanation of behavioural patterns. In J. Valsiner (ed.), *The individual subject and scientific psychology* (pp. 71–93). New York: Plenum.

Todd, J. T., and Mark, L. S. (1981). Issues related to the prediction of craniofacial growth. *American Journal of Orthodontics,* **79,** 1, 63–80.

Todd, J. T., Mark, L. S., Shaw, R. E. and Pittenger, J. (1980). The perception of human growth. *Scientific American,* **242,** 2, 132–144.

Toulmin, S., and Leary, D. E. (1985). The cult of empiricism in psychology, and beyond. In S. Koch and D. E. Leary (eds), *A century of psychology as science* (pp. 594–616). New York: McGraw-Hill.

Tourney, G. (1965). Freud and the Greeks: a study of the influence of classical Greek mythology and philosophy upon the development of Freudian thought. *Journal of the History of the Behavioral Sciences,* **3,** 67–85.

Trettien, A. (1900). Creeping and walking. *American Journal of Psychology,* **12,** 1–57.

Trevarthen, C. (1977). Descriptive analysis of infant communication behaviour. In H. R. Schaffer (ed.), *Mother–infant interaction.* London: Academic Press.

Trevarthen, C. (1979a). Communication and cooperation in early infancy. In M. Bullowa (ed.), *Before speech: the beginnings of human communication* (pp. 321–347). Cambridge: Cambridge University Press.

Trevarthen, C. (1979b). Instinct for human understanding and for cultural communication: their development in infancy. In M. Von Cranach, K. Foppa, W. Lepenies, and D. Ploog (eds), *Human ethology.* Cambridge: Cambridge University Press.

Trevarthen, C. (1982). Basic patterns of psychogenic change. In T. G. Bever (ed.), *Regressions in mental development: basic phenomena and theories* (pp. 7–46). Hillsdale, NJ: Erlbaum.

Tweney, R. D., Doherty, M. E., and Mynatt, C. R. (eds) (1981). *On scientific thinking.* New York: Columbia University Press.

Valsiner, J. (1983a). A developing child in a developing culture: a relativistic synthesis. Paper presented at the 26th Annual Meeting of the African Studies Association, Boston, December.

Valsiner, J. (1983b). Parents' strategies for the organization of child–environment relationships in home setting. Paper presented at the 7th Meeting of ISSBD, Munich, August.

Valsiner, J. (1984a). Conceptualizing intelligence: from an internal static attribution to the study of the process structure of organism–environment relationships. *International Journal of Psychology,* **19,** 363–389.

Valsiner, J. (1984b). Two alternative epistemological frameworks in psychology: the typological and variational modes of thinking. *Journal of Mind and Behavior,* **5,** 4, 449–470.

Valsiner, J. (1984c). *The childhood of the Soviet citizen: socialization for loyalty.* Ottawa: Carleton University Press (published lecture).

Valsiner, J. (1984d). Construction of the Zone of Proximal Development in adult–child joint action: the socialization of meals. *New Directions for Child Development,* **23**, 65–76.

Valsiner, J. (1985). Parental organization of children's cognitive development within home environment. *Psychologia,* **28**, 131–143.

Valsiner, J. (1986). Between groups and individuals: psychologists' and laypersons' interpretations of correlational findings. In J. Valsiner (ed.), *The individual subject and scientific psychology,* New York: Plenum.

Valsiner, J. (1987). *Developmental psychology in USSR.* Brighton: Harvester Press.

Valsiner, J., and Benigni, L. (1986). Naturalistic research and ecological thinking in the study of child development. *Developmental Review,* **6**, 203–223.

Valsiner, J., and Mackie, C. (1985). Toddlers at home: canalizatin of climbing skills through culturally organized physical environments. In T. Gärling and J. Valsiner (eds), *Children within environments; towards a psychology of accident prevention* (pp. 165–191). New York: Plenum.

Van der Daele, L. D. (1969). Qualitative models in developmental analysis. *Developmental Psychology,* **1**, 4, 303–310.

Van der Veer, R. (1984). *Cultuur en cognitie.* Groningen: Wolters-Noordhoff.

van Geert, P. (1983). *The development of perception, cognition and language.* London: Routledge & Kegan Paul.

van Geert, P. (1984). The structure of developmental theories. Paper presented at the Inaugural European Conference on Developmental Psychology, Groningen, August.

Van IJzendoorn, M. H., and Van der Veer, R. (1984). *Main currents of critical psychology.* New York: Irvington Publishers.

Von Cranach, M. (1982). The psychology of goal-directed action: basic issues. In M. Von Cranach and R. Harré (eds), *The analysis of action* (pp. 35–73). Cambridge: Cambridge University Press.

von Glasersfeld, E. (1974). *Because* and the concepts of causation. *Semiotica,* **12**, 129–144.

VonHofsten, C. (1979). Development of visually directed reaching: the approach phase. *Journal of Human Movement Studies,* **5**, 160–178.

Von Neumann, J. and Morgenstern, O. (1944). *Theory of games and economic behavior.* Princeton, NJ: Princeton University Press.

Vuyk, R. (1981). *Overview and critique of Piaget's genetic epistemology 1965–1980,* vol. 1. London: Academic Press.

Vygotsky, L. S. (1956). *Izbrannye psikhologicheskie issledovnia. Myshlenie i rech.* Moscow: Izd. APN (in Russian).

Vygotsky, L. S. (1960). *Razvitie vyshhikh psikhicheskikh funktsii,* Moscow: Izd. APN (in Russian).

Vygotsky, L. S. (1962). *Thought and language.* Cambridge, MA: MIT Press.

Vygotski, L. S. (1963). Learning and mental development at school age. In B. Simon and J. Simon (eds), *Educational psychology in the U.S.S.R.* (pp. 21–34). London: Routledge & Kegan Paul.

Vygotsky, L. S. (1966). Play and its role in the psychological development of the child. *Voprosy psikhologii,* **12**, 6, 62–76.

Vygotsky, L. S. (1978). *Mind in society.* Cambridge, MA: Harvard University Press.

Vygotsky, L. S. (1981). The genesis of higher mental functions. In J. Wertsch (ed.), *The concept of activity in Soviet psychology* (pp. 144–188). Armonk, NY: M. E. Sharpe.

Vygotsky, L. S., and Luria, A. R. (1930). *Etiudy pa istorii povedinia.* Moscow–Leningrad: Gosudarstvennoie Izdatel' stvo. (in Russian).

Waddington, C. H. (1942). Canalization of development and the inheritance of acquired characters. *Nature,* **150,** no. 3811, 563–565.

Waddington, C. H. (1966). Fields and gradients. In M. Locke (ed.), *Major problems in developmental biology* (pp. 105–124). New York–London: Academic Press.

Waddington, C. H. (1968). The basic ideas of biology. In C. H. Waddington (ed.). *Towards theoretical biology,* vol. 1 (pp. 1–41). Chicago: Aldine.

Waddington, C. H. (1970). Concepts and theories of growth, development, differentiation and morphogenesis. In C. H. Waddington (ed.), *Towards theoretical biology,* vol. 1 (pp. 1–41). Chicago: Aldine.

Weber, M. (1930). *The Protestant ethic and the spirit of capitalism.* London: Allen & Unwin.

Webster's Third New International Dictionary (1981).

Weisner, T. R., and Gallimore, R. (1977). My brother's keeper: child and sibling caregiving. *Current Anthropology,* **18,** 2, 169–180.

Weiss, P. (1969). The living system: determinism stratified. In A. Koestler and J. R. Smythies (eds), *Beyond reductionism: new perspectives in the life sciences* (pp. 3–55). London: Hutchinson.

Weiss, P. (1978). Causality: linear of systemic. In G. Miller and Elizabeth Lenneberg (eds), *Psychology and biology of language and thought.* New York: Academic Press.

Werner, H. (1937). Process and achievement—a basic problem of education and developmental psychology. *Harvard Educational Review,* **7,** 358–368.

Werner, H. (1957). The concept of development from a comparative and organismic point of view. In D. B. Harris (ed.), *The concept of development: an issue in the study of human behavior* (pp. 125–148). Minneapolis: University of Minnesota Press.

Wertheimer, M. (1981). Einstein: the thinking that led to the theory of relativity. In R. D. Tweney, M. E. Doherty, and C. R. Mynatt (eds), *On scientific thinking* (pp. 193–211). New York: Columbia University Press.

Wertsch, J. (1981). Trends in Soviet cognitive psychology. *Storia e critica della psicologia,* **2,** 2, 219–295.

Wertsch, J. (1983). The role of semiosis in L. S. Vygotsky's theory of human cognition. In B. Bain (ed.), *The sociogenesis of language and human conduct* (pp. 17–31). New York: Plenum.

Wertsch, J. (1984). The zone of proximal development: some conceptual issues. *New Directions for Child Development,* **23,** 7–18.

Wertsch, J. (1985). *Vygotsky and the social formation of the mind.* Cambridge, MA: Harvard University Press.

Wertsch, J., Minick, N., and Arns, F. J. (1984). The creation of context in joint problem-solving. In B. Rogoff and J. Lave (eds), *Everyday cognition: its development in social context* (pp. 151–171). Cambridge, MA: Harvard University Press.

Wertsch, J., and Stone, C. A. (1984). The concept of internalization in Vygotsky's account of the genesis of higher mental functions. In J. Wertsch (ed.), *Culture, communication, and cognition: Vygotskian perspectives* (pp. 162–197). Cambridge: Cambridge University Press.

West, M. J., and King, A. (1985). The inherting of parents, peers, and places in the genesis of behavior. Paper presented at the Biennial SRCD meeting, Toronto, 25 April.

Wildgen, W. (1981). Archetypal dynamics in word semantics: an application of catastrophe theory. In H.-J. Eikmeyer and H. Rieser (eds), *Words, worlds, and contexts* (pp. 234–296). Berlin–New York: Walter de Gruyter.

Wildgen, W. (1983). Modelling vagueness in catastrophe-theoretic semantics. In T.

T. Ballmer and M. Pinkal (eds), *Approaching vagueness* (pp. 317–360). Amsterdam: North Holland.
Wildgen, W. (1984). Gestalt semantics on the basis of catastrophe theory. In T. Barbe (ed.), *Semiotics unfolding*, vol. 1 (pp. 421–427). The Hague: Mouton.
Williams, L. P. (1973). Kant, Naturphilosophie and scientific method. In R. N. Giere and R. S. Westfall (eds), *Foundation of scientific method: the nineteenth century* (pp. 3–22). Bloomington, IN: Indiana University Press.
Wing, A. M., and Fraser, C. (1983). The contribution of the thumb to reaching movements. *Quarterly Journal of Experimental Psychology*, **35A**, 297–309.
Wittgenstein, L. (1958). *Philosophical investigations*. Oxford: Basil Blackwell.
Wober, M. (1972). Culture and the concept of intelligence. *Journal of Cross-Cultural Psychology*, **3**, 327–328.
Wolfenstein, M. (1951). Trends in infant care. *American Journal of Orthopsychiatry*, **23**, 120–130.
Wolfenstein, M. (1955). Fun morality: an analysis of recent American child-training literature. In M. Mead and M. Wolfenstein (ed), *Childhood in contemporary cultures*. Chicago: University of Chicago Press.
Wood, D. (1980). Teaching the young child: some relationships between social interaction, language, and thought. In D. R. Olson (ed.), *The social foundation of language and thought* (pp. 280–296). New York: W. W. Norton.
Wood, D., Bruner, J., and Ross, G. (1976). The role of tutoring in problem solving. *Journal of Child Psychology and Psychiatry*, **17**, 2, 89–100.
Wood, D., and Middleton, D. J. (1975). A study of assisted problem solving. *British Journal of Psychology*, **66**, 2, 181–191.
Wood, D., Wood, H., and Middleton, D. J. (1978). An experimental evaluation of four face-to-face teaching strategies. *International Journal of Behavioural Development*, **1**, 2, 131–147.
Wozniak, R. (1982). Metaphysics and science, reason and reality: the intellectual origins of genetic epistemology. In J. M. Broughton and D. J. Freeman-Moire (eds), *The cognitive-developmental psychology of James Mark Baldwin* (pp. 13–45). Norwood, NJ: Ablex.
Zahler, R. S., and Sussmann, H. J. (1977). Claims and accomplishments of applied catastrophe theory. *Nature*, **269**, 759–763.
Zahorsky, J. (1934). The discard of the cradle. *Journal of Pediatrics*, **4**, 660–667.
Zeeman, E. C. (1974). Primary and secondary waves in developmental biology. *Lectures on mathematics in the life sciences*, **7**, 69–161.
Zeeman, E. C. (1977). *Catastrophe theory: selected papers 1972–1977*. Reading, MA: Addson-Wesley.
Zeigarnik, B. (1927). Das Behalten erledigter und unerledigter Handlungen. *Psychologische Forschung*, **9**, 1–85.
Zeigarnik, B. (1981). *Teoria lichnosti Kurta Levina*. Moscow: Moscow University Press (in Russian, English title: *Kurt Lewin's theory of personality*).
Zempleni-Rabain, J. (1973). Food and the strategy involved in learning fraternal exchange among Wolof children. In P. Alexandre (ed.), *French perspectives in African studies* (pp. 221–233). London: Oxford University Press.

Index